The Night the Angels Came

Also by Cathy Glass

Damaged
Hidden
Cut
The Saddest Girl in the World
Happy Kids
The Girl in the Mirror
I Miss Mummy
Mummy Told Me Not to Tell
Run, Mummy, Run
My Dad's a Policeman (a Quick Reads novel)

Cathy Glass

SUNDAY TIMES BESTSELLING AUTHOR

The Night the Angels Came

The true story of a child's loss and the love that kept them alive

Certain details, including names, places and dates,
have been changed to protect the family's privacy.

HarperElement
An Imprint of HarperCollins*Publishers*
77–85 Fulham Palace Road,
Hammersmith, London W6 8JB

www.harpercollins.co.uk

and *HarperElement* are trademarks of
HarperCollins*Publishers* Ltd

First published by HarperElement 2011

1 3 5 7 9 10 8 6 4 2

© Cathy Glass 2011

Cathy Glass asserts the moral right to
be identified as the author of this work

A catalogue record of this book
is available from the British Library

ISBN 978-0-00-744262-1

Printed and bound in Great Britain by
Clays Ltd, St Ives plc

Acknowledgements

Many thanks to my editor, Anne; my agent, Andrew Lownie; and Carole and all the team at HarperCollins.

Preface

C hildren usually come into foster care as a result of abuse or severe neglect. Very occasionally, and sadly, it is as a result of one or both parents being very ill or even dying. This is the true story of Michael, whose courage, faith and strength in the face of so much sorrow will stay in the hearts of my family and me for ever.

Chapter One

It's a Cruel World

'Cathy,' Jill said quietly, 'I need to ask you something, and you must feel you can say no.'

'Sure, go ahead, Jill. I'm good at saying no,' I returned light-heartedly.

Jill gave a small laugh but I now realized she sounded subdued – not her usual cheerful self. Jill is my support social worker from Homefinders, the agency I foster for, and we get on very well.

'Cathy,' she continued, 'we need a foster home for a little boy called Michael. He's just eight. He has been looked after by his father for the last six years since his mother died when Michael was just two.' Jill paused, as though steeling herself for something she had to tell me, and I assumed it would be that the child had been badly neglected or abused, or that the father had a new partner and no longer wanted the child. I'd answered the telephone in the sitting room and I now sat on the sofa, ready to hear the details of the little boy's suffering, which would still shock me even after hearing many similar stories in the nine years I'd been fostering. However, what Jill told me shocked me in an entirely different way.

'Cathy,' Jill said sombrely, 'Michael's father, Patrick, is dying. He has contacted the social services and asked if a carer can be found to look after Michael when he's no longer able to.'

1

Jill paused and waited for my reaction. I didn't know what to say. 'Oh, I see,' I said lamely, as images and thoughts flashed through my mind and I grappled with the implications of what Jill was telling me.

'Patrick loves his son deeply,' Jill continued, 'and he has brought him up very well. Patrick has been battling against cancer for two years but the chemo has been stopped now and he's on palliative care only. He's very thin and weak, and realizes it won't be long before he has to go into a hospital or hospice. He has asked if Michael can get to know his carer before he goes to live with them when Patrick has to go into hospital.'

'I see,' I said again, quietly. 'How very, very sad. And there's no one in Michael's extended family who can look after him?' Which is usually considered the next best option for a child whose parents can't look after them, and what would have happened in my family if anything had happened to me.

'Apparently not,' Jill said. 'Both sets of grandparents are deceased and Patrick is an only child. There's an aunt who lives in Wales but Patrick has told the social worker they weren't close. She hasn't seen Michael since he was a baby and Patrick doesn't think she will want to look after him. The social services will obviously be making more enquiries about the extended family – Patrick originally came from Ireland. But that will take time, and Patrick doesn't have much time.'

'How long does he have?' I said, hardly daring to ask.

'The doctors have given him about three months.'

I fell silent and Jill was quiet too. It was one of the saddest reasons for a child coming into foster care I'd ever heard of. 'Does Michael know how ill his father is?' I asked at length.

'I'm not sure. He certainly knows his dad is very ill but I don't know if it's been explained to him that he's dying. I'll need to find out and also what counselling has been offered. Obviously, Cathy, this is a huge undertaking and I'm well aware of the commitment and emotional drain on you and your family if you agree to go ahead. Not many would want to take this on. It's bad enough if someone you know dies, but you don't go looking for bereavement.' She gave a small dry laugh.

I was silent again and I gazed through the French windows at the garden, which was now awash with spring flowers. Bright yellow daffodils mingled with blue and white hyacinths against a backdrop of fresh green grass. It seemed a cruel irony that as nature was bursting into life for another year so a life was slowly ending. And while I didn't know Michael or his father, my heart was already going out to them, especially that poor little boy who was about to lose his father and be left completely alone in the world.

'What we're looking for,' Jill clarified, 'is a carer who will get to know Michael while his father is still able to look after him, then foster him when his father goes into hospital or a hospice. Obviously if a relative isn't found who can give Michael a permanent home then we will need a long-term foster placement, but we'll cross that bridge when we come to it. His father has said he would like to meet the carer first, without Michael present, to discuss his son's needs, routine, likes and dislikes, which is sensible. The social worker will set up that meeting straight away.'

'Jill,' I said, stopping her from going any further, 'I need to think about this. I mean it's not straightforward fostering, is it? Apart from the huge emotional commitment I'm also mindful that Adrian and Paula are still coming to come to terms with their father leaving us last year. I'm not sure I can put them through this now. Adrian is the same age as Michael and sensitive; he's bound to feel Michael's loss personally. I don't think I have the right to upset my family more.'

'I completely understand,' Jill said. 'I wasn't even sure I should ask you.' At that moment I felt like saying: 'I wish you hadn't', because now I knew about Michael and his father I felt I had a responsibility towards them and I knew it was going to be difficult for me to say no.

'When do you want my answer by?' I asked Jill.

'Tomorrow, please. Can you sleep on it and let me know?'

'Yes, I will. I don't know whether I should discuss it with Adrian and Paula. Paula is only four: she doesn't understand about dying.'

'Do any of us?' Jill said quietly. And I remembered she'd lost her own brother the year before.

'It can be a cruel world sometimes,' I said. 'Let me think about it, Jill, and I'll get back to you.'

'Thanks, Cathy. Sorry if I've placed you in an awkward position. I know it's difficult.'

We said goodbye and I hung up. I stayed where I was on the sofa and stared unseeing across the room. I thought of Patrick raising his little boy alone after his wife's death and the strong bond that would have resulted from there being just the two of them. I could imagine the terror Patrick must have felt when the doctors told him he had cancer; it's a single parent's worst nightmare – the prospect of leaving your child orphaned. I marvelled at the courage and strength Patrick must have shown in dealing with the gruelling chemotherapy while looking after Michael. How he'd found the inner resources to come to terms with his dying and concentrate on making arrangements to have his son looked after when he was no longer able to I didn't know. What incredible courage, what sadness. I wouldn't have done so well, I was sure. But could I help Michael and his father? Did I have the right to bring all their sadness into my house? Did I want to? At that moment I knew I didn't. Standing, I wiped a tear from my eye, and left the room to busy myself with some housework to take my mind off the great sadness I had just heard.

Chapter Two
Proud of My Children

That afternoon when I met Adrian from school and then collected Paula from the friend she'd been playing with for the afternoon, I gave them an extra big hug and held them close. Life is so short and precious, but sometimes it takes a tragic reminder of just how fragile life is for us to really appreciate our loved ones and make the most of every day.

The April afternoon was still warm and I suggested we go to the park rather than straight home. Adrian and Paula happily agreed. Clearly other mothers had had the same idea, for when we arrived at the park it was busy, especially in the children's play area. Adrian ran over to the large slide while I went with Paula into the gated area for under-fives. I stood to one side and watched her as she ran around and then had goes on the little roundabout and rocking horse; then she called me to help her into a swing. As I lifted Paula in I heard Adrian shout, 'Look, Mum!'

I looked over to the adjacent play area, where Adrian was on the bigger swings, as usual working the swing as high as it would go. He wanted me to admire his daring feat. I smiled and nodded my appreciation of his courage, then called my usual warning, 'Hold on tight!', which made him work the swing even higher. But that's Adrian, and I guess boys in general.

Proud of My Children

Paula liked a more leisurely and genteel swing and as I pushed her I kept an eye on Adrian. He had left the swing, having jumped off while it was still moving, and was now on the rope ladder that was part of the mini assault course. My thoughts went again to Michael, as they had been doing on and off all afternoon, since Jill's phone call. Was Michael still able to enjoy simple pleasures like running free and playing in a park, I wondered, or had his life closed in to the illness of his father? With no immediate family to share the burden and help out, Michael's life must surely centre around his father's condition, especially now he was so very ill. I looked again at Adrian and for a horrendous second my thoughts flashed to a picture of him being told I was terminally ill. I shuddered and changed direction, and thought instead about the meeting Patrick had requested with the foster carer. I was sure I couldn't do it. Not meet a dying man and discuss looking after his son when he was no longer able to. Perhaps if I'd had a strong religious faith and sincerely believed Patrick was going on to a better life it would have been easier, but my faith wasn't that strong. Like many, I believed in something but I wasn't sure what, and while I hoped for a life after death I wasn't wholly convinced. Death, therefore, held a shocking finality for me and was something I avoided contemplating at all costs.

By the time we got home, despite a pleasant hour in the park, I was feeling pretty down and a failure for not being able to offer to look after Michael. Then something strange happened, portentous in its timing – a sign, almost.

Adrian and Paula were watching children's television while I made dinner. I could hear the dialogue on the television from the kitchen. It was an episode in a drama series – the children's equivalent of adult soap. It dealt with everyday issues as well as family crises. So far the series had covered a new baby in the family, a visit to the doctor, going into hospital, parents divorcing and a parent drinking too much. Now, to my amazement, it appeared to be dealing with the death of a loved one. I left the dinner cooking and joined the children on the sofa. Admittedly it wasn't a parent dying but a grandparent, but the timing of this episode didn't escape me. It showed the family visiting Grandpa while he was in hospital, him 'drifting comfortably into an endless sleep', followed by the funeral and him 'being laid to rest'. While the relatives were upset that they would not be seeing Grandpa again they rejoiced in having known him. They shared their special memories and his adult daughter said, 'He will live for ever in our memory', so the programme ended on a very positive note.

I returned to the kitchen deep in thought and finished cooking the dinner. Despite the programme I was no more convinced I had what it took to see Michael through his father dying, and indeed if I should. As I'd said to Jill, Adrian and Paula didn't need any more sadness after their father leaving, and it would be impossible that they wouldn't become involved. Then, as we ate, I decided to reverse the decision I'd made earlier – not to discuss Michael's situation with Adrian and Paula – and gently sound them out. It was, after all, their home Michael would be coming into and their lives he would be part of.

'You know the fostering we do?' I said lightly, introducing the subject.

'Yes,' Paula said. Adrian nodded.

'Are you both happy to continue and have another child come to live with us for a while?' It was a question I asked them from time to time and I didn't automatically assume they wanted to continue fostering.

Adrian nodded again, more interested in his dinner than what I was saying, while Paula glanced up at me furtively, hoping I wouldn't notice she was stacking her peas into a pile rather than eating them.

'Have a few,' I said, referring to the peas. 'You need to eat some veg.' Paula had recently gone off anything green (which obviously included most vegetables) after her best friend had told her caterpillars were green so they could hide in vegetables and she'd found a caterpillar on her plate hiding in some broccoli. 'Good girl,' I said, as she stabbed one pea on to her fork. 'And you're happy to continue fostering as well?'

'Yes, I like it,' Paula confirmed.

Now I knew that all things being equal they were happy to foster another child, I felt more confident in talking specifically about Michael's situation.

'I had a phone call from Jill earlier today,' I began, 'about a little boy called Michael who will be needing a foster home shortly.'

'A boy, great!' Adrian said, without waiting for further details. 'How old is he?'

'Same age as you – eight.'

'Fantastic! Someone to play with at home.'

'That's not fair,' Paula moaned. 'I want a girl, my age.'

'I'm afraid I can't put in an order for a specific type of child,' I said. 'It's a case of who needs a home,' which they knew really. 'And in the past you've all got along, whatever the age of the child, boy or girl, and even with the teenagers.'

'When's he coming?' Adrian said, completely won over by the prospect of having a boy his own age come to stay, while Paula gingerly lifted another pea on to her fork and scanned it for any signs of wildlife.

'I'm not sure he is coming to us yet,' I said carefully. 'Jill's asked me to think about what she's told me because it's a difficult decision to make. You see, Michael's father is very ill and he won't be able to look after Michael for much longer, which is why he will need a foster home. But I'm not sure Michael coming to live with us is right for our family.'

Adrian looked at me quizzically. 'Surely he can stay with us while his father gets better?'

I felt anxiety creep up my spine as I steeled myself to explain. 'Unfortunately Michael's father is very, very ill and I'm afraid he is not likely to get better. You know the programme you've just been watching?' I glanced at them both. 'About the grandpa dying? Well, I'm afraid that's what is likely to happen to Michael's father.'

Adrian had now stopped eating and was staring at me across the dining table, appreciating the implications of what I was saying. 'His father is dying and Michael is my age?' he asked. 'His dad can't be very old.'

'No, he's not. It's dreadfully sad.'

'His dad can only be your age,' Adrian clarified, clearly shocked.

I nodded.

'Can't his mum look after him?' Adrian asked.

'Unfortunately Michael's mother died when he was little.'

Adrian continued to stare at me, his little face serious and deeply saddened, while Paula, so innocent I could have wept, said, 'Don't worry: the doctors will make Michael's daddy better.'

I smiled sadly. 'Love, sometimes people get so very ill that the doctors do all they can, and give them lots of medicine, but in the end they can't make them better.'

'And sometimes doctors are wrong,' Adrian put in forcefully. 'There was a guy on the news last week who was told by his doctors he had only six months to live, and that was ten years ago!'

I smiled at him. 'Yes, sometimes they do get it wrong, and make the wrong diagnosis,' I agreed, 'but not often.'

'So the doctors might be wrong now,' Paula put in, feeling she should contribute something but not fully understanding the discussion. Adrian nodded.

'They might be wrong, but it's not very likely. Michael's father is very ill,' I said. While I would have liked nothing more than to believe a misdiagnosis was an option, it would have been wrong of me to give them false hope.

We all quietly returned to our food but without our previous enthusiasm, and at that moment I knew I should have just said no to Jill and waited for the next child who needed a foster home. 'Anyway,' I said after a while, 'I think I will tell Jill that we feel very sorry for Michael but we can't look after him.'

'Why?' Adrian asked.

'Because it would be too sad for us. Too much to cope with after … everything else.'

'You mean Dad going?'

'Well, yes, and having to be part of Michael's sadness. I don't want to be sad: I like to be happy.'

'I'm sure Michael does too,' Adrian said bluntly. I met his gaze and in that look I saw not an eight-year-old boy but the wisdom of a man. 'I think Michael should come here,' he said. 'We can help him. Paula and I know what it's like to lose your dad. I know divorce is different – we can still see our dad some-times – but when Dad packed all his things and left, and stopped living with us, in some ways it felt like he'd died. I think because Paula and I have been through that it will help us understand how Michael is feeling when he's very sad.'

It was at times like this I felt so proud of my children and also truly humbled. I felt my eyes fill.

'And you think the same?' I asked, turning to Paula.

She nodded. 'We can help Michael when he cries about his daddy.'

'Did you cry a lot after your daddy left?' I asked.

Paula nodded. 'At night in bed, so you couldn't see.'

It was a moment before I could find my voice to speak. 'You should have told me,' I said, putting my arm around Paula and giving her a hug. 'Thank you both for explaining how you feel. Now I've got to do some careful thinking and decide if I have what it takes to help Michael.'

'You have, Mum,' Adrian said quietly.

'Thanks, son, that's kind of you, but I'm not so sure.'

Chapter Three

Are You Going to Die Soon?

The following morning, after I'd taken Adrian to school and Paula to the nursery where she went for three hours each morning, I phoned Jill. She was expecting my call, and said a quiet, 'Hello, Cathy.'

'Has a relative been found for Michael yet?' I asked hopefully, although I knew it was highly unlikely from what Jill had told me.

'No,' Jill said.

I hesitated, my brain working overtime to find the right words for what I had to say although, goodness knows, I'd spent long enough practising it – during the night and as soon as I'd woken.

'Jill, I've obviously given a lot of thought to Patrick and Michael and I also asked Adrian and Paula what they thought.' I paused again as Jill waited patiently on the other end of the phone. 'The children think we have what it takes to look after Michael but I have huge doubts, so I've got a suggestion.'

'Yes?' Jill said.

'You know Patrick has asked to meet the carer so that he can discuss Michael's needs, routine, etc.?'

'Yes.'

'Presumably that meeting will also give him a chance to see if he feels the carer is right for his son?'

'I suppose so, although to be honest Patrick can't afford to be too choosy. We don't have many foster carers free, and he hasn't that much time, which he appreciates.'

'Well, what I'm suggesting is that I meet Patrick and then we decide if Michael coming to me is right for both of us after that meeting. What do you think?'

'I think you're delaying a difficult decision and I'm not sure it's fair on Patrick. But I'll speak to his social worker and see what she thinks. I'll get back to you as soon as I've spoken to her.'

Chastened, I said a subdued, 'Thank you.'

Remaining on the sofa in the sitting room, I returned the phone to its cradle and stared into space. As if sensing my dilemma, Toscha, our cat, jumped on to my lap and began purring gently. Jill was partly right: I was delaying the decision, possibly hoping a distant relative of Michael's might be found or that Patrick would take an instant dislike to me at the meeting. Foster carers don't normally have the luxury of a meeting with the child's parents prior to the child being placed so that all parties can decide if the proposed move is appropriate; usually the child just arrives, often at very short notice. But Michael's case wasn't usual, as Jill knew, which was presumably why she'd indulged me and was now asking his social worker what she thought about my suggestion. I hoped I wasn't being unfair to Patrick. I certainly didn't want to make his life more difficult than it must have been already.

Some time later, feeling pretty despondent, I ejected Toscha from my lap and, heaving myself off the sofa, left the sitting room. I went into the kitchen, where I began clearing away the breakfast dishes, my thoughts returning again and again to Patrick and Michael. Was I being selfish in asking to meet Patrick first before making a decision? Jill had implied I was.

The poor man had enough to cope with without a foster carer dithering about looking after his son because it would be too upsetting.

It was an hour before the phone rang again and it was Jill. 'Right, Cathy,' she said, her voice businesslike but having lost its sting of criticism. 'I've spoken to Stella, the social worker involved in Michael's case, and she's phoned Patrick. Stella put your suggestion – of meeting before you both decide if your family is right for Michael – to Patrick, and Patrick thinks it's a good idea. In fact, Stella said he sounded quite relieved. Apparently he has some concerns, one being that you are not practising Catholics as they are. So that's one issue we will need to discuss.'

I too was relieved and I felt vindicated. 'I'll look forward to meeting him, then,' I said.

'Yes, and we need to get this moving, so Stella has set up the meeting for ten a.m. tomorrow, here at the council offices. The time suits Patrick, Stella and me, and I thought it should be all right with you as Paula will be at nursery.'

'Yes, that's fine,' I said. 'I'll be there.'

'I'm not sure which room we'll be in, so I'll meet you in reception.'

'OK. Thanks, Jill.'

'And can you bring a few photos of your house, etc., to show Patrick?'

'Will do.'

When I met the children later in the day – Paula from nursery at 12 noon, and Adrian from school at 3.15 p.m. – the first question they asked me was: 'Is Michael coming to live with us?' I said I didn't know yet – that I was going to a meeting the following morning where Patrick and the social workers would be present and we'd decide after that, which they accepted. The subject of Michael wasn't mentioned again during the evening, although it didn't leave my thoughts for long. Somewhere in our community, possibly not very far from where I lived, there was a young lad, Adrian's age, who was about to lose his father; while a relatively young father was having to come to terms with saying goodbye to his son for good. It had forced me to confront my own mortality, and later I realized it had unsettled Adrian and Paula too.

At bedtime Paula gave me an extra big hug; then, as she tucked her teddy bear in beside her, she said, 'My teddy is very ill, Mummy, but the doctors are going to make him better. So he won't die.'

'Good,' I said. 'That's what usually happens.'

Then when I went into Adrian's bedroom to say goodnight he asked me outright: 'Mum, you're not going to die soon, are you?'

I bloody hope not! I thought.

I sat on the edge of his bed and looked at his pensive expression. 'No. Not for a long, long time. I'm very healthy, so don't you start worrying about me.' Clearly I didn't know when I was going to die, but Adrian needed to be reassured, not enter into a philosophical debate.

He gave a small smile, and then asked thoughtfully, 'Do you think there's a God?'

'I really don't know, love, but it would be nice to believe there is.'

'But if there is a God, why would he let horrible things happen? Like Michael's father dying, and earthquakes, and murders?'

I shook my head sadly. 'I don't know. Sometimes people who have a faith believe they are being tested – to see if their faith is strong enough.'

Adrian looked at me carefully. 'Does God test those who don't have a faith?'

'I really don't know,' I said again. I could see where this was leading.

'I hope not,' Adrian said, his face clouding again. 'I don't want to be tested by having something bad happen. I think if God is good and kind, then he should stop all the bad things happening in the world. It's not fair if bad things happen to some people.'

'Life isn't always fair,' I said gently, 'faith or no faith. And we never know what's around the corner, which is why we should make the most of every day, which I think we do.'

Adrian nodded and laid his head back on his pillow. 'Maybe I should do other things instead of watching television.'

I smiled and stroked his forehead. 'It's fine to watch your favourite programmes; you don't watch that much television. And Adrian, please don't start worrying about any of us dying; what's happened in Michael's family is very unusual. How many children do you know who lost one parent when they were little and are about to lose their other parent? Think of all the children in your school. Have you heard of anyone there?' I wanted to put Michael's situation into perspective: otherwise I knew Adrian could start worrying that he too could be left orphaned.

'I don't know anyone like that at school,' he said.

'That's right. Adults usually live for a long, long time and slowly grow old. Look at Nana and Grandpa. They are fit and healthy and they're nearly seventy.'

'Yes, they're very old,' Adrian agreed. And while I wasn't sure my parents would have appreciated being called 'very old', at least I had made my point and reassured Adrian. His face relaxed and lost its look of anguish. I continued to stroke his forehead and his eyes slowly closed. 'I hope Michael can come and stay with us,' he mumbled quietly as he drifted off to sleep.

'We'll see. But if it's not us then I know whoever it is will take very good care of him.'

Chapter Four

So Brave Yet So Ill

I usually meet the parent(s) of the child I am looking after once the child is with me. I might also meet them regularly at contact, when the child sees his or her parents; or at meetings arranged by the social services as part of the childcare proceedings. Sometimes the parents are cooperative and we work easily together with the aim of rehabilitating the child home. Other parents can be angry with the foster carer, whom they see as being part of 'the system' responsible for taking their child into care. In these cases I do all I can to form a relationship with the parent(s) so that we can work together for the benefit of their child. I've therefore had a lot of experience of meeting parents in the time I've been fostering, but I couldn't remember ever feeling so anxious and out of my depth as I did that morning when I entered the reception area at the council offices and looked around for Jill.

Thankfully I spotted her straightaway, sitting on an end seat in the waiting area on the far side. She saw me, stood and came over. 'All right?' she asked kindly, lightly touching my arm. I nodded and took a deep breath. 'Try not to worry. You'll be fine. We're in Interview Room 2. It's a small room but there's just the four of us. Stella, the social worker, is up there already with Patrick. I've said a quick hello.'

I nodded again. Jill turned and led the way back across the reception area and to the double doors that led to the staircase. There was a lift in the building but it was tiny and was usually reserved for those with prams or mobility requirements. I knew from my previous visits to the council offices that the interview rooms were grouped on the first floor, which was up two short flights of stairs. But as our shoes clipped up the stone steps I could hear my heart beating louder with every step. I was worried sick: worried that I'd say the wrong thing to Patrick and upset him, or that I might not be able to say anything at all, or even that I would take one look at him and burst into tears.

At the top of the second flight of stairs Jill pushed open a set of swing doors and I followed her into a corridor with rooms leading off, left and right. Interview Room 2 was the second door on the right. I took another deep breath as Jill gave a brief knock on the door and then opened it. My gaze went immediately to the four chairs arranged in a small circle in the centre of the room, where a man and a woman sat facing the door.

'Hi, this is Cathy,' Jill said brightly.

Stella smiled as Patrick stood to shake my hand. 'Very pleased to meet you,' he said. He was softly spoken with a mellow Irish accent.

'And you,' I said, relieved that at least I'd managed this far without embarrassing myself.

Patrick was tall, over six feet, and was smartly dressed in dark blue trousers, light blue shirt and navy blazer, but he had clearly lost weight. His clothes were too big for him and the collar on his shirt was very loose. His cheeks were sunken and his cheekbones protruded, but what I noticed most as we shook hands were his eyes. Deep blue, kind and smiling, they held none of the pain and suffering he must have gone through and indeed was probably still going through.

We sat down in the small circle. I took the chair next to Jill so that I was facing Patrick and had Jill on my right and Stella on my left.

'Shall we start by introducing ourselves?' Stella said. This is usual practice in meetings at the social services, even though we might all know each other or, as in this case, it was obvious who we were. 'I'm Stella, Patrick and Michael's social worker,' Stella began.

'I'm Jill, Cathy's support social worker from Homefinders fostering agency,' Jill said, looking at Patrick as she spoke.

'I'm Cathy,' I said, smiling at Patrick, 'foster carer.'

'Patrick, Michael's father,' Patrick said evenly.

'Thank you,' Stella said, looking around the group. 'Now, we all know why we're here: to talk about the possibility of Cathy fostering Michael. I'll take a few notes of this meeting so that we have them for future reference, but I wasn't going to produce minutes. Is that all right with everyone?'

Patrick and I nodded as Jill said, 'Yes.' Jill, as at most meetings she attended with me, had a notepad open on her lap so that she could make notes of anything that might be of help to me later and which I might forget. Now I was in the room and had met Patrick, I was starting to feel a bit calmer. My heart had stopped racing, although I still felt pretty tense. Everyone else appeared quite relaxed, even Patrick, who had his hands folded loosely in his lap.

'Cathy,' Stella said, looking at me, 'I think it would be really useful if we could start with you telling us a bit about yourself and your family. Then Patrick,' she said, looking at him, 'would you like to go next and tell Cathy about you and Michael?'

Patrick nodded, while I straightened in my chair and tried to gather my thoughts. I don't like being first to talk at meetings, although I'm a lot better now at speaking in meetings than I used to be when I first began fostering; then I used to be so nervous I became tongue-tied and unable to say what I wanted to. 'I've been a foster carer for nine years,' I began. 'I have two children of my own, a boy and a girl, aged eight and four. I was married but unfortunately I'm now separated and have been for nearly two years. My children have grown up with fostering and enjoy having children staying with us. They are very good at helping the child settle in. It's obviously very strange for the child when they first come to stay and they often talk to Adrian and Paula before they feel comfortable talking to me.' I hesitated, uncertain of what to say next.

'Could you tell us what sort of things you do at weekends?' Jill suggested.

'Oh yes. Well, we go out quite a lot – to parks, museums and places of interest. Sometimes to the cinema. And we see my parents, my brother and my cousins quite regularly. They all live within an hour's drive away.'

'It's nice to do things as a family,' Patrick said.

'Yes,' I agreed. 'We're a close family and obviously the child we look after is always included as part of our family and in family activities. I make sure all the children have a good Christmas and birthday,' I continued. 'And in the summer we try and go on a short holiday, usually to the coast in England.' Patrick nodded. 'I encourage the children in their hobbies and interests and I always make sure they are at school on time. If they have any homework I like them to do it before they play or watch television.' I stopped and racked my brains for what else I should tell him. It was difficult giving a comprehensive thumbnail sketch of our lives in a few minutes.

'Did you bring some photographs?' Jill prompted.

'Oh yes. I nearly forgot.' I delved into my bag and took out the envelope containing photos that I had hastily robbed from the albums that morning. I passed them to Patrick and we were all quiet for some moments as he looked through them. There were about a dozen, showing my family in various rooms in the house, the garden, and also our cat, Toscha. Had I had more notice I would have put a small album together and labelled the photos.

Patrick smiled. 'Thank you,' he said, returning the photos to the envelope and then handing them back to me. 'You have a lovely family and home. I'm sure if Michael stayed with you he would feel very comfortable.'

'Thank you,' I said.

'Can I have a look at the photos?' Stella asked. I passed the envelope to her. 'While I look at these,' she said to Patrick, 'perhaps you'd like to say a bit about you and Michael?'

Patrick nodded, cleared his throat and shifted slightly in his chair. He looked at me as he spoke. 'First, Cathy, I would like to thank you for coming here today and considering looking after my son when I am no longer able to. I can tell from the way you talk that you are a caring person and I know if Michael comes to stay with you, you will look after him very well.' I gave a small smile and swallowed the lump rising in my throat as Patrick continued, so brave yet so very ill. Now he was talking I could see how much effort it took. He had to pause every few words to catch his breath. 'It will come as no surprise to you to learn I was originally from Ireland,' he continued with a small smile. 'I know I haven't lost my accent, although I've been here nearly twenty years. I came here when I was nineteen to work on the railways and liked it so much I stayed.' Which made

Patrick only thirty-nine years old, I realized. 'Unfortunately I lost both my parents to cancer while I was still a young man. Cathy, you are very lucky to have your parents, and your children, grandparents. Cherish and love them dearly; parents are a very special gift from God.'

'Yes, I know,' I said, feeling my eyes mist. Get a grip, I told myself.

'Despite my deep sadness at losing both my parents so young,' Patrick continued, 'I had a good life. I earned a decent wage and went out with the lads – drinking too much and chasing women, as Irish lads do. Then I met Kathleen and she soon became my great love. I gave up chasing other women and we got married and settled down. A year later our darling son, Michael, was born. We were so very happy. Kathleen and I were both only children – unusual for an Irish family – but we both wanted a big family and planned to have at least three children, if not four. Sadly it was not to be. When Michael was one year old Kathleen was diagnosed with cancer of the uterus. She died a year later. She was only twenty-eight.'

He stopped and stared at the floor, obviously remembering bittersweet moments from the past. The room was quiet. Jill and Stella were concentrating on their notepads, pens still, while I looked at the envelope of photographs I still held in my hand. So much loss and sadness in one family, I thought; it was so unfair. But cancer seems to do that: pick on one family and leave others free.

'Anyway,' Pat said casually, after a moment. 'Clearly the good Lord wanted us early.'

I was taken aback and wanted to ask if he really believed that, but it didn't seem appropriate.

'To the present,' Patrick continued evenly. 'For the last six years, since my dear Kathleen was taken, there's just been

Michael and me. I didn't bring lots of photos with me, but I do have one of Michael which I carry everywhere. Would you like to see it?'

I nodded. He tucked his hand into his inside jacket pocket and took out a well-used brown leather wallet. I watched, so touched, as Patrick's emaciated fingers trembled slightly and he fumbled to open the wallet. Carefully sliding out the small photo, about two inches square, he passed it to me.

'Thank you,' I said. 'What a smart-looking boy!'

Patrick smiled. 'It's his most recent school photo.'

Michael sat upright in his school uniform, hair neatly combed, slightly turned towards the camera, with a posed impish grin on his face. There could be no doubt he was Patrick's son, with his father's blue eyes, pale complexion and pleasant expression: the likeness was obvious.

'He looks so much like you,' I said as I passed the photo to Jill.

Patrick nodded. 'And he's got my determination, so don't stand any nonsense. He knows not to answer back and to show adults respect. His teacher says he's a good boy.'

'I'm sure he is a real credit to you,' I said, touched that Patrick should be concerned that his son's behaviour didn't deteriorate even when he was no long able to oversee it.

Jill showed the photograph to Stella and handed it back to Patrick. Patrick then went on to talk a bit about Michael's routine, foods he liked and disliked, his school and favourite television programmes, all of which I would talk to him about in more detail if Michael came to stay with us. Patrick admitted his son hadn't really had much time to pursue interests outside the home because of Patrick's illness and having to help his father, although Michael did attend a lunchtime computer club at school. 'I'm sure there are a lot of things I should have told you that I've missed,' Patrick wound up, 'so please ask me whatever you like.'

'Perhaps I could step in here,' Stella said. We looked at her. 'I think the first issue we should address is the matter of Michael's religion. Patrick and Michael are practising Catholics and Cathy's family are not. How do you both feel about that?' She looked at Patrick first.

'Well, I won't be asking Cathy to convert,' he said with a small laugh. 'But I would like Michael to keep attending Mass on a Sunday morning. If Cathy could take and collect him, friends of mine who also go can look after him while he's there. I've been going to the same church a long time and the priest is aware of my illness, and does what he can to help.'

'Would this arrangement work?' Stella asked me.

'Yes, I don't see why not,' I said, although I realized it would curtail us going out for the day each Sunday.

'If you had something planned on a Sunday,' Patrick said, as if reading my thoughts, 'Michael could miss a week or perhaps he could go to the earlier mass at eight a.m.?'

'Yes, that's certainly possible,' I said.

'Thank you,' Patrick said. Then quietly, almost as a spoken afterthought, 'I hope Michael continues to go to church when I'm no longer here, but obviously that will be his decision.'

'So can we just confirm what we have decided?' Stella said, pausing from writing on her notepad. 'Patrick, you don't have a problem with Cathy not being a Catholic as long as Michael goes to church most Sundays?'

'That's right.' He nodded.

'And Cathy, you are happy to take Michael to church and collect him, and generally encourage and support Michael's religion?'

'Yes, I am.'

Both Jill and Stella made a note. Patrick and I exchanged a small smile as we waited for them to finish writing.

Stella looked up and at me. 'Now, if this goes ahead, and we all feel it is appropriate for Michael to come to you, I know Patrick would like to visit you with Michael before he begins staying with you. Is that all right with you, Cathy?'

'Yes.'

'Thank you, Cathy,' Patrick said. 'It will help put my mind at rest if I can picture my son in his new bed at night.'

'It'll give you both a chance to meet my children as well,' I said.

Jill and Stella both wrote again. 'Now, to the other question Michael has raised with me,' Stella said: 'hospital visiting. When Patrick is admitted to hospital or a hospice, will you be able to take Michael to visit him?'

'Yes, although I do have my own two children to think about and make arrangements for. Would it be every day?'

'I would like to see Michael every day if possible, preferably after school,' Patrick confirmed.

'And at weekends?' Jill asked.

'If possible, yes.'

It was obviously a huge undertaking, and while I could see that of course father and son would want to see as much of each other as possible I was wondering about the logistics of the arrangement, and also how Adrian and Paula would feel at being bundled into the car each day after school and driven across town to the hospital instead of going home and relaxing.

'Were you thinking Cathy would stay for visiting too?' Jill asked, clearly appreciating my unspoken concerns.

'Not necessarily,' Patrick said. 'Cathy has her own family to look after and Michael is old enough to be left in the hospital with me. It would just need someone to bring and collect him.'

'If Cathy wasn't able to do it every day,' Jill said to Patrick, 'would you be happy if we used an escort to bring and collect Michael? We use escorts for school runs sometimes. All the drivers are vetted.'

'Yes, that's fine with me,' he said. 'It shouldn't be necessary for a long time, as I intend staying in my home for as long as possible, until I am no longer able to look after myself.' Which made me feel small-minded and churlish for not agreeing to the arrangement outright.

'It's not a problem,' I said quickly. 'I'll make sure Michael visits you every day.'

'Thank you, Cathy,' Patrick said, then with a small laugh: 'And don't worry, you won't have to arrange my funeral: I've done it.'

I met Patrick's gaze and hadn't a clue what to say. I nodded dumbly. Jill and Stella made no comment either, for what could we possibly say?

'So,' Stella said, after a moment, 'do either of you have any more questions or issues you wish to explore?'

I shook my head. 'I don't think so,' I said.

'No,' Patrick said. 'I would like it if Cathy agreed to look after Michael. I would be very grateful.'

I was looking down again, concentrating on the floor.

'And what is your feeling, Cathy?' Stella asked. 'Or would you like some time to think about it?'

'No, I don't need more time,' I said. 'And Patrick deserves an answer now.' I felt everyone's eyes on me. Especially Jill on my right, who, I sensed, was cautioning me against saying something I should take time to consider. 'I will look after Michael,' I said. 'I'd be happy to.'

'Thank you,' Patrick said. 'God bless you.' And for the first time I heard his voice tremble with emotion.

Chapter Five

Treasure

U sually, once I've made a decision I'm positive and just get on with the task in hand. But now, as I left the council offices and began the drive to collect Paula from nursery, I was plagued with misgiving and doubt. Had I made the right decision in offering to look after Michael or had I simply felt sorry for Patrick? What effect would it have on Adrian and Paula? What effect would it have on me? Then I thought of Patrick and Michael and all they were going through and immediately felt guilty and selfish for thinking of myself.

I switched my thoughts and tried to concentrate on the practical. At the end of the meeting we'd arranged for Patrick and Michael to visit the following evening at 6.00. I now considered their visit and what I could do to make them feel relaxed and at home. Although I'd had parents visit prior to their child staying before, it was very unusual. One mother had visited prior to her daughter staying when she was due to go into hospital (she didn't have anyone else to look after her child); another set of parents had visited before their son (with very challenging behaviour) had begun a respite stay to give them a break. Both children were in care under a voluntary care order (now called a Section 20), where the parents retain all legal rights and responsibilities. This was how Michael would be looked after, but that was where any similarity ended: the other children had returned home to their parents. And whereas the other visits had been brief – I'd showed the family around the house and explained our routine – I thought Patrick and Michael's visit needed to be more in-depth, to give them a feeling of our home life which would, I hoped, reassure them both. I decided the best way to do this would be for us to try and carry on as 'normal', and then tormented myself by picturing Patrick and Michael sitting on the sofa and Adrian and Paula staring at them in silence.

At dinner that evening I told Adrian and Paula that Patrick and Michael would be coming for a visit the following evening to meet them and see the house. 'So let's make sure they feel welcome and the house is tidy,' I added, glancing at Adrian.

He looked at me guiltily, for even allowing for the fact that eight-year-old boys were not renowned for their tidiness the mess he managed to generate sometimes was incredible. It was often impossible to walk across his bedroom floor for toys, all of which he assured me had to remain in place, as otherwise his game would be ruined. I was never quite sure what exactly 'the game' was but it seemed to rely on all his toy cars and models – of dinosaurs, famous people and the planets – covering the carpet and being scooped up and then put down again in a different places by a large plastic dumper truck, which made a hideous hooting sound when it reversed. But the game had kept him, visiting friends and sometimes Paula occupied for hours in recent months, and had only been tidied away when I'd vacuumed.

'Suppose I'd better tidy my room,' Adrian muttered, understanding my hint.

'That would be good,' I said.

'Is Michael coming to stay, then?' Paula asked.

'Yes, but not tomorrow. Tomorrow he and his father are just coming for a visit so that they can see what our home is like before Michael has to move in.'

'When's he moving in?' Adrian asked.

'I'm not sure yet. It will depend on his father. I met him today. He's a lovely man. Sometimes he has to speak slowly to catch his breath.' I thought I should mention this so that the children wouldn't stare or, worse, comment. Adrian was old enough to know not to comment, but I could picture Paula asking Patrick, 'Why are you talking funny?' as a young child can.

'Why does he speak slowly?' Paula now asked.

'Because he's ill,' Adrian informed her.

'That's right,' I said. 'Sometimes it takes all Patrick's energy to talk, although he does very well.'

'I see,' Paula said quietly, and we continued with our meal.

The following day I took Adrian to school, and Paula to nursery, and then did a supermarket shop. I came home and by the time I'd unpacked all the bags it was time to collect Paula from nursery. The afternoon vanished in playing with Paula and housework, and it was soon time to collect Adrian from school. Those who don't have children sometimes wonder what stay-at-home mothers (or fathers) find to do all day; and indeed I was guilty of this before I gave up work to look after my children and foster. Now I know!

At 5.40 p.m. the children were eating their pudding when the doorbell rang. 'You finish your meal,' I said, standing. 'It might be Patrick and Michael arriving early.'

Although the children hadn't mentioned Michael and his father since the previous evening, they hadn't been far from my thoughts, especially when I'd prepared the spare bedroom that afternoon so that it would look welcoming when Michael saw it.

Now as I went down the hall towards the front door my heart began pounding as all my anxieties and misgivings returned. I just hoped, as I had done prior to the meeting, I didn't say anything silly or embarrassing that would upset Patrick and now Michael.

Taking a deep breath, I opened the door with a smile. 'Hello,' I said evenly. 'Good to see you both.'

'And you,' Patrick said easily. 'This is Michael.' Patrick was standing slightly behind his son and again looked very smart in a blazer and matching trousers. Michael was dressed equally smartly in his school uniform but looked as anxious as I felt.

'Hi, Michael,' I said. 'Come in. Try not to worry. It's a bit strange for me too.'

He gave a small nervous laugh and shrugged as they came into the hall. Patrick shook my hand and kissed my cheek, which I guessed was how he greeted all female friends and acquaintances. 'Lovely place you have here,' he said.

'Thank you. Come on through and meet Adrian and Paula.'

I smiled again at Michael and then led the way down the hall and to where the children were finishing their pudding.

'We've interrupted your meal,' Patrick said, concerned.

'Don't worry, they've nearly finished. This is Adrian and Paula, and this is Michael and his dad, Patrick,' I said, introducing everyone.

'Good to meet you,' Patrick said to Adrian and Paula.

'Hi,' Adrian said, glancing up from his pudding. Michael said nothing.

'Say hello, Michael,' Patrick prompted.

'Hello,' Michael said reluctantly.

'Why can't we have a girl?' Paula grumbled.

Patrick frowned, puzzled, and looked at me. 'It's Paula's little joke,' I said, throwing her a warning glance.

Patrick smiled at Paula while I asked Michael, 'Have you had a good day at school?' I wasn't sure who felt more awkward – the children or the adults.

Michael thrust his hands into his trouser pockets and shrugged.

'Answer Cathy,' Patrick said.

'Yes, thank you,' Michael said formally.

'Your dad tells me you're doing very well at school,' I said, trying to put him at ease and get some conversation going.

Michael dug his hands deeper into his trouser pockets and shrugged again.

'Take your hands out of your pockets,' Patrick said firmly, catching his breath. Then to me, 'I'm sorry, Cathy, the cat seems to have got my son's tongue. He's usually quite talkative.'

'Don't worry,' I said. 'It's a bit strange for everyone. I'm sure they'll all thaw out soon.' Adrian and Paula had finished their pudding and were now sitting staring at Michael, not unkindly, just eyeing the newcomer up and down. 'Shall I show you around the house first?' I asked Patrick. 'Then afterwards the children can play together for a while.'

'Thank you, Cathy,' Patrick said with a smile. 'That would be nice.' Michael said nothing.

Adrian and Paula stayed at the table while I turned and led the way into the kitchen. 'Very nice,' Patrick said.

'And through here,' I said going ahead, 'is the sitting room. From here you can see the garden and the swings.' Patrick joined me at the French windows while Michael hung back.

'Your garden looks lovely,' Patrick said. 'Do you do it all yourself?'

'Yes, it keeps me fit,' I said, smiling. 'I usually garden while the children are out there playing. The bottom half of the garden with the swings is for the children. There are no plants

34

or flowers there, so they can play and kick balls without doing any damage.'

'Good idea. Come and have a look, Michael,' Patrick encouraged. 'What a lovely big garden!'

Michael took a couple of steps into the centre of the room, shrugged and stayed quiet. I saw how uncomfortable Michael's sulky attitude was making Patrick feel and I felt sorry for him. Patrick was being so positive and I knew he would be wanting to create a good first impression, just as I did, but I also knew that Michael's behaviour was to be expected. Clearly Michael didn't want to be here, for this was where he would be staying when his father could no longer look after him. I wondered how much discussion Patrick had had with his son to prepare him for staying with me – it was something we would need to talk about.

'There's just the front room left downstairs,' I said, moving away from the window.

I led the way out of the sitting room, down the hall and to the front room with Patrick just behind me and Michael bringing up the rear. Then we went upstairs, where I showed them our bedrooms, toilet and bathroom. Patrick made a positive comment about each room while Michael said nothing. When we went into what was going to be Michael's bedroom Michael stayed by the door. 'Very comfortable,' Patrick said. Then to Michael: 'Come in and have a look. You'll be fine here, son.'

But Michael didn't reply. He shrugged, jabbed his hands into his trouser pockets again and refused to move. I saw Patrick's expression set and knew he was about to tell him off. I lightly touched Patrick's arm and shook my head slightly, gesturing for him not to say anything. 'Perhaps we could have a chat later?' I suggested.

Patrick nodded.

'Well, that's the tour finished,' I said lightly to Michael and Patrick. 'Let's go downstairs and find Adrian and Paula.'

I went out of the bedroom and as I passed Michael I touched his shoulder reassuringly. I wanted him to know it was all right to feel as he did – that I wasn't expecting him to be dancing and singing.

Downstairs, Adrian had thawed out and Paula seemed to be over her pique about not having a girl to stay. They had taken some board games from the cupboard and Adrian was setting up a game called Sunken Treasure. It was a good choice: I saw Michael's eyes light up. 'Would you like to play with Adrian and Paula,' I suggested, 'while your father and I have chat in the sitting room?'

Michael nodded, took his hands out of his pockets and slid into a chair at the table. 'I've played this before,' he said enthusiastically. I looked knowingly at Patrick and he winked back.

'Would you like a drink?' I asked Patrick. 'Tea, coffee?'

'Could I have a glass of water, please?'

'Of course. Michael,' I asked, 'would you like a drink? Or how about an ice cream?'

Michael looked up from the table and for the first time smiled.

'Is it all right if I give Michael an ice cream?' I asked his father.

He nodded.

'Would you like one?'

'No, just the water, please,' Patrick said. 'Thank you.'

I didn't bother asking Adrian and Paula if they wanted an ice cream because I knew what their answers would be. I went into the kitchen, took three ice creams from the freezer and, together with three strips of kitchen towel, returned to the table and handed them out. I poured a glass of water for Patrick and we went into the sitting room, where I pushed the door to so that we couldn't be easily overheard.

'Sorry about that,' Patrick said.

'Don't worry. It's to be expected.'

As Patrick sat on the sofa he let out a sigh, pleased to be sitting down. 'That's better. It's a good walk from the bus stop,' he said.

'You caught the bus here?' I asked, surprised.

He nodded, took a sip of his water, and then said easily, 'I sold my car last month. I thought it would be one less thing for Eamon and Colleen to have to worry about. Eamon and Colleen are my good friends who are executors of my will. I've been trying to make it easier for them by getting rid of what I don't need now.'

Although Patrick was talking about his death he spoke in such a practical and emotionless manner that he could have been simply making arrangements for a trip abroad, so that I didn't feel upset or emotional.

'All that side of things is taken care of,' Patrick continued. 'What money I have will be held in trust until Michael is twenty-one. I have a three-bedroom house and I was going to sell that too and rent somewhere, but I thought it would be an unnecessary upheaval for Michael. It's always been his home and he will have to move once I go into hospital, so I decided there was no point in making him move twice.'

'No,' I agreed. 'I think that was wise of you.'

There was a small silence as Patrick sipped his water and I watched him from across the room. I liked Patrick – both as a person and a man. Already I had formed the impression that he was kind and caring, as well as strong and practical, and despite his illness his charisma and charm shone through. I could picture him out drinking with the lads and chasing women in his twenties, as he'd said he had at the meeting, and then being a loyal and supportive husband and proud father.

'I think you are doing incredibly well,' I said. 'I'm sure I wouldn't cope so well.'

'You would if you had to, Cathy,' he said, looking directly at me. 'You'd be as strong as I've had to be – for the sake of your children. But believe me, in my quieter moments, in the early hours of the morning when I'm alone in my bed and I wake in pain and reach for my medication, I have my doubts. Then I can get very angry and ask the good Lord what he thinks he's playing at.' He threw me a small smile.

'And what does the good Lord say?' I asked lightly, returning his smile.

'That I must have faith, and Michael will be well looked after. And I can't disagree with that because he's sent us you.'

I felt my emotion rise and also the enormity and responsibility of what I'd taken on. 'I'll do my best,' I said, 'but I'm no angel.'

'You are to me.'

I looked away, even more uncomfortable that he was placing me on a pedestal. 'Is there really no hope of you going into remission?' I asked quietly.

'Miracles can happen,' Patrick said, 'but I'm not counting on it.'

There was silence as we both concentrated on the floor and avoided each other's gaze. 'I hope I haven't upset you,' I said after a moment, looking up.

'No.' Patrick met my gaze again. 'It's important we speak freely and you ask whatever you wish. You will become very close to me and Michael over the coming months. Not to talk of my condition would be like ignoring an elephant in the room. I wish Michael could talk more freely.'

'How much does Michael understand of the severity of your condition?' I now asked.

'I've been honest with him, Cathy. I have told him I am very ill – that unfortunately the treatment didn't work and I am unlikely to get better. But I don't think he has fully accepted it.'

'Does he talk about his worries to you?'

'No, he changes the subject. I'm sorry he was rude earlier but he didn't want to come here this evening.'

'It's understandable,' I said. 'There's no need to apologize. Coming here has forced Michael to confront a future he can't bear to think about – one without you. To be honest, since I heard about you and Michael I have tried to imagine what it would be like for Adrian and Paula to be put in Michael's position, and I can't. I can't contemplate it. So if I, as an adult, struggle, how on earth does Michael cope? He's only eight.'

'By pretending it's not happening,' Patrick said. 'He's planning our next summer holiday. We always take – I mean we used to take – a holiday together in August, but I can't see it happening this year.'

'It might,' I said. 'You never know.'

'Possibly, but I'm not giving Michael false hope.'

'No, and I won't either,' I reassured him.

A cry of laughter went up from the room next door where the children were playing Sunken Treasure, followed by a round of applause. 'I think someone has found treasure,' I said.

Patrick's eyes sparkled as he looked at me and said, 'I think Michael and I have too.'

Chapter Six

Lonely and Afraid

That evening Patrick and I continued talking for another hour while the children played. Our conversation grew easier and more natural as we both relaxed and got to know each other. We didn't talk about the future again or his illness but about our separate pasts and the many happy memories we both had. He told me of all the good times he'd had as a child in Ireland and then with his wife, Kathleen. I shared my own happy childhood memories and then told him how I'd met John, my husband, and how we'd started fostering. I also told him of the shock and disbelief I'd felt when John had suddenly left me. I was finding Patrick very easy to talk to, as I think he did me.

'Looking back,' I said speaking of John's affair, 'I guess there were warning signs: the late nights at work, the weekend conferences. Classic signs, but I chose to ignore them.'

'Which was understandable,' Patrick said. 'You trusted him. Trust is what a good marriage is based on.'

'I've let go of my anger, but it will be a long time before I forgive him,' I admitted.

Patrick nodded thoughtfully.

I made us both a cup of tea while the children continued playing board games; then when it was nearly 7.15 and the light outside was staring to fade, Patrick said, 'Well, Cathy, I could sit here all night chatting with you but we'd best be off. Michael has school in the morning and I'm sure you have plenty to do.'

'Will you be all right catching the bus?' I said. 'Or can I give you a lift?'

'No, we'll be fine, thank you. I'm sure you'd rather get started with your children's bedtime routine.'

I smiled. As a single parent – having raised Michael alone for six years – Patrick was familiar with the bedtime routine of young children: of bathing, teeth-brushing, bedtime stories, hugs and kisses goodnight, etc. He was right: I did appreciate the opportunity of settling the children into bed rather than driving across town.

We went to the table where the children were now in the middle of a game of Monopoly. 'Time to go, son,' Patrick said.

'Oh, can't I finish the game first?' Michael moaned good-humouredly. I was pleased to see he had now relaxed and was enjoying himself.

'Next time,' Patrick said. 'You've got school tomorrow.'

Michael pulled a face and reluctantly stood. 'Do you want some help packing away?' he asked Adrian, which I thought was very thoughtful.

'Don't worry,' I said. 'We'll do it. You and your dad need to get on the bus.'

Michael and his father used the bathroom first and then Adrian, Paula and I showed them to the front door and said goodbye.

'Thanks, Cathy,' Patrick said, taking my hand between his and kissing my cheek. 'We've had a nice evening, haven't we, Michael?'

Michael nodded. He looked a lot happier than he had done when he'd first arrived; his cheeks were flushed from the excitement of the games they'd played, and Adrian and Paula looked as though they'd enjoyed playing with Michael. All of which bode well for the future.

'I'll be in touch,' Patrick said as he and Michael went down the front path. 'Goodnight and God bless.'

'And you,' I called after them.

We watched them go and then I closed the front door. 'All right?' I asked the children. 'Did you have a nice evening?'

'Yes,' Adrian said. 'Michael's OK.'

'Is Michael's daddy coming to live with us?' Paula asked.

'No, only Michael,' I said. 'What made you think that?'

Paula looked thoughtful, clearly having been working something out. Then she said, 'If Michael's daddy came to live with us, you could look after him and make him better. You make me better when I'm ill. Then when he's better we can all live together, and Michael will have a mummy again, and we'll have a daddy.'

Adrian tutted.

I smiled and gave her a hug. If only life were that simple, I thought. 'It's a bit more complicated than that,' I said. 'And you have a daddy: it's just that he doesn't live with us any more.'

That evening when the children were in bed I wrote up my log notes of Patrick and Michael's visit. All foster carers have to keep a log – a daily record of the child or children they are fostering. In their log the carer records the child's progress, their physical and emotional health, their education and any significant events. The log is usually begun when the carer first meets the child and ends when the child leaves the foster home. These log notes are then placed on the social services' files and form part of the child's record, which the child can read when they are older. Not only is keeping a log a requirement of fostering: it is also a valuable and detailed record of part of the child's history. I had begun my log for Michael after meeting Patrick at the social services' offices the day before and now continued it with their visit. It was just a paragraph saying how long they had stayed, that their visit had gone well, and while Michael had been subdued to begin with he had responded to Adrian and Paula, and the three of them had played together, while Patrick and I had talked. But as I wrote I felt as though I was writing up a friend's visit in a diary rather than the log notes of a foster carer, so easily had we all bonded.

The following afternoon Jill telephoned to check on how Patrick and Michael's visit had gone. 'Very good,' I said. 'Much better than I'd expected. Michael was a bit quiet to begin with, but then he played with Adrian and Paula while Patrick and I chatted. Patrick's a lovely person and very easy to talk to. He's done a great job of bringing up Michael alone.'

Possibly Jill heard something in my voice or perhaps it was that she knew me from being my support social worker, for there was a small pause before she said: 'Good, but you might have to put some professional distance between you and Patrick. I know how involved you get with our looked-after children and their families. Patrick is likely to be very needy in his situation with no family of his own to support him.'

'He's not needy,' I said defensively. 'And although he has no immediate family he has lots of very supportive friends.'

'Good,' Jill said again, 'but just be careful. I wouldn't want you getting hurt.'

'All right, Jill. I hear what you're saying. I'll be careful.'

Jill then gave me some feedback from Stella – Patrick and Michael's social worker – who'd spoken to Patrick that morning. Stella had confirmed that the evening had gone well from

Patrick and Michael's point of view. Patrick had sent his thanks and asked if they could visit again the following Saturday, perhaps for a bit longer. Today was Friday, so it was just over a week away.

'I realize this is more introduction than we would normally do,' Jill added. 'But if it helps prepare Michael for when he moves in, when Patrick goes into hospital, then it seems appropriate.'

'Yes, that's fine with me,' I said. 'I could make us some dinner.'

'Let's set the time for their visit as two to six. Does that fit in with your plans?'

'Yes, or two to seven if they are staying for dinner.'

'OK. I'll run it past Stella and get back to you. If I can't reach her this afternoon, it'll be Monday. Have a good weekend.'

'Thanks, Jill. And you.'

When Jill phoned back on Monday afternoon she asked if we'd had a good weekend and then confirmed that Patrick and Michael would be visiting from 2.00 to 7.00 p.m. the following Saturday. She passed on Patrick's thanks and Stella's gratitude for being so accommodating, but there was no need. If they came and stayed for dinner it would be more like a social event than part of the introductions for a fostering placement, and something I would look forward to, as I thought Adrian and Paula would too. As soon as Jill had finished on the phone I began planning what I would cook for dinner on Saturday. I knew Patrick and Michael were both meat eaters because Patrick had mentioned the roasts he liked to cook after church on Sundays, so I thought roast chicken with vegetables would be a good idea, and perhaps I'd make a bread-and-butter pudding; I hadn't made one in ages and Adrian and Paula loved it.

Planning for Saturday gave me a frisson of warmth for the rest of the day and indeed most of that week.

However, it was not to be.

On Thursday afternoon when I was standing in the school playground with Paula, waiting for Adrian to come out, my mobile rang. 'Sorry,' I said to the mother I was talking to, taking my phone from my pocket. Jill's office number was displayed and I moved slightly away from the group I'd been standing with in case what Jill had to say was confidential.

'Cathy, where are you?' Jill asked as soon as I answered. 'Are you collecting Adrian from school?' She spoke quickly, suggesting it was urgent.

'I'm in the playground now, waiting for his class to come out. What's the matter?'

'Patrick has just been admitted to hospital. He collapsed at home this afternoon. A neighbour found him and called an ambulance.'

'Oh. Is he all right?' I said, which was a really silly question.

'I don't have any more details, but can you collect Michael from school and look after him for the weekend? It's what we'd been working towards but obviously it's come early. Michael's going to be very upset and shocked, as it's all happened so quickly. His teacher is looking after him until you arrive. I'll phone the school and tell them you're on your way. You know where St Joseph's school is?'

'Yes,' I said, shocked by the news. 'I'll go as soon as I've got Adrian. Is Patrick very ill?'

'I don't know. I'll phone Stella after I've phoned the school and see what I can find out. We'll need to get a change of clothes for Michael and also see about hospital visiting.'

'Yes,' I said, my thoughts reeling. The school doors opened and classes began filing out. 'I should be at Michael's school in about fifteen minutes,' I said to Jill.

'I'll phone them and let them know. Thanks. I'll be in touch.'

Saying a quick goodbye, I returned my phone to my jacket pocket and took hold of Paula's hand. I gave it a reassuring squeeze. 'That was Jill,' I said. 'I'm afraid Michael's daddy isn't very well. He's in hospital. We're going to collect Michael from school and he's staying the weekend.' I took some comfort from Jill's words, which suggested Patrick would be coming out of hospital again after the weekend.

'Aren't they coming for dinner on Saturday?' Paula asked as Adrian's class began streaming out.

'No. Well, Michael will be with us but his daddy isn't well enough.'

I spotted Adrian and gave a little wave. He bounded over. 'Can Jack come to tea? He's free tonight.'

'I'm sorry, not tonight,' I said as Jack dragged his mother over. 'Can we make it next week?'

'Sure,' Jack's mother said. 'I told Jack it was too short notice.'

Adrian pulled a face.

'I'll speak to you next week and arrange something,' I confirmed to Jack's mother.

'That's fine,' she said. 'Come on, Jack.'

I began across the playground with a disgruntled Adrian on one side and Paula on the other. 'I'm sorry,' I said to Adrian, 'but it would have been a good idea to ask me first before you invited Jack for tea. I've just had a call from Jill and –'

'Michael's daddy is in hospital,' Paula put in.

'Thank you, Paula,' I said a little tersely. 'I can tell Adrian.' I could feel myself getting stressed.

'We're going to Michael's school now,' I clarified. 'His daddy was taken to hospital this afternoon. Michael will be staying with us for the weekend. I know it's all a bit short notice but it can't be helped. Michael's obviously going to be very worried and upset.'

Adrian didn't say anything but his face had lost its grumpiness and disappointment at not having Jack to tea and was now showing concern for Michael.

We went round the corner to where I'd parked the car and the children clambered into the back. I helped Paula fasten her seatbelt as Adrian fastened his. I then drove to Michael's school – St Joseph's Roman Catholic primary school – on the other side of the town centre, although I used the back route to avoid going through the town itself. During the drive we were all quiet, concerned for Michael and his father and feeling the sadness Michael must be feeling.

The road outside the school was clear, most of the children having gone home, so I was able to park where the zigzag lines ended outside the school. The building was a typical Victorian church school with high windows, a stone-arched entrance porch and a small playground at the front, now protected by a tall wire-netting fence. Although I'd driven past the school before, I'd never been inside. Someone in the school must have seen us cross the playground, for as I opened the heavy outer wooden door and entered the enclosed dark porch, the inner door suddenly opened. I was startled as a priest in a full-length black cassock stood before us. Adrian and Paula had stopped short too.

'You've come to collect Michael?' the priest asked.

'Yes. I'm Cathy Glass.'

'Come this way. Michael is waiting in the head teacher's office.' He turned and led the way.

We followed the priest down a dark wood-panelled corridor, which was lined with huge gilt-framed religious pictures – of Mary, Christ and hosts of angels. It was like stepping back in

47

time and a complete contrast to the bright modern school with wall displays of children's artwork that Adrian went to. It had an air of strict religious and moral observance, and discipline, and if I'm honest I found it a bit intimidating. I saw Adrian and Paula cautiously looking around too.

'Patrick has kept the school informed of his condition,' the priest said as we arrived outside another massive wooden door with a brass plaque announcing 'Head Teacher'. 'He and Michael are in our prayers.'

I nodded.

The priest opened the door and we entered a spacious but cluttered room, which looked as though it hadn't changed since the Victorian era. Beneath the one window was a huge oak desk; the chair behind it was empty, but over to the right, lost in the centre of a large leather captain's chair, sat Michael. As he turned to face us our eyes met. He looked so lonely and afraid I could have wept.

Chapter Seven
Comfortable

I wanted to rush over and take Michael in my arms and comfort him, but I felt inhibited by the presence of the priest and the formality of the head teacher's office. Instead I said, 'Are you all right, love?' I crossed the room to where Michael sat, so alone.

He gave a small nod and I touched his shoulder reassuringly.

'You're going home with Cathy,' the priest said, remaining by the door.

'How's my dad?' Michael asked me.

'He's being well looked after in hospital,' I said. 'I'm expecting to hear more soon, love. Try not to worry.'

'Can I go and see him now?' Michael asked. I wasn't sure. Jill had told me to collect Michael from school and take him home. I didn't know if it was appropriate to take Michael to the hospital now.

'Not straight from school,' I said, 'but I'll find out when you can visit.' Michael nodded.

'Don't forget your bag,' the priest said.

Michael picked up his school bag, which was propped beside the chair, and slowly stood.

'Will you be bringing Michael to school tomorrow?' the priest asked. 'I think it's better for him to be in school than moping around.'

'I'll have to wait until I hear from Michael's social worker,' I said, 'but I think she'll probably say Michael should come to school if he feels up to it. What time does school start?'

'The doors open at eight a.m. and registration is at eight fifteen sharp.' Which meant I would have time to bring Michael to school before taking Adrian to his school for its 8.50 a.m. start, and then continue as usual to Paula's nursery for 9.00.

Michael heaved his school bag on to one shoulder and the four of us crossed the room to where the priest waited by the door. We went out of the head's office and then followed the priest down the corridor to the main entrance. He opened the inner and outer doors. 'Take care, Michael,' he said as we passed through the dark lobby and into the light and air. 'I'll visit your dad when I get a chance. He is in our prayers.'

'Thank you, Father,' Michael said respectfully. Adrian and Paula glanced at me and I knew I would have to explain later that priests in the Catholic Church were referred to as 'father'.

'When will I be able to see my dad?' Michael asked as we crossed the playground.

'I'm not sure yet. I'm waiting to hear from your social worker and I'll tell you as soon as I do.' I was hoping Jill or Stella would phone before too long so that I could reassure Michael, and I also needed to know what arrangements would be made to collect the clothes Michael needed for the weekend.

'If you can't take me I could go to the hospital on the bus,' Michael offered.

I gave a small smile. 'There's no need for that, love. I'll take you just as soon as I hear from Stella about visiting times.' Of course I also needed confirmation that it was advisable for Michael to visit tonight – that Patrick was well enough – although I wasn't going to alarm Michael by saying so.

Comfortable

'You don't have to keep to visiting times when someone is terminally ill,' Michael said, and I was saddened that an eight-year-old knew this.

'What's a terminal?' Paula asked innocently.

'Terminally ill is when someone is very ill,' I said. I guessed Michael probably knew the full definition but he didn't say.

'Have you visited your dad before in hospital?' Adrian asked.

Michael shook his head. 'Dad had to go to the hospital for chemo but he always came home again afterwards. Sometimes he was sick and I held his hand and got him a glass of water.'

My heart ached at the touching image of Michael caring for his father. 'Chemo can make you sick,' I said, and I wondered how long it would be before Paula asked what chemo was.

'What's a chemo?' she said a second later.

'It's a very strong medicine that can help people get better,' I said.

'It hasn't helped my dad,' Michael said quietly.

I didn't say anything and Paula and Adrian fell quiet too, and I thought how much Michael had had to cope with in his short life compared to the average child.

We arrived at the car and I opened the rear door and the children climbed in. The children were quiet on the journey home and I was deep in thought. Not only was I concerned and sad for Michael but I was also thinking about Patrick. How ill was he? Jill had said he'd collapsed and a neighbour had found him, which could mean anything from a faint to a coma. Would he be able to leave hospital after the weekend, as Jill's comment had suggested, or was he going to need a longer stay? Patrick had been doing so well on the two occasions I'd met him and should have been coming to dinner on Saturday instead of being rushed to hospital. I knew I was going to have to be very strong for Michael, for if I was worrying goodness knew what Michael must be thinking as he sat silently next to Adrian staring through the side window.

It would be nice to say that when we arrived home Adrian's and Paula's naturally happy disposition took over and we all brightened up, but that didn't happen. As I unlocked the front door and we filed into the house the cloud of Michael's sadness came with us. Michael stood in the hall with his bag on one shoulder looking so very sad, lost and alone, while Adrian and Paula, who usually ran off playing before I'd closed the front door, stood subdued on either side of him.

'Take your shoes and coats off,' I encouraged. 'Michael, you can leave your school bag here in the hall, love, or take it up to your room. It's up to you.'

He dropped it where I pointed, in the recess in the hall; then he took off his shoes and jacket, which I hung on the coat stand. Adrian and Paula took off their shoes and coats and the three of them looked at me.

'Adrian, would you like to get a game from the cupboard while I make dinner?' I suggested.

He shrugged. 'Can't we watch television?'

'Yes, if that's what you'd all like to do.'

They nodded. 'Does anyone want a drink and a snack first?'

They looked at each other and shrugged again; then Adrian led the way into the sitting room to watch television while I went to the kitchen to make dinner.

Not having any news of Patrick was in some ways worse than having bad news because my thoughts went into overdrive and I kept imagining the worst. I could hear the television in the background as I worked in the kitchen and I assumed the children's thoughts were safely occupied with the programme. But after fifteen minutes as I was peeling potatoes Adrian rushed in.

Comfortable

'Mum, come quickly,' he said. 'Michael and Paula are crying.'

I left what I was doing and flew into the sitting room. Michael was sitting on the sofa, staring blindly at the television, with tears streaming silently down his cheeks. Paula sat next to him, her little arms looped around his shoulders, trying to comfort him but also in tears.

'Adrian, can you turn off the television for now, please?' I said. I went over to the sofa and, lifting Paula to one side, positioned myself between the two of them. I linked one arm around Michael's waist, who remained sitting stiffly upright, and my other arm around Paula, who snuggled into my side.

'It's all right,' I soothed gently. 'It's OK to be upset. I understand.'

'I miss my dad,' Michael said. 'I want to be with him.'

'I know you do, love. If I haven't heard anything from Stella soon I'll phone and see if there is any news, and ask her when you can visit.'

'My dad needs me,' Michael said, his brow creasing. 'We're never apart.' As well as hearing Michael's deep sadness at their separation I heard his anxiety and sense of responsibility for his father.

'Your dad is being very well looked after by the doctors and nurses,' I reassured him. 'You've done so much caring for your dad and now it's their turn to help.'

'Why didn't they phone me instead of taking him to hospital?' Michael asked, as though he was responsible for his dad being admitted to hospital. 'I look after him when he's unwell.'

'I know you do, love, and you do a fantastic job, but sometimes people need what a hospital can offer. The doctors and nurses can do more there.' Michael was still sitting upright and rigid, as though trying to keep his grief under control and accepting my hug would be a sign of weakness.

'Are the doctors making Michael's daddy better?' Paula asked, still snuggled into my side. Her tears were subsiding now she'd had some reassurance from me.

'The doctors are making sure Patrick is very comfortable,' I said carefully, for in truth I'd no idea how Patrick was.

'And you'll phone?' Michael asked.

'Yes, I'm expecting your social worker to phone me but if she doesn't by the time I've finished preparing dinner, then I'll phone her.'

'Mum will,' Adrian confirmed. He was sitting in the chair opposite, sombrely watching us. 'Mum always does what she says.' Which I thought was sweet and showed Adrian had confidence in me despite my failings.

'What time will you phone?' Michael persisted.

I glanced at the clock. 'If I haven't heard anything I'll phone at five thirty,' which seemed to reassure Michael at little. He gave a small nod and then wiped his eyes on the back of his sleeve. 'I'll get you a tissue,' I said.

Giving them both a little hug, which Michael resisted, I stood and fetched the box of tissues, and Michael and Paula took a few each.

'Do you want the television on?' Adrian asked Michael. 'Or do you want to play something?'

Michael shrugged. 'Don't mind.'

'Why don't you and Paula take Michael to where all the toys are and the three of you can choose something?' I said to Adrian. I thought that hunting through the cupboards, drawers and boxes of toys and games would provide a distraction and occupy their thoughts if nothing else.

Adrian stood, Michael and Paula followed, and the three of them went off to the conservatory-cum-playroom, where most of the toys were kept, while I returned to the kitchen to continue with the preparation of dinner. It was nearly 5.15 before the phone rang and I grabbed the extension in the kitchen. My stomach churned as I heard Stella's voice.

'Good and bad news,' she said. 'Patrick has regained consciousness but he doesn't want Michael to visit him.'

Chapter Eight
Michael's Daddy

'Patrick's red blood cell count is very low, which is why he collapsed,' Stella continued. 'He's having a blood transfusion. He's feeling pretty rough at present and is on a ward with some very ill people. He doesn't want Michael to see him there, as he thinks it will worry him more. If all goes well Patrick should be out of hospital on Monday. Apparently Michael has never seen his dad in hospital before and Patrick wants to keep it that way for as long as is possible.'

'I see,' I said doubtfully. 'I'm not sure stopping Michael from visiting is a good idea. Michael is desperate to see his dad. I think seeing him on a hospital ward with other ill people won't be as bad as not seeing him at all.'

'Yes, I know, I tend to agree, but Patrick wants to protect Michael for as long as he can. And we have to respect his wishes.' Which I had to accept. 'Patrick would like to phone Michael later this evening. Is it all right if I give him your landline number?'

'Yes, of course.'

'Will you explain to Michael what I've told you? And also tell him that I'll bring him a change of school clothes and what he needs for the weekend this evening. Patrick gave me a list of what Michael needs over the phone. I'm going to their house now; a neighbour has a key. Then I'll come on to you. I won't be there for another hour or so. Is that all right with you?'

'Yes. Does Patrick have what he needs in hospital?' I asked, mindful that he had been rushed in unconscious without time to pack an overnight bag.

'The neighbour's husband is taking in what he needs. I won't speak to Michael now, as I have to get going. Explain to him, please, and I'll see him later.'

'I will.'

I replaced the phone in its cradle on the kitchen wall and was about to go through to the sitting room to tell the children what was happening when Michael appeared, having heard the phone ring. His face was tight and anxious and I knew he was expecting bad news. 'It's all right,' I reassured him quickly. 'Your dad is doing fine. He's having a blood transfusion and should be able to leave hospital on Monday.' His face brightened a little. 'Do you know what a blood transfusion is?' I asked.

He nodded. 'When can I see him?'

'Your dad is going to phone you later, here, but as he's only in hospital for the weekend he's told Stella there's no need for you to visit him. He'll see you at home as soon as he comes out.'

I'd phrased it as best I could, but predictably Michael said, 'But I want to see him tonight, or tomorrow. You said we would.'

I hadn't said we would but that wasn't the issue. 'I have to do what your father thinks is best for you,' I said gently. 'I can't go against his wishes. He thinks it's best if he phones you instead of you visiting, as it's just for the weekend. He's given Stella a list of what you'll need for tomorrow and the weekend and she's bringing your things here later. She'll be able to tell us more when we see her and so will your father when he phones. Is that all right, love?' Michael gave a small nod and seemed to accept what I was saying. 'Could you tell Adrian and Paula dinner is ready, please?'

Giving another small nod Michael turned and went off to tell Adrian and Paula. A few moments later the three of them came into the kitchen/diner. As they entered I heard Michael telling Adrian and Paula that his dad was getting better and he would be phoning later. While Michael probably understood that his use of the phrase 'getting better' referred to a temporary remission in an otherwise poor prognosis, I wondered if Paula and Adrian might assume Patrick was now making a full recovery, for in their limited experience of illness people who were sick got better.

I was right. 'Michael's daddy is getting better,' Paula announced as we sat at the table to eat. 'He's not going to die.'

'Not yet,' Michael put in quickly, which saved me from a very difficult and painful conversation.

I looked at him with a reassuring smile. He returned my smile, the tension having eased a little from his face. Even if Patrick's remission was only temporary, like Michael I rejoiced in it, and there was always hope. 'We'll have a nice weekend,' I said to him. 'What would you like to do?'

Michael looked thoughtful for a second and then asked quietly, 'Can we go swimming? I used to go swimming every Saturday with my dad but he hasn't been well enough this year.'

'Yes,' I said, pleased that he was showing enthusiasm, and honoured that I was being allowed to take over an activity that had hitherto been one he did with his dad. 'That sounds good to me.' Adrian and Paula were nodding in agreement. 'We'll go on Saturday morning,' I said. 'I don't suppose Stella will be bringing your swimming shorts so I'll buy another pair while you're at school tomorrow. You're the same size as Adrian.'

Michael's Daddy

Michael smiled again, his blue eyes creasing at the corners exactly as Patrick's did. 'Thanks, Cathy. Is that what I call you? Or is it Mrs Glass?'

'Cathy's fine,' I said as Adrian and Paula sniggered, but not unkindly.

I'm pleased to say that Michael ate well and once dinner was finished he played with Adrian and Paula while I cleared away. At 6.45 when the doorbell rang I guessed it was Stella. The children stopped playing and joined me in the hall as I opened the front door.

'What a welcoming committee!' Stella said, laughing. 'How are you all?'

'Good,' the children chorused.

Stella hadn't met Adrian and Paula before, so I introduced them as she carried a large canvas holdall into the hall.

'That's my bag,' Michael said, a little surprised. It must have seemed strange to him seeing his bag arrive in my hall, although he knew Stella was bringing him a change of clothes.

'Yes,' Stella said. 'Your dad told me where to find it and the things you need. I think I've remembered everything. Your neighbour, Mrs Harvey, let me into your house and she sends her love. Her husband, Jack, wasn't there, but he sends his love too. He was visiting your dad.'

'So why can't I visit Dad?' Michael asked.

Stella glanced at me. 'I have explained,' I said. We were still standing in the hall. 'Shall we go through to the sitting room?' I suggested.

'Just for a few minutes,' Stella said. 'It's getting late and I have to write a report for tomorrow when I get home.'

We went into the sitting room. Michael sat on the sofa between Adrian and Paula, and Stella squatted on the floor in front of them as she spoke. She explained, as I had, that Patrick had said there was no need for Michael to visit as he was only in hospital for the weekend. Also, as I had done, Stella omitted the other reason for Patrick not wanting Michael to visit: that seeing him looking so poorly and surrounded by other very sick people would be unnecessarily upsetting for Michael. Seated in a line on the sofa all three children nodded as Stella spoke and Stella ended up addressing them all.

'Your dad is phoning later,' Stella concluded, looking at Michael. 'Visiting ends at seven thirty, so I guess once Jack has gone your dad will phone. There's a portable payphone on the ward. I don't think you're allowed to use a mobile in hospital.'

The children nodded and Paula took Michael's hand between hers and patted it, as I did hers when she was worried. 'Your dad has a portable payphone,' she reassured him. Then looking at Stella, asked, 'What's a portable payphone?'

'It's a phone that can be moved around the ward so that all the patients can use it,' Stella explained.

'That's good, isn't it, Michael?' Paula said. 'All the patients use it.'

Michael smiled indulgently and nodded. He was very good with Paula, especially I thought as he didn't have any brothers or sisters of his own.

'Well, I can see you're being well looked after,' Stella said, straightening as she got up from the floor. 'Your dad is doing fine, so try not to worry. He's assuming you'll be going to school as usual tomorrow.' Michael nodded. 'Well, if there's nothing else I'll be going.' Stella paused, allowing Michael the chance to think of anything he wanted to ask, but he didn't. 'All right, then,' she said. 'I'll phone Cathy on Monday to confirm that your dad is out of hospital.'

Michael's Daddy

Michael nodded and then said cheerfully, 'We're going swimming on Saturday, like I used to with my dad.'

'Fantastic,' Stella said. 'You have a lovely weekend, and don't worry about your dad: he's being very well looked after.'

She said goodbye to the children and we left them sitting on the sofa as I saw Stella to the front door. We could hear Adrian and Michael telling each other of the daring diving stunts they were going to perform when we went swimming, while Paula, less sure of the water, sat quietly listening.

'It'll do Michael good to have a weekend away from all the responsibility,' Stella confided as I saw her out. 'I haven't seen him look so excited about anything in a long while. Usually all his talk is of his dad's medication – which tablets he has to take and when. This will give him a complete break and a chance to be a child again. Thanks for all you're doing.'

'There's no need to thank me,' I said, embarrassed. 'Michael's a lovely lad. I just wish I was looking after him in different circumstances.'

Stella nodded. 'So do I, Cathy. So do I. It's all so very sad.'

Having seen Stella out I returned to the sitting room and announced it was Paula's bedtime. 'School and nursery tomorrow,' I reminded them, 'so no one is going to be very late.' Adrian and Michael pulled a face. 'Boys,' I continued, 'once Paula is clear of the bathroom and is in bed, I would like you two to start getting ready. Adrian is usually in bed at eight on a school night,' I added, addressing Michael.

'So am I,' Michael admitted, 'but what if my dad phones when I'm in bed?'

'I'll get you up. Don't worry, you will speak to your dad when he phones: of course you will. I'll take your bag up now and put it in your room. Paula, say goodnight to Adrian and Michael.'

'Good night,' she said reluctantly, not wanting to leave them. She stood and offered her cheek for kissing – first to Adrian as she usually did, and then to Michael, who gave her a little peck.

'Good girl,' I said.

She came over and gave a little wave. 'Night, night,' she called as we left the sitting room.

'Night,' the boys chorused behind us. 'Sleep tight. Sweet dreams,' Michael added, which I guessed was probably what his father said to him at night.

Upstairs, I put Michael's holdall in his room and then ran Paula's bath, all the while listening out for the phone. It was 7.15 and Stella had said she thought Patrick would phone at the end of visiting time – about 7.30. I hoped he didn't leave it too late as, in my experience, children can become very fretful, with worries and sadness escalating if they become over-tired. Problems and anxieties always seem more manageable in the morning after a good night's sleep. Fortunately at 7.45, just as I was tucking Paula into bed, the phone rang.

'Cathy! The phone!' Michael shouted from downstairs. 'Shall I answer it?'

I was already on the landing, going to my bedroom to answer the extension. 'Just a moment,' I called down to him. I wanted to make sure it was Patrick.

I picked up the extension and said hello. Even before he spoke I knew it was him, for I heard the small gasp as he caught his breath before he spoke.

'Hi, Patrick. How are you?' I bubbled. 'Good to hear from you.'

'And you, Cathy,' he said, taking another breath. 'Thank you for looking after Michael at such short notice.'

'No problem.'

'I think I'm going to have to postpone our dinner date on Saturday,' he said with a small laugh. 'Pity, because I'd bought a nice bottle of wine especially.'

'The lengths some people will go to to avoid my cooking!' I said. He laughed again but I could hear it was a lot of effort for him to talk and his breathing was more laboured than when I'd seen him before. 'I'll put Michael on,' I said. 'He's waiting by the phone downstairs. Perhaps we could have a chat when you've finished talking to him?'

There was another pause in which Patrick took a long-drawn-in breath before he spoke. 'Would it be all right if we had a chat tomorrow, Cathy?' he said. 'I'm not so good at present. I'm exhausted. The doctors have told me that once I've have this blood I'll feel much better.'

'Yes, of course. You look after yourself. I'll put Michael on.'

'Thank you. Did the social worker bring Michael's clothes?'

'Yes. Don't worry. He's fine. He's got everything he needs. I'll fetch him.'

'Thank you.'

Replacing the receiver in my bedroom, I went on to the landing and called down to Michael, who was waiting patiently at the foot of the stairs. 'Pick up the phone on the hall table.' I said. 'It's your dad.' I waited until he had done so and had said hello, before I returned to Paula to say goodnight.

'Is that Michael's daddy?' she asked.

'Yes, love.'

'Is he using the portable payphone?'

I smiled. 'Yes. Now I want you to go to sleep. It's getting late and you have nursery tomorrow.'

She snuggled down and we hugged and kissed each other goodnight; then I came out and hovered for a moment on the landing. I could see Michael in the hall below. He was standing with his back to me and was very quiet as he listened to his father on the phone. I couldn't hear what Patrick was saying, but I guessed he was trying to reassure his son, for as I went downstairs and past Michael he was saying: 'So you promise you will be home on Monday?'

Chapter Nine

A Prayer Answered

I continued into the sitting room, where Adrian was reading a magazine. I pushed the door to so that Michael could speak to his father in private. There was no need for me to observe or monitor his father's phone call, as I was sometimes asked to do by the social services with some of the children I fostered. Michael wasn't an abused child who needed protecting from abusing parents – far from it: he couldn't have been more loved and cared for, which made it all the more sad.

Michael was only on the phone for about five minutes before he joined Adrian and me in the sitting room. I could tell as soon as he walked in he was sad and anxious again. Gone was the little boy eagerly looking forward to swimming on Saturday and in his place stood the child carer weighed down with worrying and the responsibility of his father's illness.

'Dad's very tired,' he said, standing aimlessly in the middle of the room. 'He couldn't talk for long.'

I stood and went over and rested my hand lightly on his shoulder. 'I know, love. He isn't feeling so good right now, but once the blood transfusion takes effect he'll feel much better.'

Michael gave a small nod but didn't say anything. It was just after eight o'clock and I thought the best thing for Michael now was for him to try to get some sleep; as well as looking sad he was looking very tired. I told the boys I wanted them to start getting ready for bed. Adrian closed his magazine and I went with them upstairs. While Adrian showered I went with Michael to his bedroom with the intention of unpacking his bag, but as soon as I began taking out his clothes to hang in the wardrobe Michael grew more anxious.

'Can't my things stay in my bag?' he asked, worried. 'I'm only here for the weekend.' Perhaps he saw finality in unpacking, as though it might prolong his visit, and possibly his father's stay in hospital.

'Yes, if you prefer,' I said. 'Shall we just take out what you need for tonight and tomorrow?' He nodded. I took out his pyjamas, wash bag and a change of school uniform for the following day. As I straightened, Michael quickly zipped the bag shut, leaving his other things inside.

Adrian finished showering and I went with Michael to the bathroom, showed him how to work the control on the shower and made sure he had everything he needed. I came out, leaving him to wash and change into his pyjamas. I checked on Paula, who was fast asleep on her side, her little mouth slightly open, and breathing gently; then I went through to Adrian's room. He was propped up in bed reading, as he did most nights. I kissed him goodnight and reminded him to switch off his light by 9.00. I then went in to my bedroom, which is next to the bathroom, and sat on the bed and waited for Michael to finish. A strange house with new routines can be very unsettling for any child, and it would be even more so for Michael, who was already very anxious about his father.

A few minutes later he came out of the bathroom, clutching his wash bag, and hesitated.

'Do you want to leave your wash bag in the bathroom for morning?' I asked.

Michael shook his head.

'OK. I'll see you into bed and say goodnight. If you need anything in the night, knock on my door. I'm in here.' I pointed behind me to my bedroom.

Michael nodded and I led the way round the landing and to his bedroom. 'It's bound to be a bit strange on your first night,' I said, 'so if you wake and wonder where you are, call me. Do you sleep with your curtains open or closed?'

'Closed,' Michael said, unzipping his holdall and tucking in his wash bag before zipping it shut again. 'But I usually have a gap in the middle of the curtains so I can see the stars. Can I have that here?'

'Yes, of course, love.' I drew the curtains, leaving a gap in the centre. It was pitch dark outside, but a clear night, so many of the stars were visible, twinkling and glowing brightly in the inky-black sky.

Michael joined me at the window and looked up. 'My dad likes the stars,' he said quietly. 'He says they make him think of heaven.'

A lump immediately rose in my throat. 'They are certainly very beautiful,' I agreed. 'And for me seeing something so wonderful and vast helps me put my own problems into perspective.'

'Do you believe in heaven?' Michael suddenly asked, turning to look at me.

I knew he was looking for reassurance. 'I like to think there is a heaven,' I said. 'Do you believe there is?'

'Yes,' Michael said firmly. 'My mummy is there. And when it's my daddy's turn the angels will come from heaven and take him to be with her. That's what my daddy believes and I do too.'

I smiled sadly, and we stood side by side for a moment, looking up at the night sky, so vast, so unfathomable, while beside me stood a little boy who believed his daddy would be going to join his mummy in heaven. It was one of those moments that touches the soul and stays with you for ever.

Presently Michael moved away from the window and towards the bed. 'I'll say my prayers now and go to sleep,' he said. I stood to one side as he crossed himself and then knelt on the floor beside the bed. Resting his elbows on the bed itself he said:

'Bless this family that I love and comfort them each day.
As daytime turns to night-time please bring them peace, I pray.
When morning comes tomorrow, may all their cares be small.
Guide us with Your wisdom, Lord. Bless us one and all.'

It was a very touching prayer that Michael knew by heart and I was moved by his sincerity. Michael paused and with his eyes still closed and his hands clasped together finished his prayer by saying: 'Dear Lord, I know you want my daddy, but I'm staying at Cathy's and haven't said goodbye. So please don't send your angels for him yet.'

Michael crossed himself again, stood and climbed into bed, while I had never before felt so humbled by a young child's faith and courage. Michael was being so brave and I could see his faith was playing a big part in helping him through. It was then I realized I didn't know if I was supposed to be taking Michael to church on Sunday as Patrick had asked at the meeting. I made a mental note to ask Stella if she phoned the following day or Patrick, when he phoned the following evening.

'Good night, love,' I said, tucking Michael in.

'Night, Cathy. Thank you for looking after me.'

'There's no need to thank me,' I said. 'I'm very pleased to have you. Now try to get some sleep and I'll wake you in plenty of time in the morning. If you need anything in the night, call me.'

He nodded. I kissed his forehead and began towards the door.

'Cathy,' he called.

I paused. 'Yes, love?'

'Where's Adrian and Paula's daddy? Is he in heaven?'

Not in a million years, I thought unkindly, but didn't say. 'No, he doesn't live with us any more, although Adrian and Paula still see him.'

'That's sad. My friend at school lives with his mummy because his dad left them. They're getting divorced.'

I gave a small nod, said goodnight again and came out. Michael had touched a raw nerve, for before long I too would have to start divorce proceedings so that I could draw a line under my marriage legally, as I'd had to emotionally, and begin to move on.

Michael must have been exhausted, for he didn't wake or call out in the night and was still asleep the following morning at 7.00. I gently woke him and said it was time to get ready for school. He stretched and yawned, said good morning and got up straight away. He washed and dressed quickly and was the first one down to breakfast. He was also the first one to finish breakfast, brush his teeth, and be ready with his coat and school bag in the hall. I guessed he was used to getting himself ready on time in the morning, while Adrian and Paula, like many children of their age, still needed cajoling and reminding of the time if we weren't going to be late.

Michael seemed relaxed and was quite chatty as I drove across town to his school. We arrived at 8.00, and I found a place in the street to park a little way past the main entrance to the school. We all got out and saw Michael into the playground, where we said goodbye. He joined other children, who were playing under the watchful eye of a playground supervisor until the bell went. Returning to my car, I drove back across town to Adrian's school, which was only five minutes from our home. Paula and I waited with Adrian in the playground until the whistle went at 8.50, when Paula and I said goodbye to Adrian, and continued round the back of the school to where Paula's nursery was housed in a separate building. I took Paula into the nursery, kissed her goodbye and returned to my car.

I drove to the high street, where among other things I bought a pair of swimming shorts for Michael. Fortunately, as it was April the shops had their swimwear in, ready for summer. Not knowing Michael's choice I opted for a plain dark-blue pair of fashionable boxer-style shorts rather than anything bright or patterned. It was nearly 10.45 by the time I arrived home and I was looking forward to a cup of coffee before I had to return in an hour to collect Paula from nursery. But as I opened the front door the phone began ringing. Picking it up with one hand, I slipped off my coat with the other. It was Jill, asking how Michael had been.

'He was a bit tearful to begin with, yesterday evening,' I said, 'but he brightened up and ate a good dinner. He slept well and seems more relaxed this morning.'

'And he's at school?'

'Yes. Patrick wanted him to go in. Michael's very good at getting himself up and ready in the morning.'

'I expect he's had to be with his dad being so ill,' Jill said. 'I've got the paperwork to cover Michael's stay, so I'll let you have a copy next time I see you. I'm treating this weekend as respite, so there'll just be the one form.' The paperwork Jill referred to was a legal requirement for all foster carers looking after a child. Because Michael was only with me for the weekend (on this occasion) Jill had classified his stay as 'respite', which was a single form, compared to the more extensive paperwork needed if a child was staying for longer. 'Have a good weekend and I'll phone on Monday,' Jill concluded. 'Obviously if you do need us over the weekend phone the emergency number, but I can't see Michael causing you any problems.'

'No,' I agreed. 'Far from it.' The usual reasons for phoning the agency's emergency number were a child behaving very badly and the carer needing advice, or a teenager not being home when they were supposed to be and therefore missing. Neither of which would apply to Michael.

We said goodbye and I put down the phone; but as I hung my coat on the hall stand, the phone rang again. This time it was Stella, asking, as Jill had done, how Michael was. I repeated what I'd told Jill and then asked, 'Do you want me to take Michael to church on Sunday?'

'I'm not sure,' Stella said. 'I'll be phoning Patrick later. I'll ask him and phone you back if he wants you to.'

As it turned out, there was no need for Stella to call me back, for ten minutes after Stella had phoned, when the kettle hadn't quite boiled, the phone rang again, and it was Patrick. I knew immediately he was feeling a bit better.

'Top of the morning to you, Cathy,' he chirped, his Irish accent shining through. 'How are you on this glorious spring day?' In truth, I'd been so busy I hadn't actually noticed what a fine morning it was.

'I'm very good,' I said, relieved to hear him sounding so bright. 'And I can hear you're pretty good too.'

'To be sure, I am. Whatever they're giving me is good stuff. All I need now is a pint of Guinness and I'll be perfect.' I laughed. 'In fact I'm thinking of coming home before Monday,' he added.

'You do as the doctors tell you,' I lightly cautioned.

'I will, Cathy. So how's my little man?'

'Michael's fine. After you'd spoken last night he went to bed, said his prayers and slept well. He had porridge for breakfast and was in school in good time.'

'You wonderful woman! How soon can I marry you?' Patrick joked.

'Calm down,' I laughed. 'You don't want a relapse.'

'Ah, Cathy, it would be worth it, that's for sure,' he sighed.

I laughed again; then said seriously, 'I'm so pleased you're feeling better. You gave us all a shock yesterday.'

'I gave myself a shock too, Cathy, I can tell you. I thought my days were numbered – more than they are all ready. But clearly the dear Lord doesn't want me yet.'

'That might be something to do with Michael's prayer,' I said.

'Oh yes? What's he been saying now?'

'He explained he was staying with me and hadn't had a chance to say goodbye to you, so not to send the angels yet.'

'His prayers are usually about me getting better, poor kid. You'd have thought his faith would have been shaken by now.'

'Well, clearly someone up there was listening, for here you are fighting fit and raring to go.'

'Possibly,' Patrick said and changed the subject, so that I wondered if he questioned his faith sometimes, which would have been understandable.

We continued talking easily and I asked Patrick if he wanted me to take Michael to church on Sunday. He said again he hoped to be out of hospital by then but if he wasn't Michael could miss one week and they would go to church together the following Sunday. We chatted about lots of things, just as we had before when we'd met, and were on the phone for over half an hour. Doubtless we could have continued chatting all day, for Patrick was very easy to talk to, but I checked my watch and realized I needed to leave in five minutes to collect Paula from nursery.

'You have to go straight away?' Patrick asked, sounding disappointed.

'I'm afraid so.'

'All right, I'll phone this evening to speak to Michael. I'll try and make it earlier if possible.'

'That's fine.'

We said goodbye and I grabbed my coat from the hall stand, at the same time pushing my feet into my shoes. I liked to walk to collect Paula from nursery whenever possible, only now it would need to be a very brisk walk if I wasn't to be late. I checked my keys were still in my coat pocket and came out of the house, pulling the door to behind me. Patrick was right: it was a beautiful day, and I could have almost got away without wearing a coat.

As I walked and felt the warm sun on my face and smelt the fresh spring air, I could still hear Patrick's voice – snippets from our conversation. His gentle Irish accent caressed the words and sentences as he spoke, producing a gentle sing-song lilt. I couldn't imagine him ever shouting or saying harsh things. His was the voice of calm and caring, of someone who empathized and appreciated another person's point of view. It was also the voice of someone who'd experienced sorrow and had suffered. Yet he'd sounded so well and full of life on the phone it was impossible to believe his future would be any different. I heard again his disappointment when I'd had to bring our conversation to an end. Then I heard Jill's words of warning: 'Patrick is likely to be very needy ... I wouldn't want you getting hurt.' But I wasn't daft and there was no harm in Patrick and me taking pleasure from each other's company, was there?

Chapter Ten

A Child Again

Friday continued pretty much as planned. I collected Paula from nursery (I wasn't late), and then two hours later I collected Michael and Adrian from their schools. Both boys were pleased it was Friday and the start of the weekend. I told Michael his father had phoned and would be phoning again in the evening to speak to him. I said how much better he'd sounded, although I didn't say he was hoping to leave hospital before Monday, as I didn't want to build up Michael's hopes if there was a chance he could be disappointed. When we arrived home I showed Michael the swimming shorts I'd bought and he didn't laugh or cringe, so I assumed I'd made a reasonable choice and he wouldn't feel embarrassed wearing them. I knew from Adrian how fashion conscious boys can be, even at the age of eight.

Patrick phoned at 5.00 p.m. and chatted to Michael for over half an hour while I made dinner. When Michael finally said goodbye he was a different child to the one who'd spoken on the phone to his father the evening before, when he'd come away depressed, weighed down and anxious he might never seen his father again. Now he was smiling and relaxed, as a child should be, and scampered off to continue playing with Adrian and Paula.

The three children played together before and after dinner, and then when I took Paula upstairs to bed, the boys continued playing downstairs with a construction kit and board games. As there was no need to be up early for school the following day, I let the boys stay up well past their bedtime. Clearly Adrian was enjoying Michael's company as much as Michael was enjoying his, for while Adrian was very good with Paula and often played with her, it was nice for him to have the companionship of a boy his age with similar interests. It was nearly 10.00 before I finally said it was time for bed and sent them upstairs with the caution that they should be quiet, as Paula was fast asleep. Once they were washed and changed I went up to say goodnight, first to Adrian and then to Michael. Tonight Michael's prayers were different from those of the night before when he'd been so very worried. Now, he knelt beside his bed and, crossing himself, said simply: 'Thank you, Lord, for making my daddy better and letting me have fun.'

The following morning we weren't all up and dressed until nearly 11.00. We had a light breakfast and then I drove to the leisure centre for swimming. It was the same pool Michael used to go to regularly when his father had been well enough to take him and the lady on reception recognized Michael and asked how his father was. 'Fine,' Michael said, eager to get into the pool. Then remembering his manners added, 'Thank you for asking. I'll tell Dad.'

Once changed we walked through the footbath and then into the pool. Paula and I stayed in the shallow end and swam widths while Adrian and Michael went deeper and practised diving off the edge. They were both reasonably good swimmers but nevertheless I watched them carefully, for I know that when boys get together bravado can sometimes result in safety and wisdom being left behind. Paula could swim but only recently without armbands, so she felt happier staying in the shallow end, where she could put her feet down and touch the bottom if necessary.

We stayed in the water for an hour and a half and then Paula gave a little shiver. 'Are you getting cold?' I asked. She nodded and her teeth began to chatter. I helped her climb out, wrapped her in her towel, and then we walked along the side of the pool until we were parallel with the boys in the water. I'm sure they could have stayed in the pool all day but when I called them over they came. I suggested we had lunch in the cafeteria and they admitted they were hungry and scrambled out.

It was about 3.00 p.m. when we arrived home and as it was still a fine day we went into the garden. The boys kicked a ball around while Paula helped me do some gardening. We swept up the fallen leaves from winter, pulled up some weeds, and then I cut the daffodils and tulips, which had finished blooming and were now being replaced by carnations and other late April flowers. The earth smelt fresh and clean. The grass was overdue for its first cut of the year and when Paula joined the boys, who were now playing in the sandpit, I decided to cut it.

Hauling the lawnmower from the shed, I found the oil can and began oiling the moving parts, as I'd seen John do. I then unwound the extension lead, plugged in the external circuit breaker and, warning the children not to come close, began cutting the lawn. Mowing the grass had always been one of John's jobs (he'd said he liked doing it), but as with the other jobs that had been 'his', since he'd left it had become my job. And while I continually surprised myself at just what I could do – including unblocking sinks and drains, minor electrical repairs and, most commonly, repairing broken toys, my self-sufficiency was a double-edged sword. For while I took pride in my achievements, I no longer had anyone with whom to share responsibility or just chat and discuss problems, which I greatly missed, as I'm sure most single parents do.

When I'd finished cutting the grass and Michael saw me cleaning and collapsing the lawnmower, he said admiringly, 'You're like my dad: he can do everything too.'

I smiled and said quietly, 'It's a case of having to, love.'

Patrick phoned at about 6.00 and Michael chatted happily, telling him all the things he'd done that day. When he'd finished talking to his father he called me to the phone. 'Dad says can he talk to you if you're not busy?'

'Which I'm sure you are,' Patrick said as I picked up the phone.

I laughed. 'No, not too busy, more exhausted. We've had a fun but tiring day.'

'Yes, Michael was telling me. Thank you very much. He sounds so happy.'

'We all enjoyed it,' I said.

'Look, Cathy,' Patrick said, 'I haven't said anything to Michael but if my blood test is clear I can come out tomorrow.'

'Fantastic,' I said.

'I don't want to interfere with your plans but I was thinking of collecting Michael late morning. As soon as I've got a time I'll call you and then come over in a cab. How would that fit in? I don't want you waiting in if you were going out.'

'That's fine,' I said. 'We'll be in. I was planning a relaxing day tomorrow and I think Michael has some homework to do. But instead of you taking a cab why don't I bring Michael home in my car? It's only a fifteen-minute drive.'

'I don't want to put you to any trouble.'

'It's no trouble,' I assured him.

'Well, if you're sure that would be a great help. I'll give you something for petrol.'

'No, you won't,' I said.

'All right, I'll buy you flowers instead.'

I laughed. 'Well, if you insist.'

'I do. I'll say goodbye now and let you get on. I'll phone you in the morning as soon as I've got the all-clear.'

'OK. Take care and see you tomorrow.'

As a foster carer I wouldn't normally suggest I take a child home unless the social worker had specifically asked me to, but looking after Michael wasn't a 'normal' fostering placement. Michael was in care on a voluntary basis, and with no concerns for his safety there weren't the same constraints, so there was no reason why I couldn't help out Patrick by returning Michael home.

After we'd had dinner the four of us watched television together. There was a game show on which Michael liked and watched with his father. When the programme had finished I told Paula to say goodnight and I took her up to bed as Adrian and Michael began a game of Monopoly.

'Why can't I play?' Paula moaned as we went upstairs.

'It's well past your bedtime. How about I read you extra stories instead?' Which seemed to appease Paula. I find parenting is often about compromise.

Paula washed and changed into her nightdress and then I read to her for half an hour. When I returned downstairs the boys, now seasoned property developers, were doing very well in their game of Monopoly. Adrian owned three houses, one on each of three sites, while Michael had concentrated on one site on which he had a hotel. Unfortunately neither of the boys was able to collect the income from their properties, as both were languishing in jail. I sat on the sofa with the newspaper, occasionally glancing up, as the game progressed. Michael came out of jail on the next throw of the dice and Adrian followed two throws later. Adrian then landed on Mayfair but Michael wanted it, as he already owned Park Lane, so he tried to do a deal with Adrian. The air was charged as they bargained, so that I could have believed they were talking about real money rather than paper Monopoly money. It's always nice to see children enjoying themselves, but Michael's joy was especially poignant given what was happening in the rest of his life. Michael finally bought Mayfair at an inflated price and the game continued for another two hours, with both boys having to sell property to pay for repairs. Eventually, when it was after 10.00 and there was still no sign of an outright winner, I announced a draw, which allowed both boys to proclaim themselves the winner to whoops of joy.

They were still excited as they ran upstairs to get changed, ready for bed, and I had to remind them to be quiet as Paula was asleep. When I went into Michael's room to say goodnight he was changed, ready for bed and about to say his prayers before getting in. I waited by the door. He crossed himself, knelt by the bed and put his hands together. 'Thank you, Lord, for making my daddy better and for all the nice things I've done today. I hope you don't mind me being happy. I still love my daddy but it's nice to play sometimes.'

I was deeply moved.

The following morning, Sunday, after breakfast I suggested to Michael he did his homework before he started playing. He pulled a face but nevertheless fetched his school bag from where we'd left it in the hall on Friday. He sat at the dining table and got on with it, while Adrian read his school book and I washed Paula's hair.

A Child Again

When Michael had finished his homework he asked me to check it, which he said his father normally did. He'd had to write a story about a dog's adventures, based on a Lassie storybook the class had been reading. Michael had written a full page and it was of a good standard; apart from a couple of spelling mistakes the rest was fine. 'Well done,' I said. He made the corrections, returned his homework book to his bag, and his bag to the hall, ready for Monday, when he thought I would be taking him to school.

The boys then went into the garden and kicked a football around, while Paula played with the farmyard set and I cleared up in the kitchen, listening out for the phone. Although Patrick had said he didn't know what time he'd be discharged from hospital he'd seemed to think it would be late morning, so I guessed I'd be taking Michael home before lunch. But as twelve noon came and went and Patrick hadn't phoned I decided to make some lunch. I was also starting to worry. While logic told me that Patrick's discharge from hospital had simply been delayed – possibly because of the test results not being back – there was always the nagging doubt that he had had a relapse and was ill again, or worse. So that when the phone finally rang shortly after 1.00 p.m. when we were having lunch I jumped up from the table and ran down the hall to answer it.

'Hello?' I gasped, chewing and swallowing.

'Cathy?'

'Yes.' It was Patrick. I breathed a sign of relief.

'You sound different.'

I swallowed again. 'Sorry. I was eating.'

'Oh, I've disturbed you.'

'Don't worry. How are you?'

'Good. My blood results have just come back from the lab. They're fine and the doc says I can go.'

'Fantastic.'

'I'm just waiting for some tablets to be made up and then I'll be on my way.'

'How are you getting home?' I asked, for I now realized that while I'd offered to take Michael home, I hadn't offered to collect Patrick from hospital.

'My friends Eamon and Colleen are collecting me. I'm going to phone them now.'

'Good. What time shall I bring Michael home?'

'I'm not sure how long my meds will be. Shall we say three o'clock, to be on the safe side?'

'Yes, that's fine with me.'

Patrick paused thoughtfully before he said, 'Cathy, do you have my address?'

I laughed. 'No. Good thinking.' Because Michael had come to me on Friday as an emergency I hadn't been given the placement forms I would normally have by the social services, which, with other details, contained the child's home address. Although Patrick and I had swapped telephone numbers at our first meeting, and I knew the road where he lived from talking to him, I didn't have the house number.

'Forty-six Queen's Road,' he said, also laughing.

I jotted '46' on the notepad by the phone. 'See you at three, then.'

'Thanks, Cathy.'

I do so like being the messenger of good news and as I returned to the dining table to finish my lunch I had a huge grin on my face. The children looked at me expectantly, wondering why I'd fled from the table and then returned grinning inanely.

'Good news,' I announced unnecessarily. I looked at Michael. 'That was your dad on the phone. The doctor has said he is well enough to leave. I am taking you home this afternoon.'

A Child Again

Michael stopped eating and looked at me, his expression pleased but not as happy as I would have anticipated. 'So I can't stay and play this afternoon?' he asked after a moment.

'Until two forty-five, yes, and then we need to go.'

'You can come and play again another time,' Adrian said, seeing Michael's disappointment.

Michael nodded but was quiet. He put down his sandwich and stopped eating. I could see the conflict of emotions he was experiencing. Of course he wanted to be home with his father – they had a strong bond, and loved each other dearly – but at the same time being with us over the weekend had allowed Michael to let go of his worries and responsibilities and just play as a child should. Despite Patrick's sensitivity and wish to protect Michael as much as he could, life at home would doubtless be very different from the weekend Michael had spent with us. Yet while I was aware how confusing these conflicting emotions must be for Michael, just as I think Adrian was, there was little I could say to help beyond, 'Finish your lunch, good boy, and then you'll have time to play before we go.'

Chapter Eleven

Friends and Neighbours

I rang the doorbell at 46 Queen's Road a few minutes after three o'clock. Michael was standing on one side of me, holding his school bag and coat, Adrian stood just behind him, carrying the holdall, and Paula stood by my other side, holding my hand tightly, a little nervous at going to a new house.

The children had played after lunch and when I'd told Michael it was time to go he'd exclaimed happily, 'I'm seeing my dad soon!' In the car Paula and Adrian had asked Michael about his house. Did he have a garden? Any pets? What was his bedroom like? Michael had said he would show us around his house, but I wasn't so sure we would be invited in. 'Your dad might be too tired to have us all in now,' I cautioned.

But as the door now opened, an attractive woman in her early forties said, 'Hi, come in. You must be Cathy.' For a second I thought it must be Patrick's girlfriend, the existence of whom he'd forgotten to mention, until she said, 'I'm Colleen. Pleased to meet you all.'

'And you,' I said going in. 'These are my children, Adrian and Paula.' Colleen smiled at them and then kissed and hugged Michael.

'Good to see you again,' she said to him, and then to me, 'How's he been?'

'He did very well,' I confirmed. 'We kept him busy. How's Patrick?' I looked down the hall to where Michael was taking Adrian.

'He's in the sitting room. Come through.'

With Paula still holding my hand I followed Colleen down the hall to the room at the rear of the house. Patrick and another man were in the sitting room and stood as we entered. Michael fell into his father's arms and they hugged each other hard. After a moment Patrick let go of Michael and shook Adrian's hand; then coming over gave me a big kiss on the cheek before bending down to Paula, 'And how are you, little miss?' he said.

Paula, still shy, snuggled into my side. 'She's good, thank you,' I confirmed. 'You look well.'

'Yes, I feel it,' Patrick said. His skin had a healthy colour and his breathing was even, so that apart from still being thin there was no other indication he was so ill. 'You've met Colleen,' Patrick said. 'This is Colleen's husband, Eamon.' The other man, of a similar age to Patrick, now shook my hand.

'Good to meet you, Cathy,' he said. 'We've heard a lot about you.'

'Oh, have you?' I said, embarrassed.

'Would you like some tea?' Colleen asked me.

'Yes please.'

'What would your children like? I've been shopping and bought in apple, orange and pineapple juice, which I know Michael likes.'

I looked at Adrian and Paula. 'Apple, please,' Adrian said, while Paula, still shy, just nodded.

'She'll have apple too, please,' I said. 'Thank you.'

Patrick waved me to the sofa and I sat down. Paula nestled into my side while Patrick and Eamon returned to the armchairs they'd been sitting in as we'd arrived. 'Shall I show you my bedroom?' Michael asked Adrian.

Adrian nodded.

'Do you want to come?' Michael asked Paula, but she shook her head.

'You two go,' I said. 'Paula can stay with me until she thaws out.'

Adrian followed Michael out of the sitting room and when they were out of earshot Patrick asked me, 'How's he been, really?'

'He's been fine,' I confirmed. 'The first evening he was a bit tearful to begin with, but once he'd spoken to you on the phone and knew you were getting better he brightened up.'

Patrick nodded thoughtfully. 'To be honest I wondered afterwards if I'd made the right decision in not letting him visit me in hospital. There was an elderly man in the bed next to me who had Alzheimer's and kept crying out. I thought it would be upsetting for Michael. But on the other hand it would have given him the experience of visiting me in hospital, which he will have to do one day.'

I didn't immediately reply. At that point, with Patrick having just come out of hospital and looking so well, nothing was further from my mind than him having to be re-admitted. Eamon apparently felt the same way too, for he said, 'You are well now, Pat; that's all that matters. Michael is fine and has clearly had a nice time at Cathy's. But haven't you forgotten something?'

Patrick looked questioningly at Eamon, who then nodded towards me.

'Oh yes,' Patrick exclaimed, standing. 'Thanks. I'd forgotten.' Patrick left the sitting room and then returned a minute later, carrying a bunch of red roses, which he placed in my lap.

'Thanks for everything,' he said, kissing my cheek. 'I'm sorry I couldn't make dinner on Saturday.'

I smiled. 'Thank you,' I said. 'They're beautiful.' I was really touched. 'Do you think I could leave them in water until we go? They may wilt in this warm room.'

'Of course,' Colleen said, having returned with a tray of drinks and a plate of biscuits. 'I'll stand them in water in the kitchen.'

I thanked Patrick again as Colleen set the tray on the coffee table, and then took the flowers to the kitchen. Patrick went to the coffee table and, bending over, lifted the lid on the teapot and stirred the tea.

'Milk and sugar?' he asked me.

'Just milk, please.'

He stirred the tea again and then began carefully pouring it into the cups before adding milk. I found something very touching in watching Patrick leaning over the coffee table, intent on this homely task: something comfortable, warm and secure. It might have been simply that a man was making me a cup of tea, which hadn't happened in a long time, or it might have been the care and gentleness with which Patrick performed this task, as he appeared to perform all tasks. Whatever it was, I felt I was being well looked after, pampered almost, as he handed me the cup and saucer, and then began pouring Paula a glass of juice.

'Here, let me help,' Colleen said to Patrick, returning from taking the flowers to the kitchen.

'No,' Patrick said. 'I'm not helpless. You could tell the boys their drinks are ready and then sit yourself down on the sofa. You've done enough for me today.'

Colleen did as Patrick asked and went into the hall, where she called upstairs to the boys that their drinks were ready when they were. 'Thanks. Be down soon,' they called. Colleen returned to the sitting room and Patrick handed her a cup of tea and then passed round the plate of biscuits.

As I sipped my tea I glanced around Patrick's neat sitting room, which was very comfortable and almost had a 'woman's touch'. There were china ornaments on the mantelpiece above an ornate gas fire; framed pictures on the walls, including photographs of Michael and Patrick; a large potted plant in one corner of the room; and a bowl of fresh fruit in the centre of the coffee table.

'He keeps the place very nice, doesn't he?' Colleen said, almost reading my thoughts.

'Yes, very,' I agreed.

'Thank you, ladies,' Patrick said, laughing. 'I do my best.'

'So how long have you been fostering?' Eamon asked me. 'My sister in Ireland fosters.'

'Oh, does she?' I asked, interested. It is always good to meet or hear of others who foster.

'She's been doing it for nearly ten years now. She's had some very sad cases and also some very difficult children. One lad's been with her for five years and calls her Mum. It will be dreadful if he has to leave.'

I agreed it was always difficult saying goodbye to a child and I said I wished more was done to try to keep foster children in touch with their carers. We then chatted generally about fostering – the highs and lows, the rewards and frustrations. Having a sister who fostered, Eamon had some sad stories to tell, for child abuse is worldwide and Ireland was no exception.

Time passed. Michael and Adrian came downstairs for their drinks and then returned to play upstairs, taking Paula, who'd finally thawed out, with them. Colleen talked about her job in a travel agency and then Eamon said that they were thinking of going on a cruise the following winter. I understood from their conversation that they didn't have any children, although they'd been married for fifteen years. When Patrick left the room to go to the toilet, Colleen turned to me and said quietly, 'It's so sad. First Kathleen and now Patrick. I can't believe it.'

'Did you know Patrick's wife?' I asked her.

'Yes, very well. The four of us were close. Eamon was Patrick's best man at his wedding and we're Michael's godparents.' Colleen shook her head sadly and looked as though she was about to say more – possibly share her memories or sadness – but the doorbell rang. 'I wonder who that is?' she said, standing and crossing the room.

A few seconds later Eamon and I heard the front door open and Colleen exclaim, 'Hello, good to see you again. How are you both?' So I guessed she knew the visitors.

A male and female voice replied and Eamon said, 'It's Pat's neighbours, Jack and Nora Harvey.' I remembered Stella mentioning a Mr and Mrs Harvey: Mrs Harvey had let Stella into the house to collect Michael's clothes while Jack had visited Patrick in hospital. I wondered if it was the same neighbour who'd found Patrick unconscious and had called the ambulance.

A couple in their late sixties came into the sitting room and Eamon and I stood to greet them. Colleen introduced me, while Eamon clearly knew them very well.

'Ah, so you're Cathy,' Nora said kindly to me. 'Pleased to meet you.'

'And you,' I said. Jack shook my hand warmly.

Patrick came down from upstairs and Jack and Nora Harvey turned to greet him. 'You gave me quite a shock, young man,' Nora said as Patrick hugged her. 'Me, coming in with some soup for you and finding you on the floor like that.'

Patrick laughed at the admonishment. 'I'll try not to do it again, Nora.'

'No, you'd better not!'

Aware these people were old and dear friends of Patrick's and I was a newcomer, I thought I should go now and leave them all to chat together. I waited until Patrick had finished answering Nora's question about how he felt, and then I said, 'Well, it's been nice meeting you all, but I think I should call the children and go now.'

'Must you?' Patrick asked, clearly disappointed. 'Can't you stay a while longer? I would like it if you could.' It was a heart-felt request, not a polite formality. 'Do you have something you have to go to?' he added.

'Well, no,' I said. 'But I don't want to outstay my welcome.'

'You won't do that,' Patrick said quickly. 'Sit yourself down. The children are playing happily: I checked on them while I was upstairs. I'd like you to get to know my good friends better.'

So I did as I was told and sat on the sofa and chatted with Patrick's close friends: Colleen, Eamon, Nora and Jack. They were lovely people, so warm and welcoming, open and honest, and I quickly felt I had known them for years rather than a few hours. To begin with the conversation centred mainly on Patrick's stay in hospital and how he was feeling, but it soon became clear he didn't want to dwell on his illness and deflected further questions about his health and what the doctors had said by changing the subject. We talked about holidays, work, fostering and the children. Shortly after five o'clock Colleen disappeared into the kitchen to make another pot of tea and returned with the tea, two plates of sandwiches and a sponge cake, which was unexpected but very nice. The children joined us to eat and then disappeared again to play. Finally, when it was after 6.30 p.m. I said we really had to be going, as I needed to get the children bathed and into bed, ready for school the following day. I also thought Patrick was starting to look tired.

'Yes, I should get Michael into the shower and his bag unpacked,' Patrick agreed.

'Don't worry about his bag. I'll unpack it,' Colleen offered.

'Thank you,' Patrick said.

'I'll call up to Adrian and Paula,' I said. Standing, I left the sitting room and went to the foot of the stairs. 'Adrian. Paula,' I called up the staircase. 'We need to go now.'

There was no reply, so I guessed they were playing in Michael's room with the door closed. I called up again, slightly louder, but there was still no reply.

'Go up, Cathy,' Patrick said from the sitting room. 'Michael's room is at the front of the house. You can't miss it.'

I went up the carpeted stairs and turned on to the landing. Straight in front, at the end of the landing, was a closed door covered in cut-out pictures and stickers of boys' action heroes: Batman, Superman, Spiderman, Power Rangers, etc. The door to the bedroom on my left was slightly open and as I passed I glanced in and saw it was Patrick's bedroom. Emulsion light-grey walls matched the grey-striped duvet, and there were framed photographs on the bedside cabinet. In front of the cabinet and within easy reach of the bed was an oxygen cylinder with a mask. It was a harsh reminder of Patrick's illness and just for a moment I caught a glimpse of Patrick waking in the night gasping for breath and desperately grabbing the mask.

I knocked on Michael's door and turned the handle. 'Hi,' I said, going in. 'It's time to go now.'

The children looked up from where they sat cross-legged on the floor around a large Scalextric racing-car circuit. The track was looped in a figure 8 and three electric cars, controlled by the handsets they held, raced around the track.

'Can't they stay a while longer?' Michael asked, glancing up.

'Not today, love. It's gone six thirty and I know your dad wants to get you into the shower. School tomorrow.'

Michael and Adrian groaned, although I knew they both liked school, and then Paula, feeling it was the thing to do, gave a little groan too. The cars completed another two circuits and then slowly and reluctantly drew to a halt.

'I think you should help Michael pack away,' I said.

'It's OK,' Michael said. 'I'm allowed to leave my Scalextric up. I play with it after school.'

'Well, if you're sure,' I said. Then to Adrian and Paula, 'Say goodbye to Michael.' For no one was making any move to go.

The children reluctantly put down their handsets and stood. 'Bye,' Adrian and Paula said.

'I'll come down and see you out,' Michael said, which I thought was very polite.

I asked Paula if she needed the bathroom before we left but she said she didn't, so the three children and I went downstairs and into the sitting room, where I introduced Adrian and Paula to Nora and Jack Harvey, as they hadn't met them yet. We all said goodbye and then Patrick and Michael saw us to the front door while Patrick's friends stayed and chatted in the sitting room.

'Thanks for everything, Cathy,' Patrick said again, kissing my cheek. 'I'll phone you during the week and perhaps we can all get together?'

'Yes, that would be nice, and it was good meeting your friends. I've enjoyed it. They are lovely people.'

'Yes, I'm very lucky,' Patrick agreed.

Adrian and Paula said goodbye and then just as we were about to leave Colleen's voice called from the sitting room, 'Wait! You've forgotten the flowers.'

We waited in the hall as Colleen went into the kitchen and returned with the flowers. 'Thanks,' I said to her, and then to Patrick, 'The flowers are lovely. It was very thoughtful of you.'

'It was nothing.'

Colleen returned to the sitting room while Patrick opened the front door and then came with us down the path. He stood at his front gate, slightly leaning against it, as the three of us climbed into the car.

'Drive safely,' he called.

'I will. Take care of yourself.'

We all waved as I pulled away, and seeing Patrick standing there so very healthy, albeit a little tired, I began to think that a little miracle might have happened and the doctors had been wrong in their prognosis.

Chapter Twelve
Good and Bad News

Jill phoned as promised on Monday for an update and I told her very enthusiastically of our weekend, culminating in my taking Michael home and meeting his family's friends. 'Patrick looks so well,' I gushed, 'I'm wondering if he's gone into remission. I've read of cases of spontaneous remission, where the doctors had tried everything and given a person only a few months to live and miraculously the person is cured. There was a case in the paper a couple of weeks ago where a woman had an inoperable brain tumour and was only given weeks to live. That was ten years ago and she's still alive today. When the doctors X-rayed her the tumour had completely gone.'

'Really,' Jill said doubtfully as I finished. 'As far as I'm aware Patrick's prognosis is unchanged.'

'But doctors can be wrong. It does happen,' I insisted.

'Yes, but not very often, which is why these cases make news.'

Although I respected Jill as my support social worker and we had a good professional working relationship, I sometimes found her too practical and down to earth, pessimistic almost. I guessed her attitude had come from years of being a social worker and having to deal with child-abuse cases. They had taken the shine out of her. But I thrive on optimism and see my glass as half full whereas Jill sees hers half empty.

'There's always hope,' I said. 'In every situation.'

'Agreed, and as long as it doesn't affect your judgement there shouldn't be a problem. As I said at the beginning of this case, when I first approached you about looking after Michael, it is very unusual and I don't want you and the kids getting hurt more than you have to.'

'No, I'll remember what you said. Thanks, Jill.' Although of course Patrick was no longer 'a case' but my friend and confidant, to whom I already felt very close.

Shortly after Jill phoned Stella phoned to see how the weekend had gone and I repeated what I'd said to Jill, omitting my hope that Patrick could possibly be in remission.

'He looks well,' I ended.

'Yes, I phoned Patrick this morning and he said the blood transfusion had helped a lot and he felt better than he had done in a long while. I've also spoken to your support social worker, Jill, and explained I'm not sure when we will be needing you to have Michael again. It will depend on how well Patrick does.'

'Yes, I understand that.'

'Well, thanks for having Michael at such short notice,' Stella wound up. 'Hopefully next time he stays with you we'll have a bit more notice.'

'No problem,' I said, and then hesitated. 'Stella, I assume you have no objection if Patrick and I meet up with the children before Michael stays again?'

'No, not at all. That's very kind of you. Keeping the contact going now will make it easier for Michael if or when he does have to stay with you again.'

'Good. That's what we thought,' I said. And in that 'we' – Patrick and I – I heard a unit, a small bond, of a couple, that I hadn't heard in a long while, although, of course, as far as Stella was concerned I was simply a conscientious foster carer doing her job.

While Patrick had said he'd phone me during the week he hadn't said when, so it was a complete surprise when shortly before 1.00 p.m. on that Monday I answered the phone to hear Patrick's voice, bright and breezy with its sing-song Irish accent: 'Hello, Cathy. How are you doing?'

'I'm doing very well,' I said. 'How are you?'

'Good. Very good indeed. In fact I'm feeling so well I was thinking of taking you out to dinner one evening this week, as a thank you.'

'Oh,' I said. 'Oh, I see. What, without the children, you mean?'

He gave a small laugh. 'Yes. Will they let you out alone? Do you have a babysitter?'

I thought; not about finding a babysitter – I had plenty of friends I could ask – but that I hadn't been out with a man since John had left; indeed I hadn't been out socially in the evening without the children at all. I thought for longer than I should, which led Patrick to say, 'It's all right to say no. I'll understand if you don't want to.'

'No, it's not that,' I said quickly. 'I'd like to, really I would.'

'Sure?'

'Yes.'

'I'll let you choose which evening would suit you best and then I'll ask Nora or Colleen to sit with Michael.'

I thought again. 'I think Wednesday or Thursday will probably be best but I'll need to check with my sitter first.'

'OK. Speak to her and then give me a ring and we'll take it from there.'

I said I would and, still reeling from the shock of being asked out and now struggling with the thought of trying to find something in my wardrobe to wear, I made conversation as best I could. Patrick asked me how Monday morning had gone and if we'd got to school on time, and then said Michael hadn't stopped talking about his weekend with us.

'You'd be surprised how much I know about you,' Patrick teased.

'Oh yes? What's Michael been telling you?' I laughed.

'That you always go downstairs for a mug of coffee before you shower and dress in the morning. And when you stir your tea you give the spoon a little clink on the side of the mug to clear the droplet, just as I do.'

'Michael noticed that?' I said, surprised.

'Yes. He also said you always try to be cheerful and look on the bright side but if something upsets you your eyes water as though you're about to cry. And if you're worried about something you don't say anything but you chew your bottom lip, and your favourite expression is: "Come on, best foot forward," as on the TV series *Dad's Army*.'

I laughed again. 'That's not fair. I only say that when I'm trying to get the children to hurry up, if we have to be somewhere.'

'I know. I told Michael I hoped you didn't have to say it to him too often.'

'No, he was great. They all were.'

We chatted for about another twenty minutes and then wound up. Patrick was going to the shops to buy Colleen and Nora a box of chocolates each to thank them for their help at the weekend, and I had things to do in the house before I collected Paula, who'd gone to a friend's for lunch after nursery. We said goodbye and before we hung up Patrick reminded me to phone him as soon as I'd spoken to my sitter – as if I was likely to forget!

The Night the Angels Came

With a mixture of apprehension and excitement, as soon as we'd finished on the phone I ran upstairs and into my bedroom, where I flung open my wardrobe doors and confronted the rail of clothes. What should I wear for my dinner out with Patrick? What could I wear? Most of my clothes were practical everyday garments – jeans, trousers, tops and plain skirts. There were a couple of smart suits for meetings and I had two evening dresses which clearly weren't suitable, plus what I called my Sunday best clothes for special family occasions, none of which seemed right for dinner out with Patrick. I hadn't bought myself any new clothes in a long while and I decided now might be a good opportunity. Then I caught myself and thought that I'd better find a sitter for Adrian and Paula first – otherwise new clothes wouldn't be necessary.

I had a couple of very close friends, Rose and Jenny, whom I could ask to sit. They were friends I'd known from before my marriage and whom I'd stayed in touch with. Rose and Jenny had been encouraging me to start going out in the evening and had offered to babysit before. I phoned Rose first but her line was busy, so I tried Jenny's number and she answered after a few rings.

'Hi, Cath. How are you?' she said on hearing my voice.

'Good. Are you?'

'Yes, Ben and I booked a holiday to Egypt at the weekend.'

'Fantastic. When are you going?'

'Not until the October half-term break, another six months. But the boys are already very excited at the thought of seeing the pyramids and the pharaohs' tombs in the Valley of the Kings.'

Jenny and her husband, Ben, had two boys aged eight and six. When Jenny had finished telling me about the holiday they'd booked I asked her if she could babysit: 'Wednesday or Thursday would be good for me,' I said.

'Sure,' Jenny said without hesitation. 'Thursday would be best. Ben works in head office on Wednesday and doesn't get home until late.'

'Thanks very much,' I said.

There was a small pause before Jenny laughed and then asked, 'So who is he?'

I also laughed. 'It's not like that.'

'No?'

'No. You remember I said I was going to foster a boy called Michael whose father was ill?'

'Yes. They came for a visit, didn't they?'

'That's right. Then at very short notice Michael stayed last weekend when his father, Patrick, went into hospital. Well, he's out now and wants to take me to dinner to say thank you.'

'Great,' Jenny enthused. 'So he's not as ill as the doctors thought he was?'

'He's very much better at present,' I said.

'Good. What time do you want me on Thursday?'

'I'm not sure yet. I'll phone Patrick and get back to you. Is that OK?'

'Sure. Any time after six is fine with me.'

'Thanks, Jenny.'

'You're welcome.'

With only a few minutes before I had to leave to collect Paula from her friend's, I quickly dialled Patrick's landline number, but he didn't pick up, so I guessed he'd already left to go the shops. I hung up and, slipping on my shoes and coat, let myself out, texting Patrick as I went: *I hve a sitter 4 Thrsdy. Wht time? Cathy x*

In the car I slotted my mobile into the hands-free attachment on the dashboard and started the engine, but before I'd reversed off the drive my phone bleeped with an incoming text message.

Taking the car out of gear, I picked up the phone and pressed to read the text. It was from Patrick: *Great. 7pm ok? I'll collect u by cab, save u drivn. P x*

I texted back: *Thanks. Lookin 4wrd to it. C x*

And the thought that Patrick was going to the trouble of arranging a cab so I didn't have to drive made the evening even more special.

I've found in the past that good news is often tempered by bad and vice versa, as if the powers that be want to give you a reality check. Feeling good and looking forward to Thursday, I arrived home with the children shortly after 4.00 p.m. and the landline went. It was Jill. Having spoken to her that morning and updated her on the weekend, I knew she must be phoning with some news. I was right, and it wasn't good news.

'I've been speaking to Stella,' she said. 'You remember we were told that Patrick had an aunt living in Wales – his mother's sister?'

'Yes.'

'Apparently Patrick has contacted her about the possibility of her looking after Michael long term if it becomes necessary, and she is adamant she can't. I'm not sure of the reason. Patrick has told Stella that the only other relatives he has are two distant cousins in America and he hasn't addresses for either of them, so they are non-starters. Stella has therefore explained to Patrick that when it becomes necessary the department will start family finding to find a long-term foster family for Michael.'

'I see,' I said slowly.

If a child cannot be looked after by his or her parents then a member of the wider family is usually considered to be the next best option; this is called kinship caring in fostering. If there is no suitable family member, then a long-term foster family is found. I was (and still am) a short-term carer, although the definition is flexible and children have stayed with me for years. However, if a child is placed permanently at the outset with a foster family, that has to be approved by the permanency panel, which also oversees adoption. This is to ensure the family is a good match for the child, which is vital if the child is to successfully integrate and bond with the family.

It was sad that there was no one in Michael's family to look after him (when it became necessary, as Jill put it) and even sadder that Michael would be moved from us and have to get to know another foster family. However, I realized what a huge commitment it would be if I offered to keep Michael, and I also acknowledged that it might not be considered the best option for him. I was now a one-parent family, and had a son the same age as Michael, which isn't usually considered ideal, but that didn't stop me from staying: 'Patrick is very well at present, but should Michael ever need a permanent family then I think we should be considered.'

'I thought you might say that,' Jill said, 'but I think we will wait and see what happens in the short term first. See how Michael settles with you if Patrick has to go into hospital again. Stella won't be starting family finding until nearer the ...' She stopped but I knew she had been about to say 'the end'.

'All right, Jill. I understand. Was there anything else? I'm just about to start making dinner.'

'No, that's all.'

I felt down after speaking to Jill: the talk of 'when it becomes necessary', and 'near the –', and knowing Michael was without relatives, made me so sad. I thought of my own family – my parents, brother, aunts, uncles, cousins and even, begrudgingly, John, all of whom would have given Adrian and Paula a home if anything happened to me. Yet Michael had no one apart from his father, and how dreadfully worrying must that be for Patrick in his situation.

Chapter Thirteen

An Evening Out

By Tuesday morning I was back on course. I find you can't stay down for very long when you have young children around you. I took Adrian to school and Paula to nursery and then went into town to shop for something to wear for Thursday. Although it was only the end of April, the shops were full of summer clothes to the exclusion of all else: swimwear, beachwear, shorts, T-shirts, sandals, brightly patterned cotton dresses and lightweight knee-length combat trousers. I went from shop to shop and was beginning to think I'd forget about buying new and find something to wear in my wardrobe when I spotted a rail of 'new season' linen dresses. Mindful I had to collect Paula in half an hour, I grabbed four, quickly tried them on and came out triumphant with a pale-yellow dress. Paying, I drove straight to Paula's nursery with a minute to spare. On returning home I spent the afternoon doing what I should have done in the morning – housework and clearing up after the weekend – while Paula amused herself with puzzles and games.

We collected Adrian from school at 3.30 and then the children watched some television while I made dinner. During the meal I told them I would be going out on Thursday evening.

'Patrick is taking me to dinner,' I said, 'as a thank you for looking after Michael at the weekend.'

'Can we come?' Paula asked. 'We helped look after Michael too.'

I smiled. 'I know you did, love, and it was nice of you. But it's too late for you and Adrian: you'll both be in bed.'

'Is Michael going?' Paula asked.

'No, just Patrick and me. Adults go out in the evening some-times without their children,' I added, and was about to illus-trate the point by saying, 'Your father and I used to,' but decided against it. It would have been an unnecessary reminder of the past and Paula had been too young to remember her father and me going out in the evening. Instead I said: 'You go to your friends without me and when you see your dad.'

'Can you come with us when we see Daddy?' Paula asked, as she had asked before.

'No,' Adrian put in, slightly embarrassed, 'Mum and Dad are getting divorced.'

My heart ached for them and I wished things could have been different.

'Michael's Scalextric is whiz,' Adrian said, changing the subject. 'I was thinking that perhaps I could have one for my birthday or Christmas?'

'Yes, good idea,' I said.

Adrian grinned.

That evening I phoned Jenny to confirm the time for Thursday and she said she'd be with me by 6.50 p.m. Then a while later Patrick texted: *I hope u and the kids had a good day? P x* I texted back: *Yes thnks. And u? C x* He replied: *Yes. Very good. P x*

The evening continued as normal with the children's baths, bedtime stories, and hugs and kisses goodnight; then before I went to bed I tried on the new dress with a pair of heels – I'd been wearing trainers in the shop. I looked at myself in the mirror and thought the dress had been a good choice. The few extra pounds around my stomach which I'd been carrying since the birth of Adrian and Paula didn't show, and with a bit of make-up I'd look quite presentable, maybe even attractive, I thought.

I consider myself a level-headed, sensible person but it is true to say that for the next few days – the Tuesday and Wednesday leading up to Thursday evening – I was like a schoolgirl about to go on her first date. It wasn't only that I was looking forward to spending time with Patrick but also the novelty of getting ready to go out socially in the evening, which I hadn't done for so long.

On Thursday I made dinner early for Adrian and Paula, and while they were eating I showered and washed and dried my hair. When they'd finished their meal I helped Paula change into her nightdress, ready for bed, and she went downstairs in her dressing gown; Adrian, four years older, would get himself ready for bed later, after I'd gone. I then returned upstairs and carefully put on new stockings, the new dress, make-up and the heeled shoes, and giving my hair a final brush I was ready to answer the front door when the bell rang at 6.45 p.m.

'Hi, Cath,' Jenny said as I opened the door. 'You look lovely.'

'Thank you.'

'Doesn't your mum look nice?' Jenny said to the children, who'd come with me to the door.

They both looked at me and nodded, and then Paula said: 'Mummy's going out with Patrick tonight. Adults can go out without their children sometimes, you know.'

Jenny and I both smiled. 'Yes, that's right,' Jenny said. 'And your mum should be doing it more often.'

The children came with me as I led the way through to the kitchen and showed Jenny where the tea, coffee and biscuits were kept. 'Help yourself to whatever you want,' I said. 'If you can't find it, Adrian knows where things are.'

'So do I,' Paula put in.

'I know, love, but you'll be in bed,' I reminded her.

We went into the sitting room and chatted for a while, although my mind was only partly on the conversation and more on the clock as I anticipated Patrick's arrival. At exactly 7.00. the bell rang and I stood.

'Can I say hello to Patrick?' Paula asked, also standing.

'Yes. Come on, but quickly: Patrick has a cab waiting.'

Adrian and Paula came with me down the hall while Jenny took a magazine from the rack and waited in the sitting room.

'What a welcome party!' Patrick exclaimed as I opened the front door with a child either side of me. 'Hello, Cathy, you look very nice,' he said, kissing my cheek.

'Thank you.' I felt myself blush.

'Is your sitter here or shall I tell the cab to wait?' Patrick asked.

'No, she's here. The children just wanted to say hello.'

Patrick nodded to them. 'You be good for your sitter,' he said. 'I'll look after your mum and I promise she won't be out too late.'

'She's allowed a late pass,' Jenny called from the sitting room.

I laughed. 'Come in and say a quick hi to my sitter,' I said. 'She's one of my oldest friends.'

'Not so much of the old!' Jenny called, appearing in the hall.

Patrick met her halfway down the hall. 'Good to meet you,' he said, shaking her hand and kissing her cheek.

'And you,' Jenny said; then to Adrian and Paula, who were rooted either side of me, 'Come on, let's say goodbye to your mum and Patrick and we'll find some stories to read.'

An Evening Out

Jenny took Paula's hand and the three of them came with Patrick and me to the front door. I kissed the children goodnight, thanked Jenny again and then followed Patrick down the path to the cab waiting at the kerb. Like a true gentleman, Patrick opened the rear door for me to get in and closed it again before going round and getting in the other side.

'Have a good time,' Jenny called.

'I will.' I waved.

But as the cab pulled away and I looked at Jenny standing on the doorstep I felt a sudden stab of sadness mingled with anger and regret. It reminded me of the last time Jenny had babysat for me: it had been for John's office party the Christmas before he'd left. Jenny had said then as she had now how nice I looked and wished us a good time. And I'd had a good time, but some months later I found out that a girl John had introduced me to – his new PA – was the woman he'd been having an affair with and subsequently left me for.

'You OK?' Patrick asked, lightly touching my arm.

'Yes.' I looked at him. 'Just remembering.'

'As long as they are good memories. You know what the Irish say: "May you never forget what is worth remembering, nor ever remember what is best forgotten."'

I laughed. 'Perfect! That is so true.'

Chapter Fourteen
'May Joy and Peace Surround You'

Patrick had reserved a table at a very nice, but pricey, restaurant called the Old Manor. It was a seventeenth-century manor house and retained many of its original features, including exposed beams, a huge inglenook fireplace and little alcoves with ornate lattice windows.

'This is lovely,' I said to Patrick as the waitress showed us to our table, nestled in one of the alcoves.

'I'm glad you like it. Have you been here before?'

'Not for a long while.'

Each table had a starched white tablecloth with a centrepiece containing a lit candle and flowers. Exactly the type of place you avoid with young children for fear of staining the cloth or them overturning the flowers and candle.

The waitress handed us each a menu, pointed out the chef's specials which were chalked on a blackboard and then asked us if we'd like a pre-dinner drink. I ordered an orange juice and Patrick had a scotch with ice.

'How's Michael?' I asked after the waitress had left to fetch our drinks and we studied the menu.

'Good. I've left him playing Scalextric with Nora. I don't think she knows what she's let herself in for.'

I smiled. 'Adrian is asking for a Scalextric for a present for his birthday or Christmas.'

Patrick nodded. 'I think all boys have an electric train set at some time in their childhoods. I did.'

'My brother still has his,' I agreed. 'It's in the loft at my parents' house with his Matchbox cars. He was talking about those the other day: he thinks they might be worth something now.'

'They could well be. Matchbox cars are collector's items. He should get them valued.'

We returned to the menu. 'So have you decided what you would like to eat?' Patrick asked after a few moments. 'The steaks used to be very good here, if you're a meat eater.'

'I'm not really but the salmon sounds nice.'

'Yes, it is. Kathleen used to like that.'

I glanced up. 'Did you and Kathleen come here often?'

'Only for special occasions: birthdays, wedding anniversary, etc. Eamon and Colleen came with us a few times. The last time was to celebrate the birth of Michael. Kathleen became ill soon after and didn't feel up to restaurants and eating out.'

The waitress returned with our drinks and took our orders. Neither of us wanted a starter, so Patrick ordered the steak – medium rare – and I ordered the poached salmon; both came with new potatoes and a selection of vegetables. Patrick asked for the wine menu and chose a bottle of Sauvignon, which he said would go with my salmon. 'We're not driving, so we may as well have some wine,' he said, and I agreed.

As we sipped our drinks and waited for the food we talked, as parents often do, about our children. Patrick said Michael was good at maths but didn't like reading or writing. He said he hoped Michael would start enjoying books soon because he (Patrick) could sit for hours with a good book, lost in a different world. I said I could too, given the time. Patrick liked science fiction and one of his favourite authors was Arthur C. Clarke. We then spent some time talking about *2001: A Space Odyssey* and the film, which had become a classic, and whether robots could ever become so sophisticated that they could think and feel for themselves.

The food arrived and with it the wine, and we continued talking as we ate. We covered many subjects – the weather, unemployment, holidays, our schooling compared to our children's, etc. The only topic we didn't touch on was Patrick's illness – until we neared the end of the meal. We'd finished eating and, having refused the sweet menu, we were finishing the wine while waiting for the coffees to arrive, when Patrick said: 'I phoned my aunt last weekend. She lives in Wales. She was my mother's sister.' I nodded. 'The last time I saw her was at Kathleen's funeral. Strange woman.'

I looked at him questioningly.

He shrugged. 'She's a devout Presbyterian and tries to convert everyone she meets. It's difficult holding a conversation with her with all that hellfire and damnation.' He gave a small dismissive laugh. 'Stella suggested I contact her, to see if she would be willing to look after Michael long term. She didn't, and to be honest I was quietly relieved. I'd prefer Michael going to a long-term foster carer than her. Do you know she actually told me I should have remarried when Michael was little and then I wouldn't have this problem?'

'What!' I gasped, amazed. 'You're not serious?'

He laughed. 'I am. What was I supposed to do? Place an ad in the Classifieds: wife and mother wanted in case I pop my clogs.'

We both laughed, and then I said more seriously, 'Your aunt doesn't sound like the type of person I'd want to look after my children.'

'She's not,' Patrick said bluntly. 'And I don't.'

Despite Jill's advice and warning, I now knew I had to say what was in my heart. Setting my glass on the table, I leant slightly forward. Patrick was gazing into the candlelight, deep in thought.

'Pat, I don't want to talk about your illness tonight. We've had a lovely evening, but I do want to say one thing.' He looked up and met my gaze questioningly. 'If you ever become too ill to look after Michael and he has to come and live with me, I would make it permanent if that is what you and he wanted. You mustn't worry; I would look after Michael.'

There was a moment's pause before he said, 'Would you, Cathy? Would you really? What a good kind woman you are!' I saw his eyes mist and he looked away.

'Anyway,' I said quickly, 'let's talk about something more cheerful. If you're not doing anything this weekend, would you and Michael like to come for that dinner you missed when you took yourself off to hospital?'

'Love to,' he said, brightening. 'I'll look forward to it.'

We drank our coffees, refused the offer of a liqueur from the waitress and then Patrick said if we'd finished he'd call for the bill.

'Can we split the bill?' I asked as he took out his wallet.

'Certainly not,' he said firmly. 'I wouldn't hear of it.'

'Well, thank you very much,' I said. 'I've really enjoyed myself.'

'So have I. Thank *you*.'

We stood and he helped me into my coat.

Outside two cabs were parked on the far side of the restaurant's carriage driveway with their engines off but lights on, waiting for diners who might need a cab. Patrick signalled to the first to come over, and when it had pulled round he gave my address to the driver and then opened the rear door for me to get in.

'Nice restaurant,' the cab driver remarked as Patrick climbed in beside me and we pulled away.

'Very,' Patrick and I agreed.

'It changed owners a while back but the standard hasn't dropped,' the driver said and then continued making intermittent conversation during the fifteen-minute drive to my house. But as he spoke I noticed he seemed to be looking more at me in his rear-view mirror than at Patrick. Then as we turned into my road he said: 'I know this road. I thought you looked familiar.'

Patrick and I both met his gaze in the interior mirror.

'You looked after my neighbour's kiddie for a few weeks,' he said to me. 'It was a couple of years ago when she went through a bad patch.'

'Did I?' I said, taken aback.

'His name's Carl. Mum is Chrissie. He'd have been three then.'

'Oh yes, I remember,' I said, wondering how the cabbie knew me. 'How are they?'

'Very well. They still live next door to me. I gave his mum a lift when she came to collect him from you.'

'Oh, I see,' I said. 'You've got a good memory.' For while I remembered Carl and his mother I certainly wouldn't have recognized the cab driver who had collected them.

'I'll tell Chrissie I saw you.'

'Yes, please do and give them my love. I'm so pleased they're doing well.'

We drew up outside my house and although I was tired I felt I should ask Patrick in for coffee. I was quietly relieved when he refused, saying it was after eleven o'clock and we both had to be up in the morning to get the children to school. Patrick told the cab driver to wait and he got out and opened my door and then walked with me down the path to my front door.

'Thanks again for a lovely evening,' I said as we stood on the doorstep and he kissed my cheek.

'The pleasure is mine,' he said. 'Sleep tight and I'll phone you tomorrow, if that's all right?'

'Of course.'

He kissed my cheek again and then returned to the cab as I quietly let myself in so that I didn't wake the children. Closing the front door, I slipped off my shoes and padded along the hall and to the sitting room, where Jenny had the door open and the television on low so that she would hear the children if they woke.

'Good evening?' she asked quietly as I went in.

'Perfect. We went to the Old Manor.'

'Oh yes, very nice. Ben and I took his parents there last year for his mum's birthday.'

I sat on the sofa as Jenny told me Adrian and Paula had been fine and had gone to bed on time and fallen asleep straight away. She said there'd been one phone call – from a double-glazing salesman whom she'd had difficulty getting rid of, despite telling him she wasn't the homeowner. He'd said he'd phone back. Jenny then stood and said she'd go and let me get to bed. I thanked her again and went with her to the front door. I waited until she was safely in her car before I closed and then locked the door.

Switching off all the downstairs lights, I went upstairs, exhausted but with my thoughts still full of the evening. I was pleased I'd said what I had to Patrick about looking after Michael permanently should it ever be necessary. Hopefully Patrick would continue to stay well and my offer wouldn't be necessary, but I knew it had reassured him and he'd appeared relieved. However, I also knew that when Jill found out I'd receive a 'ticking off', for although Patrick and I had become friends, I was still a foster carer and my offer should have been approved by the fostering agency first.

It was nearly midnight by the time I finally climbed into bed and it was a real struggle to get up when the alarm went at 6.00 the following morning. Hauling myself from under the duvet, I showered and dressed before waking Adrian and Paula at 7.00. Over breakfast they asked if I'd had a nice time with Patrick and when could they see Michael?'

'Sunday,' I said. 'I've invited them for dinner. They're coming after they've been to church.'

'Can we go to church with them?' Paula asked.

'No, love,' I said. 'They go to a Catholic church.'

'What's a Catholic church?' Paula predictably asked. 'Don't they believe in Jesus?'

'Yes, they believe in Jesus but they put more emphasis on Mary, the Virgin Mother.' I knew the moment I'd said it that it was the wrong thing to say.

'What's a virgin mother?' Paula asked.

Adrian smirked.

'The lady who had baby Jesus, but without a husband,' I said. Adrian smirked some more.

'You haven't got a husband now,' Paula said innocently. 'Are you a virgin mother?'

Adrian exploded into laughter, sputtering a mouthful of half-chewed cornflakes back into his bowl.

'Enough!' I said to Adrian. Then to Paula: 'No, I'm not a virgin mother. There is only one and she was the mother of Jesus. Now, we haven't got time to talk about this now, so please get on with your breakfast – otherwise we'll be late for school

114

and nursery.' Apart from which, if I was honest, I was slightly hung over and didn't feel up to explaining exactly what a virgin was, which doubtless would have been Paula's next question. One glass of wine with my dinner on a Sunday is my maximum and last night I'd had half a bottle.

On Saturday morning we went shopping at the supermarket, where I bought what I needed for Sunday and also topped up on essentials – bread, milk, fruit and toilet tissue, which seemed to vanish before my eyes. On Saturday afternoon we visited my parents, whom we usually saw every two weeks. I'd always been close to my parents, but since John had left we'd become closer, with my father providing a male role model for the children as well as simply being a loving grandpa.

Before I went to bed that night I took the chicken from the freezer to defrost, the best china and cutlery from the top cupboard, and the linen napkins from the drawer. I was up again by eight o'clock the next morning to begin the preparations for when Patrick and Michael arrived at one o'clock. As it was Sunday, the children weren't up and dressed until after nine, and when they'd had breakfast I suggested to Adrian he might like to tidy his room, as I'd noticed Michael's bedroom was very tidy. He said he would, without argument, and thirty minutes later called me up to have a look. I gasped with admiration as I entered his room. 'Fantastic!' I said. 'Well done. I am impressed.' Paula then wanted me to look at her bedroom, which I did and admired, although it was always reasonably tidy.

Just before eleven o'clock the phone rang and for a moment I thought it might be Patrick cancelling, but it was John to speak to the children. He'd seen them at the beginning of the month and was due to see them again the following Sunday. I said a courteous if a little stiff hello and then called Adrian and Paula to the phone. I left them speaking to their father while I went into the kitchen to continue the preparations for dinner. The doors were open, so I could hear them if they called but not their actual conversation. They both spoke to their father for about ten minutes each and then, having said goodbye, came through to find me in the kitchen.

'Dad says to remind you he'll be taking us out next Sunday,' Adrian said.

'Yes, don't worry: I won't forget.' Although why John couldn't have said that to me when I'd answered the phone instead of sending a message with the children I didn't know.

At one o'clock when the doorbell rang we were ready for our guests. The house was clean and tidy, the chicken was roasting in the oven and the vegetables were prepared and ready for cooking in their pans.

'Don't you two look the smart pair!' I exclaimed as I opened the front door. Having come straight from church Patrick and Michael were wearing suits and ties.

'Dress to impress,' Patrick said, smiling and placing a bottle of wine and a large box of chocolates in my arms.

'Thank you very much, but you shouldn't have done that,' I said.

'My pleasure,' Patrick smiled, and then kissed my cheek.

They came into the hall, where Patrick and Michael both took off the jackets to their suits and Patrick hung them on the hall stand. 'You won't mind if I take off my tie?' he said to me.

'Of course not.' Michael had already taken off his and was undoing the top button on his shirt. Patrick did likewise and then tucked the two ties into his jacket pocket.

The children disappeared upstairs to play while Patrick came with me into the kitchen. 'Mmm, something smells good,' he said.

'May Joy and Peace Surround You'

'I hope it's the dinner,' I said. 'Would you like to open the wine while I check the oven? The corkscrew is in that drawer' – I nodded to a cabinet – 'and the glasses are in the cupboard above.'

While Patrick opened the drawer and rummaged for the corkscrew I took the oven gloves and opened the oven door. Partially sliding out the roasting tray I began basting the chicken and potatoes as Patrick uncorked the wine behind me. I heard the cork come out of the bottle with a small plop followed by a gentle glug-glug as he poured the wine into the glasses. For a moment I couldn't see what I was doing for emotion, as my eyes misted and I swallowed the lump rising in my throat. This cosy domestic scene of a man uncorking the wine while I cooked and which had been missing from my life touched a raw nerve. Returning the pan to the oven, I quickly composed myself as Patrick said: 'A toast.'

I straightened and turned to face him. He handed me a glass of wine and raised his own. 'Another of my Irish sayings,' he said. 'To Cathy:

> May joy and peace surround you
> Contentment latch your door
> And happiness be with you now
> And bless you evermore.'

'Thank you, that's lovely,' I said. 'And you.'

Chapter Fifteen

Boyfriend

Sunday was a huge success. We ate dinner around the dining table like one big happy family, with the children grouped along one side and Patrick and me on the other. There was lots of talking and laughing as we ate and Patrick was very complimentary about my cooking, which was nice. When I took the pudding – fresh cream chocolate trifle – from the fridge and placed it on the table they clapped and cheered, and I took a small bow. As the weather was good, after we'd eaten we went into the garden for the rest of the afternoon. Patrick and I sat on the garden bench talking while the children played various games and then impressed us with their handstands and cartwheels.

'Look, Mum!' Adrian and Paula called.

'Look, Dad,' Michael said.

'Well done! Very daring,' we praised.

By five o'clock Adrian was saying he was hungry again, so leaving Patrick watching the children in the garden I went into the kitchen and made cheese and ham sandwiches, which we ate on the lawn in the garden with a drink of lemonade like a mini picnic. It was nearly 7.00 p.m. before the air began to chill and we finally put away the garden toys and went indoors. Patrick said they should be going. He offered to do the washing up but I refused. He called for a cab and when it arrived Adrian, Paula and I waved them off at door to shouts of 'See you soon'. It was a truly lovely day and one I still think of fondly.

The children and I saw Patrick and Michael regularly throughout the following month of May: all together at weekends and just Patrick and me one evening mid-week. Sometimes Patrick came to my house, when Nora or Colleen would babysit Michael, and sometimes I went to his house, when Jenny or Rose sat for me. Patrick and I also went out for a couple of evenings: for a walk by the lake, and to the cinema, where we ate popcorn and chocolates from wrappers that crinkled and we laughed just like children. There was a sense of carefree abandonment when there were just the two of us out alone and we'd left the responsibilities of single parenting behind us for a few hours. Likewise when we were all together we were light-hearted and laughed a lot. We went on family outings, to the park and to the swimming pool, where I went in the water with the children while Patrick watched from the tiered seating at the side, and we all had hot chocolate afterwards.

Patrick and I didn't talk about his illness when we were together and for my part I rarely thought about it either. Patrick appeared well and although he was still very thin he was eating, so I was expecting him to start gaining weight. Sometimes he became breathless but recovered after a short sit-down. Only once did he mention the hospital – that he'd been to the hospital in the morning for some tests. He told me the doctor had said he was very pleased he was 'still holding his own'. I smiled and said, 'Of course you are. You're doing very well.' I didn't hear the limitation of time suggested in the doctor's comment 'still holding his own': the implication that there could be another outcome. To me the doctor's words simply confirmed Patrick was staying well and would continue to do so indefinitely.

I suppose it was inevitable that at some point John would hear of Patrick's existence, and although I was doing nothing wrong, when he phoned he tried to make me believe I was. Paula must have said something to her father when he'd taken her and Adrian out on the Sunday after Patrick and Michael had come for dinner. I could picture her innocently mentioning Patrick and Michael and John seizing on her remark and questioning her. The first I knew that Patrick had been spoken of was when I answered the phone on Monday morning – the Monday after John had seen the children.

'Cathy, it's John,' he said tightly. 'There's something I need to discuss with you.' I was surprised to hear his voice, as usually he phoned only at the weekends to speak to the children, so I thought he must want to talk about the divorce. I'd been putting off finding a solicitor and starting the divorce process, although I knew John wanted a divorce so that he could remarry. But it wasn't the divorce John wanted to discuss, although he did mention it, and indeed he didn't want to 'discuss' anything but accuse me.

'I understand you've moved your boyfriend into the house,' he began, 'so you can forget about maintenance or me paying half the mortgage. I've spoken to my solicitor and he has advised me that as we're still technically married you've committed adultery, so we're equally to blame now. I therefore want a divorce on two years' separation, not my adultery –'

'John!' I said, recovering. 'Patrick is not a boyfriend. He's a friend, and he never stays the night.'

'Pull the other one,' John sneered. 'He's there when the children go to bed.'

'Yes, occasionally he comes here in the evening. But he always goes home before eleven o'clock.'

'So who's looking after my children while you two are canoodling on the sofa?' he said changing tack.

'They're in bed, and we don't canoodle. We talk.' I was upset, and struggling to defend myself, but I stopped short of telling him Patrick was the father of a child I would be fostering. It was none of his business and he was being so irrational it wouldn't have made any difference.

'If you give me any reason to believe my children are being neglected, I'll apply for custody,' John said. It was the worst threat he could have issued and he knew it. I felt hot and sick and my heart pounded with fear. John had always been a tower of strength but now he had turned against me I was no match for him.

'The children are fine,' I said, struggling to keep my voice steady. 'You know I always put them first. If you really don't want Patrick to come to the house then he won't until everything is sorted out. I'll find a solicitor tomorrow and make an appointment to start the divorce process.' Which seemed to placate him.

'So I can tell my solicitor he can expect to hear from your solicitor soon? And the divorce will be by mutual consent not my adultery?'

'Yes,' I said quietly.

'Good. I'll phone at the weekend to speak to the children. Goodbye.' And he hung up.

I stayed where I was on the sofa in the sitting room and slowly replaced the handset. My heart was pounding and tears stung the back of my eyes. It wasn't only the injustice of John's false accusations – that I was neglecting the children and 'canoodling' with Patrick – that had upset me, but the manner in which he'd spoken to me. I knew I couldn't put off finding a solicitor any longer, for to do so would antagonize him further and he would seize on everything I did or didn't do to make life difficult. As I sat on the sofa staring unseeing across the room I finally had to admit my marriage was over and the loving person I thought I'd be with for life had gone for good.

On a lighter note it wasn't only John Paula had mentioned Patrick to. The next time my parents visited Mum and I were in the kitchen preparing dinner when Mum sidled up to me and asked conspiratorially, 'So who's this Patrick Paula's told us about?'

I smiled. Mum wanted nothing more than for me to have a 'companion', as she put it. 'He's a friend,' I said, slightly defensively, but then realized I could say more. 'He's a widower, the father of the boy I fostered for a weekend last month.'

'Oh, I see,' she said, her eyes lighting up and doubtless marrying me off on the spot. 'When can we meet him?'

'Not for a long while. When my divorce is through.'

'So why were you fostering his son?' she asked after a moment, pausing from chopping the carrots.

'Patrick has been ill. He was taken into hospital and there was no one else to look after Michael.'

'How sad. That was very nice of you, though, dear,' which is what Mum says whenever I tell her about a child I've looked after – although it's my parents who deserve the praise for unreservedly welcoming every child I foster into their home and hearts.

I didn't hear from Jill or Stella during May. I wasn't surprised. There was no need for them to contact me, as I wasn't fostering Michael. What was unusual, though, was that as a foster carer I was left without a child to look after for a whole month. There is always a shortage of foster carers and beds are not usually left empty for long, so that as one child leaves another arrives. However, I was still technically on 'standby' to look after Michael so, although Patrick was well, the bed had to be kept free. Assuming Patrick continued to make the progress he had been making, I knew I would soon be taken off standby so that I could foster another child.

It was the first Sunday in June and Adrian and Paula were out with their father for the day. The weather was fantastic, with the sun shining in a cloudless blue sky and a gentle warm breeze stirring the leaves on the trees. I was in the back garden, pulling up some weeds, breathing in the smell of the grass I had just cut and feeling life was pretty good, when the phone rang indoors. I straightened and, brushing the dirt from my hands, left my shoes at the French windows and went into the sitting room, where I answered the phone.

'Mrs Glass?' a male voice asked.

'Yes. Speaking.'

'It's the duty social worker. I understand you are the foster carer for Michael Byrne?'

'Yes, but he's not here now. He went back to his father,' I said, wondering why the duty social worker was phoning me. The 'out of hours' duty social workers are often supplied by agencies who do not always have access to the latest information.

There was a short pause before he asked, 'When was Michael with you?'

'Last month. He came for a weekend. Why?'

Ignoring my question he said: 'You are listed as the foster carer for Michael on an "as and when" basis.'

'Yes, that's right.'

'Can you collect him now? He's been taken to St Mary's hospital with his father.'

Finally I realized why the duty social worker was phoning me. 'Michael's father is ill?'

'Yes. I understand he collapsed on his way home from church. A passer-by called an ambulance and Michael went with his father in the ambulance. How long will it take you to get there?'

'I'll leave straight away. I can be there in twenty minutes.'

'I'll phone the hospital and tell them you're on your way. It's St Mary's.'

'Yes. Tell Michael I'll be with him soon.'

Chapter Sixteen

An Empty House

Quickly closing the French windows in the sitting room, I flew round to the kitchen and locked the back door. I then tore down the hall, pushed my feet into my shoes and, grabbing my handbag, rushed out the front door. My heart was thumping and my thoughts were racing. Patrick, who'd sounded so well when I'd spoken to him on the phone the evening before, was now in hospital and poor little Michael, who'd seen his father collapse, was waiting for me. How ill was Patrick? The duty social worker hadn't said, but I reassured myself that like the last time Patrick had collapsed it was probably as a result of a low blood-cell count and a blood transfusion would see him well again.

Fortunately the traffic was light on Sunday and I pulled into the hospital car park fifteen minutes later. I then wasted five minutes trying to find an empty space to park and another couple of minutes buying a ticket and placing it on the dashboard of my car. I hurried across the car park and entered the hospital through the revolving doors of the main entrance. I didn't know where Patrick and Michael were, but given Patrick had been admitted as an emergency A & E (Accident and Emergency) seemed the best bet, and I followed the sign to A & E to my right. I'd been to A & E some years before when a child I was fostering had an asthma attack, but the building had been modernized since then and as I now entered it I saw the layout had completely changed. It took me a moment to spot the reception/admission desk set back in an alcove.

I hurried over. Two women in white uniforms sat behind computer screens at the desk. Neither looked up as I approached and then waited by the desk. There was no one waiting to be seen in front of me, although there were a dozen or so people in the seated area behind me. In my anxious state – worried about Patrick and Michael – I was short on patience.

'Excuse me,' I said, more loudly than I should have done. Both women looked up. 'I received a phone call from the duty social worker a short while ago. Patrick Byrne has been admitted and I'm here to collect his son, Michael.'

'And you are?' the receptionist directly in front of me asked haughtily, clearly put out by my intrusion. The other receptionist returned to her computer.

'Cathy Glass. I'm Michael's foster carer. Someone here should be expecting me.'

She looked at her computer screen as she typed. 'Patrick Byrne?' she asked.

'Yes.'

'B-y-r-n-e?' she confirmed, spelling out his surname.

'Yes.'

She typed some more and then picked up her phone and pressed for an extension. 'Hi. It's Anna on reception here,' she said. 'I've got a Mrs Glass with me. She's come to collect Michael Byrne.' She paused and waited. I waited too, watching her and willing whoever was on the other end to hurry up. A minute passed and then the receptionist said into the phone, 'OK, thanks. I'll send her through now.'

An Empty House

Replacing the receiver, she looked at me. 'Go through those double doors over there.' I looked to where she was pointing on the far side of the waiting area. 'Then go straight and first right.'

'Thank you,' I said, and immediately headed off in the direction she'd pointed to.

On the other side of the double doors was a corridor with consultation rooms on both sides. I turned right as directed and into another shorter corridor, which opened out into a large square treatment area. A nurse's station was in the centre and curtained cubicles lined three walls. Nurses bustled in and out of the cubicles, while another was standing with a doctor poring over a patient's notes. I looked around, but there was no sign of Michael. I quickly crossed to the nurse's station and then waited for the nurse to finish on the phone.

'Michael Byrne?' I asked as the nurse finished the call. 'I'm Cathy Glass, his foster carer.'

She nodded, stood, and then came out from behind the nurse's station. 'Come with me. He's keeping his father company. In fact he wouldn't leave his side.' She gave a small smile and led the way to the corner cubicle, where she pulled back the curtain far enough for us to enter.

As I stepped into the cubicle my eyes went straight to the bed and my heart clenched. Propped on two white pillows, with an oxygen mask covering his mouth and nose, lay Patrick; his eyes were closed and his skin was a sickly grey. A drip had been inserted in the back of his left hand, and wires came from pads stuck to his chest, which led to a heart monitor on a trolley beside the bed. On the other side of the bed, with his chair as close to the bedhead as he could get it, sat Michael. Seeing him hunched slightly forward, looking so lost and afraid, I was reminded of the time I'd collected him from the head's office when Patrick had collapsed before.

Michael looked at me, stood, and then rushing over, fell into my arms, sobbing.

I held him close, his head resting against my chest, his arms wrapped around my waist. 'It's all right, love,' I gently soothed. 'It's OK now.'

As I held and comforted Michael I looked at Patrick. His eyes were still closed, so I wasn't sure if he was asleep or unconscious. His shirt had been removed to allow the stick-on pads for the heart monitor to be placed on his chest and his bare chest rose and fell in laboured breath.

'How is he?' I asked the nurse, as Michael still clung to me.

'Comfortable. We've given him something for the pain. He'll sleep for a while.'

'And his blood-cell count?' I asked. 'Are you going to give him a blood transfusion? That's what he had last time.' For I'd noticed that the bag on the drip stand contained clear fluid, not blood.

'We're running tests,' the nurse said. 'We'll notify his social worker and family when we know more.'

I realized she was politely telling me that as I wasn't a relative confidentiality forbade her from discussing Patrick's medical condition with me.

'Patrick doesn't have family apart from Michael and a distant aunt,' I said, unsure if they knew.

She nodded. 'We have Mr and Mrs Doyle listed as next of kin. Colleen has been informed that Patrick has been admitted to hospital and she is bringing his night things later.'

'So Patrick has to stay in just for tonight?' I asked, wanting to know as much as possible so that I could reassure Michael.

'We'll know more tomorrow when the test results are back,' she said a little stiffly, and held the curtain open for Michael and me to leave.

An Empty House

I looked again at Patrick. The jacket to his suit was draped over the back of the chair on which Michael had sat. There was a dusty scuff mark on the jacket sleeve, presumably from where he'd collapsed on the pavement. It seemed ridiculous that I should notice that when Patrick was so ill, but he was always so smartly dressed that the mark seemed to undermine his pride and dignity.

'Do you want to kiss your dad goodbye before we go?' I asked Michael, who still had his arms around my waist, holding tight.

I felt his arms loosen and he slowly raised his tear-stained face and nodded. Together we took the few steps to the bed and I stood beside Michael as he bent forward and kissed his dad on the forehead. 'Get better soon, Dad,' Michael said quietly. 'I'll say my prayers very well tonight, I promise. I'm sorry I didn't say them properly in church but I'll make up for it tonight.' I felt a lump rise in my throat and my eyes mist.

Michael gave his dad another kiss, but Patrick didn't stir. His eyes remained closed and his mouth stayed slightly open under the transparent oxygen mask. As Michael stepped away from the bed, I went forward. Leaning over, I kissed Patrick's forehead. His skin felt unnaturally cool and damp. 'Get better soon,' I whispered close to his ear. 'I'll take good care of Michael, so don't worry.' Straightening, I took Michael's hand and led him away from the bed, past the nurse and out of the cubicle.

I could hardly see for the tears welling in my eyes as I crossed the treatment area with Michael beside me, holding my hand. Michael was quietly sniffing back tears and I saw a nurse we passed glance in our direction. I knew I had to be strong for Michael, but with no idea how ill Patrick was it was difficult to know what to say to reassure him.

'Daddy's being well looked after,' I finally said, giving Michael's hand a reassuring squeeze. 'I'll phone Colleen later and find out more.'

We went down the corridor, through the A & E waiting area and then out of the main doors. We crossed the car park in silence, but before we got in the car Michael paused and looked at me, his face pained. 'I should have said my prayers better in church,' he said, his face creasing, as though he was responsible for his father collapsing.

I stopped and, placing my hands on his shoulder, gently turned him towards me. 'Michael, love, there is no way that not saying your prayers led to this. The God you believe in is good and kind. He wouldn't punish a young boy by making his father ill because he didn't say his prayers properly.'

Michael gave a small shrug and climbed into the back of the car. I got into the driver's seat. I would reinforce what I'd said to Michael later – that there was no link between his lack of devotion in church and his father collapsing – for I knew how guilt could fester in a young mind without the objective reasoning that comes with adulthood. The other thought I had as I started the car and drove slowly across the car park was that none of the staff in the hospital had asked to see my ID. I'd walked in and declared I was Cathy Glass and had been allowed to take away a small child who wasn't mine without anyone asking me to verify who I was. As a foster carer I'm obliged to carry ID whenever I am working with or responsible for children; the card was in my handbag. And while Michael had recognized me in the cubicle – presumably if he hadn't the nurse wouldn't have let him go with me – it would have been reassuring if someone – the receptionist or the nurse – had asked to see my ID when I'd first arrived or before I'd left.

An Empty House

Michael sat quietly in the rear of the car as I pulled out of the car park and joined the main road. I realized he hadn't any of his belongings with him and while I could have found a change of clothes for him at home I didn't have his school things for tomorrow. I knew Nora, his neighbour, had a key to Patrick's house and although his house was a couple of miles in the opposite direction to mine I had plenty of time before Adrian and Paula returned home to go there and pick up what Michael needed. Having met Nora and Jack previously at Patrick's, I felt reasonably comfortable about arriving unexpectedly and asking for their help.

'Michael, are you all right, love?' I asked, glancing at him in the interior mirror. He nodded. 'Do you know if Nora is likely to be at home? I was thinking of stopping by and getting some of your things for tonight and tomorrow.'

'She should be. Dad said we were going there for dinner after church.'

'Oh, I see. I wonder if anyone at the hospital phoned Nora to tell her what happened?'

'I don't think so,' Michael said.

Ten minutes later I pulled up outside Michael's house, aware that I might have to break the news that Patrick had collapsed to Nora and Jack. It is often said by those who work in fostering that when you foster it isn't just the child you look after and become involved with but the whole family. This is very true and often, as with Michael, the child's social network spreads outside the family and includes family friends and neighbours.

Someone in Nora and Jack's house must have seen us arrive, for as Michael and I got out of the car the front door to the house opened and Jack appeared on the doorstep.

'Dad's in hospital, Uncle Jack,' Michael cried, leaving my side and rushing up their front path. Although Michael wasn't related to Jack, like many young children, he referred to his father's friends as Uncle and Aunt.

'I know, lad,' Jack said. 'Your Auntie Colleen phoned a few minutes ago.' Then looking at me, 'How's Pat doing? We'll go and see him later.'

I had followed Michael up the path and Jack was now ushering me inside. 'The nurse didn't say much,' I said. 'Only that they've done some tests and would know more when the results come back in the morning. Dad was asleep, wasn't he?' I added positively, smiling at Michael.

Nora appeared in the hall, wearing an apron, 'Hello, lovey,' she said to Michael, spreading her arms wide for a hug. Michael went up and gave her a big hug, as he had done with Jack.

'I was expecting the two of them for dinner,' Nora said to me. 'Then Colleen phoned to say Patrick was in hospital and you were on your way to collect Michael. Why don't you sit down and I'll make you a cup of tea?'

I appreciated Nora's hospitality and didn't want to appear rude, but I was mindful of the time. I didn't know how long it would take to sort out Michael's belongings and sometimes Adrian and Paula were returned home early.

'That's kind of you,' I said, 'but I really came to collect some of Michael things and then I need to be getting home.'

'Of course,' Nora said, not the least bit offended. 'Jack, watch the dinner, please, while I take Cathy and Michael next door.'

Jack headed down the hall towards the kitchen while Nora took off her apron and then unhooked a set of keys from the key rack on the wall by the front door. I thanked Nora, and Michael and I followed her out of the door, down her front-garden path and then up the garden path next door to Patrick's and Michael's house. Nora unlocked the front door, and then led the way in.

An Empty House

It was strange going into Patrick's house without him being there. Previously when I'd visited – in the evenings – the house had always felt warm and inviting; now it was unnaturally quiet and there was an emptiness, a hollowness, as though the house had been abandoned. The Sunday newspaper lay folded on the hall table as if Patrick was about to return and pick it up. Patrick and Michael's slippers, which they always wore in the house, were paired in the hall, and Michael automatically kicked off his shoes and pushed his feet into his slippers before going upstairs.

'I know what I need to pack,' he called over his shoulder.

'We'll be up in a minute to help,' Nora called after him. 'I'll find you a case for your things.'

I followed Nora a little way down the hall and to the cupboard under the stairs. Opening the door, Nora switched on the light and as the cupboard illuminated I felt a pang of nostalgia at seeing Patrick's possessions. Patrick clearly used his understairs cupboard much as I did – for storing items that were used occasionally or had sentimental value and he didn't want to throw away. Among other things there was a 1950s standard lamp, a pretty but obsolete fireguard, a vacuum cleaner, an ironing board, a large china vase, an oil painting, various cardboard boxes, a suitcase and the holdall Michael had had his belongings in when he'd stayed with me before.

'I think we'll use this again.' Nora said, reaching in and taking out the holdall. 'If I send Michael with the big suitcase he'll think he's not coming home again.'

She set the holdall on the floor, turned and looked at me, and in that look I saw all her worries and fears about Patrick. 'Pat will be coming home again, won't he, Cathy?' she asked, her brow furrowing.

'Of course he will,' I said without a second thought. 'And soon. They'll give him a blood transfusion like they did last time and he'll be fine.'

'Yes, I'm sure you're right,' Nora said, recovering. 'Jack and I will visit him later. Will you be taking Michael to visit this evening?'

I paused and thought. 'I don't think so, not tonight. I think I'll wait until tomorrow when Patrick is feeling better. What do you think?'

'Yes. Pat worries about the effect his illness is having on Michael. He wouldn't want him seeing him poorly.'

'No, so I'll wait until tomorrow when he's awake and talking. He might even be coming out of hospital then.'

Nora nodded. 'Would you like me to phone you after we've seen him this evening? Then you can reassure Michael.'

'Yes please. I'll leave you my number before I go and it might be a good idea if I had your phone number too.'

'Yes, of course.'

I picked up the holdall and followed Nora upstairs, past Patrick's bedroom, where the door was now closed, and into Michael's room. Michael was busy taking toys and games from the cupboard and placing them in a pile in the centre of the bed, ready to pack. 'Adrian will like playing with this,' he said, holding up a sophisticated Transformer action figure with vivid green flashing eyes. 'And can I take my Scalextric?' he asked me. I was pleased that the prospect of playing with Adrian was helping keep his mind off his father's illness.

'It's fine with me,' I said. 'What do you think, Nora? Would Patrick be happy with the Scalextric leaving the house?'

'Yes, I'm sure,' she said. 'Michael's careful with his toys. I'll tell Patrick tonight you've taken it with you. But Michael,' Nora said, looking at the growing pile of toys on the bed, 'I think we need to be packing some of your clothes as well as your toys.'

'Oh yes,' Michael said, grinning.

'I tell you what,' Nora said to Michael. 'you get out the Scalextric box and pack that while Cathy and I sort out your clothes.'

I followed Nora to the built-in wardrobe with the holdall as Michael delved under the bed and retrieved the original Scalextric box. While he sat on the floor dismantling his racing car set and carefully laying it in the box, Nora took Michael's clothes from the wardrobe and handed them to me, and I folded and packed them into the holdall. Michael must have been watching us and noting how much we were packing, for when we'd put in two changes of school uniform, a couple of sets of casual clothes, and some pants and socks, he said: 'That's enough. I'll be back soon.'

Nora and I agreed. She put his school shoes into a plastic carrier bag to stop them from dirtying his clothes and I tucked the bag into the holdall. Nora then went to the bathroom to fetch Michael's flannel and toothbrush while I filled the rest of the holdall with the toys from the bed. I closed the zip. The bag was bulging and when Nora returned with Michael's wash bag I tucked it into a side compartment.

'School bag?' I asked Michael.

'Oh yes,' he said. Delving under the bed again, he pulled out his school bag. I thought that Michael's storage system appeared to be similar to Adrian's, with most things being pushed out of sight under the bed.

With Michael carrying the boxed Scalextric, Nora the school bag and me the holdall, we went downstairs and stacked everything in the hall.

'Which coat are you taking?' Nora asked Michael. There were a number of coats and jackets hanging on the wooden coat rail in the hall.

Michael unhooked his school blazer and also a casual jacket.

'I can't think of anything else,' Nora said, glancing round. 'I'll pop back later and check everything is switched off.'

Outside we packed the bags into my car and then returned briefly to Nora and Jack's house to swap telephone numbers and say goodbye. Nora and Jack gave Michael a big hug and then did the same to me, which was sweet.

'Don't worry,' Jack called to Michael as we got into the car. 'Dad will be out soon, and we'll all be round your place partying.'

Chapter Seventeen

Attached

On the way home from Patrick's I explained to Michael that Adrian and Paula were out with their father and would be home at about five o'clock. It was now just after three o'clock, and Michael said he would use the time before they returned to set up his Scalextric and he asked which room he should put it in.

'How about your bedroom?' I suggested. 'That's where you have it at home and it will be safe there. Then Adrian and Paula can come into your room to play with it.' Michael agreed. The Scalextric could have been set up downstairs but I thought it would make Michael feel more at home if he had it with him in his room; also, it would be less likely to be trodden on or damaged than downstairs in the living room.

Michael was quiet in the car for the rest of the journey and I regularly glanced at him in the interior mirror. He was gazing through his side window, deep in thought.

'Nora will phone us this evening after she's seen your dad,' I reassured him.

'Dad will want to phone and speak to me as soon as he can,' Michael said. 'He knows I worry when he falls over and doesn't wake up.'

'Does it happen often?' I asked, concerned, glancing at him in the interior mirror.

Michael nodded. 'Last week he fell over twice at home, but he woke up after a minute so I didn't have to call an ambulance or get Nora or Jack.'

Again I was reminded of the huge responsibility Michael and other child carers carry for their disabled or sick parent, but I wondered why Patrick hadn't mentioned he'd collapsed to me the week before, or gone to the hospital for tests. Perhaps he had seen a doctor but hadn't wanted to worry me. Obviously Michael didn't have the luxury of not knowing as he was living with and looking after his father. 'The doctors will have your dad up and about very soon,' I said.

Michael nodded and continued to gaze through the side window, deep in thought.

When we arrived home Michael helped me to unload the car and we carried his bags up to his room. He seemed more relaxed and 'at home' compared with the first time he'd stayed. I guessed that was a result of all the time Patrick and I had spent together with the children: Michael was familiar with the house and knew me better. He was keen to set up his Scalextric straight away, so I suggested he did that while I made us something to eat, as neither of us had eaten since breakfast. He nodded, and leaving him unpacking his Scalextric I went downstairs and made a quick pasta bake for the two of us. Adrian and Paula usually ate with their father and just wanted a snack in the evening when they returned.

Michael and I ate together, and then when we'd finished he returned upstairs to put the finishing touches to his race track while I cleared away the dishes. I then went upstairs with the intention of seeing if I could persuade Michael to unpack some of his clothes. The last time he'd stayed he'd been reluctant to unpack his clothes, viewing it, I thought, as too permanent when he was hoping to go home as soon as possible. Now, however, as I entered his bedroom not only was the Scalextric nearly complete but his holdall was lying empty on the bed.

'Have you unpacked?' I asked, surprised.

Michael nodded. Leaving the Scalextric he opened the wardrobe door to show me.

'Well done,' I said. 'Excellent. I'll put your bag out of the way up here.' I took the holdall from the bed and pushed it on top of the wardrobe, pleased that Michael had felt comfortable enough staying with us to unpack. 'Adrian and Paula should be home in half an hour,' I said. It was now 4.30.

Michael had returned to the Scalextric and was sitting cross-legged on the floor, his head lowered as if concentrating on the car he held, but he didn't say anything.

'I'll be downstairs if you need anything,' I added.

He nodded, but again didn't reply.

I took the couple of steps to where he sat and squatted down beside him. 'Michael?' I said quietly, trying to see his face. 'Are you all right, love?'

He looked up at me, his expression serious. 'Do you think it's OK if I play with my Scalextric while Dad's in hospital?' he asked anxiously.

'Yes, of course,' I said, not fully appreciating what he was trying to say. 'You look after your toys and it'll be safe up here. I know your dad won't mind.'

'Dad won't mind,' he said. 'Dad wants me to play and be happy, but what about God? Will he mind?'

I was taken aback. 'Of course not. God would want you to be happy too, not feel guilty about playing.' I didn't know where Michael had got his feelings of religious guilt from, it certainly wasn't from Patrick, and I didn't think it was healthy. I remembered Michael's bedtime prayer when he'd stayed with us before: 'Lord … I hope you don't mind me being happy. I still love my daddy but it's nice to play sometimes.' Then there'd been his worry earlier at the hospital that his lack of devotion had caused his father to collapse on the way home from church; and now this comment. Although I didn't know much about the Catholic religion, I was sure its faith wasn't based on, or fuelled by, guilt.

'I'll say an extra prayer tonight,' Michael said, obviously still thinking about it.

'If you wish, and you can blame it on me,' I said lightly. 'Explain it was my decision to bring your Scalextric here and let you play with it, not yours. I take full responsibility,' which seemed to help, as Michael grinned at me conspiratorially.

'All right,' he said, and more happily set the car on the track.

Leaving Michael putting the finishing touches to the layout of the track, I went downstairs. I wondered if it was Michael's school which had taught the children to fear God, or perhaps it was something he'd heard and had misinterpreted in the Catholic teachings at church. But either way I didn't want him saddled with the added burden of guilt for being happy, and if my taking responsibility for his playing helped then I was more than willing to do so. I was sure the God who watched over me, whoever he was, would continue to forgive my transgressions, just as I hoped he had done in the past.

At five o'clock I was looking out from behind the net curtains in the front room, watching out for Adrian and Paula. Although I had faith in John's ability to look after the children and keep them safe, I was always relieved when they were home again safely. Michael now had his Scalextric fully operational and I could hear the electric cars racing around the track upstairs. I'd offered to play with him but he'd said he'd wait for Adrian, although first I would have to explain to Adrian and Paula why

Attached

Michael was here, preferably after John had said goodbye and I'd closed the front door.

A few minutes later John's car drew up and parked outside the house. I still found it strange seeing him park and get out, knowing that he wouldn't be coming in or staying. I watched him unseen from behind the net curtains and I wondered if he too felt uncomfortable returning to the house that had previously been his home. As the children began down the garden path I left the front room and went into the hall, ready to answer the door as soon as the bell rang.

'Hi!' I said, smiling at all three of them. 'Have you had a good time?'

Paula as usual fell straight into my arms and gave me a big hug, while Adrian, more reserved in showing his emotions, nodded and grinned at me.

'We've had a lovely time, haven't we?' John said to the children. They nodded.

'Good,' I said, smiling at John.

'Bye, then. I'll phone next weekend,' John said to the children, who were now in the hall.

'Say goodbye,' I reminded them. This was always the most difficult part, and part of me felt sorry for John. I couldn't have said goodbye to my children knowing I wouldn't be seeing them again for another month, but that was his decision.

Adrian and Paula returned to the doorstep and hugged their father at the same time as Michael appeared on the landing and then began down the stairs. The staircase leads off the hall, so halfway down Michael was clearly visible from the front door.

'Michael's here,' I said to Adrian and Paula as they finished saying goodbye to their father. They were as pleased to see Michael as he was to see them.

141

'Is Patrick here?' John asked, quick as a flash.

'No,' I said. 'He doesn't come in any more.' Which seemed to defuse him.

'Bye, kids,' he called after Adrian and Paula as they scampered upstairs with Michael.

'Bye, Dad,' they called down.

'Goodbye.' I smiled politely.

John took a couple of steps down the path and then paused and turned. 'Have you seen your solicitor yet?' he asked.

'I have an appointment next week.'

He nodded stiffly and then continued down the path as I closed the front door and breathed a sigh of relief. I hoped that once he had the divorce he wanted and was free to remarry our conversations would become easier.

I had wanted to explain to Adrian and Paula that Michael was here before they saw him but I hadn't had the chance, so I now went upstairs and into Michael's bedroom. The children were grouped around the Scalextric, with the boys working a hand-held control each and Paula watching and waiting for her turn.

'Patrick's had to go into hospital, so Michael is staying with us for a few days,' I said redundantly, as it must have been obvious to Adrian and Paula why Michael was here.

Adrian nodded, intent on the game, while Paula said, 'Don't worry, Mum, Michael's fine with us.'

'I'm fine,' Michael confirmed without taking his eyes from the cars.

I smiled and came away, pleased that as a result of all the time Patrick and I had spent together with the children they were relaxed in each other's company and Michael felt 'at home'. However, and I hadn't given it much thought, the downside of this comfort and familiarity the children felt was that as well as bonding with Michael, Adrian and Paula had grown attached to Patrick, and would fret and worry that he was ill – although this didn't come out until later, when they were tired and getting ready for bed.

I made a light supper at six o'clock and then at seven I began the bath and bedtime routine, ready for school and nursery the following day. As usual, I took Paula, the youngest, up first and helped her into the bath, and then washed her back while she did the rest. I thought she was quieter than usual; normally she loves her bath and there are usually lots of squeals of delight as she plays in the foaming bubble bath.

'Are you all right?' I asked her after a while.

'Yes.' But a moment later Paula suddenly asked, 'Does Patrick sleep in a bed in hospital?' Having never been in a hospital, she wouldn't know.

'Yes,' I said. 'There are beds in what are called wards. Each patient – that's the name for someone who stays in hospital – has their own bed, just like at home.'

'Will someone look after Patrick at night, while he is in bed?' she asked.

'Yes, the nurses. There are nurses on the wards to look after the patients during the day and the night. You know what a nurse is, don't you?'

She nodded. 'Is there a toilet in the ward?'

'Yes, and a bathroom. You're not worrying about Patrick, are you?'

'No.' But a few seconds later she asked,' 'Will Patrick have dinner and breakfast there?'

'Yes, love. Please don't worry. He'll have plenty to eat. Meals are brought to the ward on a special trolley that keeps the food warm.'

She thought about this, and then said, 'I wish Patrick wasn't in hospital. I wish he was at his house or here with us.'

'I know, love, but sometimes people have to stay in hospital if they are poorly. He's being well looked after by the nurses, so please stop worrying.'

She finished washing and I helped her out of the bath and wrapped a towel around her. As I helped her dry herself, she said more lightly, 'When will we see Patrick again?'

'In a few days. When he comes out of hospital.'

'Good. I like Patrick. I mean I love Daddy but I like Patrick. That's OK, isn't it?'

'Of course, love,' I said, smiling. 'That's just fine.'

Adrian and Michael went up to get ready for bed together and then took turns in the shower. Once they were in their pyjamas and in their respective bedrooms I went in to say goodnight, Michael first. He seemed very relaxed and, with his clothes unpacked and in the wardrobe, and the Scalextric on the floor at the foot of his bed, quite at home. He was placing the racing cars in their pit stops for the night and I noticed he'd even taken the plug from the wall socket. Before climbing into bed he knelt and clasped his hands together, ready to say his prayers. I respectfully looked away as I usually did but Michael's prayer was quick and light tonight: 'God bless Mummy, Daddy, Nora, Jack, Colleen, Eamon, my friend David at school, Cathy, Adrian, Paula and their daddy. Amen.' Opening his eyes, he sprang into bed.

'That was nice,' I said, pleased his prayers hadn't been laden with guilt and asking for forgiveness for enjoying himself. 'Night,' I said, kissing his forehead and straightening the duvet.

'Night, Cathy,' he said, smiling. 'Can you open my curtains a bit like you did last time, so I can see the stars?'

'Yes, of course.' I went to the curtains and parted them slightly in the middle, although the stars weren't visible yet as the sky hadn't fully darkened. 'Is that all right?' I asked.

He smiled and nodded. 'Dad will be looking at the sky too,' Michael said, clearly finding comfort in this. I said goodnight again and left him lying in bed, gazing towards the window with a contented smile on his face.

However, it was a different matter in Adrian's room. He was changed and about to get into bed, but I knew immediately from his expression there was something worrying him. I also knew that unlike Paula, who voiced her concerns, I would need to coax whatever was worrying Adrian out of him.

'You look a bit sad,' I said as he got into bed and I perched on the edge. 'Is there something bothering you?'

He gave a small dismissive shrug, which I knew translated as yes.

'Can you tell me what it is?' I asked. Adrian shrugged. 'You know the saying,' I persisted: 'a problem shared is a problem halved. Telling me will help.'

There was a small pause when Adrian looked down and fiddled with the duvet before he admitted, 'It's Patrick. And you.'

I looked at him, puzzled. 'Patrick and me? What's the matter? Can you explain?'

He fiddled some more with the duvet, clearly finding if very difficult to say what he was thinking, while my thoughts worked overtime on what could possibly be worrying him about Patrick and me.

'Adrian, love, can you try and explain what you mean?' I tried again. 'And then I can help.'

He took a small breath and without looking at me said, 'Michael said his daddy has lung cancer.'

145

'Yes, that's right.' I hadn't explained the exact nature of Patrick's illness to the children – that he had cancer, which had begun in the lungs. It seemed enough for them to know that Patrick was ill with what I'd described as a nasty disease.

'Michael said his dad's lung cancer was because he used to smoke,' Adrian said anxiously.

'It's possible,' I said. 'A lot more is known now about the dangers of smoking than when Patrick smoked in his twenties.'

There was another pause before Adrian said, without looking up, 'Dad told me you used to smoke. Will you get lung cancer like Patrick?'

Thank you, John, I thought: I need help like that. 'No,' I said. 'That was years ago, before I had you and Paula. And I didn't smoke much. I'm fine, and it's possible Patrick's illness wasn't caused by smoking. People who have never smoked sometimes get lung cancer.' For I didn't want Adrian to feel that Patrick was to blame for his illness and therefore Michael's suffering. 'When did your dad tell you I smoked?' I asked, wondering why he had felt the need to tell the children.

'A few months ago. We saw some boys smoking in the park and Dad gave me a lecture on not smoking. I told him I wouldn't ever smoke. It's disgusting and makes you smell.'

'Good,' I said and thought that my son was clearly far more sensible than I had been.

Then Adrian looked at me and said quietly, 'Mum, Patrick will come out of hospital, won't he?'

I took his hand between mine. 'Yes, of course. Once the test results are back the doctors will give Patrick the medicine he needs and he'll be out in a few days.'

'Good,' Adrian said, at last smiling. 'I like Patrick and Michael.'

'So do I, love.

Attached

Having spent some time reassuring Paula and Adrian, it was after 8.30 when I went downstairs. I tidied up and then went into the lounge with a cup of tea. I knew visiting at the hospital was 6.00–8.00 p.m., so I was expecting Nora's phone call any time. In fact it was nearly ten o'clock before she phoned – when I'd been about to phone her. The poor woman sounded exhausted; I also knew straight away there was something badly wrong.

Chapter Eighteen
News and NO News

'Sorry I didn't phone sooner,' Nora began, her voice strained. 'I've only just got in. Colleen and Eamon were at the hospital and we waited behind to talk to a nurse.'

'How is Patrick?' I broke in, eager for news.

She sighed. 'The nurse didn't really say more than we already knew – that they would know more when the test results are back in the morning – but I ...' Nora paused, trying to find the right words to voice her thoughts. 'I know I can say this to you, Cathy, and obviously don't say anything to Michael, but I have a bad feeling about this – about how ill Patrick really is.'

'What do you mean?' I asked, a cold chill running up my spine.

'I think Pat's illness could have progressed further than he's been letting on. Jack does too.'

'You think he's purposely not told us?'

'Yes. I could be wrong but Pat's a great one for protecting others, especially Michael.'

'I don't know,' I said, searching for every reason to disbelieve her. 'I've seen quite a lot of Patrick recently and he was fine until yesterday. What makes you think he's worse than he's been saying?'

'It's difficult to explain. He was lying too still; he barely stirred in the whole two hours we were there, and his colour is dreadful. He wasn't like that when he was ill before – even when he collapsed and was taken to hospital. Perhaps it's the medication they're giving him, but when I saw him, so still and pale, it reminded me of the last time I saw my father in the nursing home.'

I felt my stomach clench. 'He didn't wake at all the whole time you were there?' I asked.

'Once, sort of. He half opened his eyes and seemed to focus on us. I took the opportunity to tell him Michael was with you and you'd collected his things.'

'Good.'

'I don't know if he heard me. He didn't say anything and his eyes closed again almost immediately. The four of us stayed until the end of visiting but I don't think he knew we were there. How is Michael?' Nora finished.

'All right, considering. He's asleep now. He's had a good evening. I'll take him to school in the morning. What do you think I should tell him about his dad?'

Nora let out another small sigh. 'Just reassure him for now, until we know more. Patrick wouldn't want him being upset unnecessarily. Hopefully once the test results return they'll be able to give Pat something to get him back on his feet.'

'Will you phone me again as soon as you know anything?' I asked. 'It's no good me phoning the hospital: they won't tell me anything as I'm not family.'

'Nor me. I'm just the neighbour as far as they're concerned, although Jack and I have been close friends of Pat's for twenty years. Colleen and Eamon are down as next of kin. Colleen is going to phone the hospital tomorrow morning, and then phone me. Either she or I will phone you.'

'Thank you,' I said. 'And thank goodness Patrick has friends like you.'

We said goodbye and I hung up. I remained where I was, sitting on the sofa, and stared into space. I ran through all Nora had said, which wasn't a lot, still searching for hope. I knew what Nora had meant when she'd said Patrick was very still and pale. I'd seen that earlier when I'd collected Michael from the hospital. Usually Patrick had a ruddy complexion but he'd looked almost grey. He was also an active man, even since his illness, and seeing him lying so still seemed unnatural. Whether or not his condition was worse than he'd let on, as Nora and Jack thought, I didn't know. I'd have hoped Patrick would have confided in me – we'd shared a lot in the time we'd known each other. I also had no idea when Michael would be able to see his father again and I knew that that would be one of the first questions he'd ask in the morning. It was therefore with a very heavy heart that half an hour later I switched off the television and went up to bed, hoping the following day would bring better news.

I didn't sleep. I thought of Patrick as I'd seen him in A & E, with the oxygen mask covering his mouth and nose, and poor Michael sitting beside his bed looking so very sad and alone. I thought of Patrick's jacket hanging over the chair back and the scuff mark on the shoulder, which he would have immediately brushed off had he been able to. I pictured Pat unconscious in the street with Michael kneeling beside him waiting for help; then refusing to be parted from his dad until I'd arrived at the hospital. I also remembered Michael's words when he'd stayed with me before and we'd looked out of his bedroom window at the night sky: 'When it's my daddy's turn the angels will come from heaven and take him to be with my mummy.' Tears filled my eyes as I remembered the way Michael had finished his prayer that night: 'I know you want my daddy, but I'm staying at Cathy's and haven't said goodbye. So please don't send your angels for him yet.'

'No, don't send your angels yet,' I now said quietly, making the prayer my own. 'None of us has said goodbye.'

The first thing Michael said when I woke him at 7.00 the following morning was, 'Did Nora phone? How's my dad?'

'Yes, Nora phoned,' I said brightly. 'She and Jack, and Auntie Colleen and Uncle Eamon, went to see your dad. Nora said he was having a good sleep but he woke once and Nora was able to tell him you were fine and with me. Dad sends his love.' Which I knew Patrick would have done had he been well enough.

'When can I see him?' Michael asked.

'As soon as your dad is feeling a bit better. Auntie Colleen or Nora will phone later when they've spoken to the doctors.'

'OK,' Michael said, reassured and getting out of bed. 'School today.'

Leaving Michael to dress in his school uniform, I went to Paula's bedroom to wake her.

'Is Patrick better?' Paula asked as soon as she opened her eyes.

'The nurses are looking after him,' I said, laying her clothes on her bed.

'When's he coming out of hospital?'

'Soon, I hope.'

'Good.'

And when I went into Adrian's room the first thing he asked was: 'Any news?'

'Nora phoned last night and said Patrick was comfortable. She will phone again later when the test results are back.'

The Night the Angels Came

Leaving Adrian to dress, I checked on Paula's progress and then went downstairs to make breakfast – toast and cereal. Despite my waking the children in plenty of time to wash, dress and have breakfast there wasn't a moment to spare, and I had to remind them all to eat rather than talk at the breakfast table if we weren't going to be late for school, which we weren't.

We arrived at Michael's school at 8.05, ready for his 8.15 start. I saw him into the playground and then turned the car around and headed back to Adrian's school for his 8.50 start. Then I took Paula to nursery for 9.00, and once I'd seen her in and said goodbye I went straight home.

Although I knew it was probably too early for the test results and Nora's phone call, as soon as I let myself into the hall my eyes went to the answerphone in the hall, which showed no messages. I slipped off my shoes and jacket and concentrated on the tasks in hand. There's always plenty of clearing up to do on a Monday morning, after the weekend. I also wanted to fill in a job-application form that had arrived in the post on Saturday. With Paula starting full-time school in September I'd started searching the job section in the local paper for any position that would fit in with school hours. So, it appeared, had many others: the last post I'd applied for – a classroom assistant in a local school, hours 9.15 a.m.–3.00 p.m. – had had 175 applicants, and the one before that, a part-time clerical post, over 200.

But as I sat at the dining table and began filling in this application form for part-time supermarket work my thoughts were a long way from what I was writing and I kept making mistakes and having to Tipp-Ex them out. At 11.40 I had to leave to collect Paula from nursery and when I returned at 12.15 there were still no messages on the answerphone. I made Paula and me a sandwich lunch and after we'd eaten she played while I had another attempt at the job application, still anxiously awaiting news. Surely the test results would be back from the lab now? I thought. Nora had said Colleen was going to phone the hospital in the morning and the morning had officially ended at twelve noon. I didn't want to phone Nora and make a nuisance of myself, but I was desperate to hear and, without news to the contrary, I began to imagine the worst.

When the phone did eventually ring just after 1.00. I pounced on the extension in the kitchen, nearly tripping over the chair leg.

'Hello?'

'Cathy, it's Jill. Stella has just phoned. I understand Michael is with you?'

Disappointed that it wasn't Nora, I hoped that Jill might have more information. 'Yes, I collected him yesterday. Have you heard anything?'

'Stella phoned the hospital this morning and was told they were waiting for some test results,' Jill said.

'Yes, that's all I know.'

'How's Michael? He'll need his clothes.'

'I collected them yesterday on the way back from the hospital. A neighbour let me in. Sorry, Jill, I should have phoned and updated you, but I've been so worried waiting for news. Didn't the doctors give Stella any more details? Is Patrick still unconscious?'

'All Stella said was that Patrick had collapsed, was in hospital, and they were running tests. What have you told Michael?'

'Only that his dad is being well looked after and we should know more later today. He's coping well, considering. Adrian and Paula have been keeping him occupied.'

'Good. And how are you and the children?' Jill asked.

I appreciated her concern. 'Worried, obviously. I'll be happier when I know more.'

I heard Jill's silence. 'Cathy,' she said sombrely after a moment, 'it may be that the test results are not what any of us want to hear. It may be we have to start preparing Michael for saying goodbye to his father.'

'It's only your optimism that keeps you going,' I said curtly and unprofessionally. 'Let's wait and see what the hospital has to say tomorrow.'

'I agree,' Jill said, unperturbed. 'But bear in mind what I said. Let me know if you hear anything further. I understand you are in contact with Patrick's friends?'

'Yes.'

'And Cathy?'

'Yes?'

'The bereavement counselling that Michael will be offered will also be extended to you and the children if you want it.'

'Thanks, Jill,' I said stiffly. 'I'll remember that.'

All manner of thoughts and emotions went through my mind as I said goodbye to Jill and hung up. While I knew she had Michael's, my and my children's welfare at heart, talking about bereavement counselling was unnecessary and unhelpful at present. Also, I thought, presumptive. Jill hadn't met Patrick since that first meeting. She didn't know him and hadn't seen how well he'd been dong. Had she known him better, she would have realized that with his strength of character he wouldn't let one setback get the better of him.

Still anxious and now somewhat annoyed by Jill's comment, I hid my feelings from Paula and put away the job-application form again; there was no way I could concentrate on it now. Jill hadn't been able to tell me any more than I already knew and I was still waiting to hear from Nora. It was now nearly 1.30 and in an hour I would have to leave to collect Michael from school. I couldn't arrive at the school gates without any news of his father, so I decided that if Nora hadn't phoned by 2.00 I'd phone her. I played a few card games with Paula and then she went upstairs to play with her dolls' house in her bedroom. Finally at 1.50 the phone rang and it was Nora.

'How is he?' I asked immediately on hearing her voice.

'Much the same. Colleen has only just managed to contact someone at the hospital. I've just finished speaking to her. Patrick's blood-cell count is very low, so they are giving him more blood, and a saline solution so that he doesn't become dehydrated. Colleen and I are going to the hospital this evening, so hopefully he'll be awake by then.'

'Michael was hoping to see his father tonight but I'm not sure that's a good idea, are you?'

'No, I should wait. If he's awake tonight then you can take him tomorrow. I'll phone you either way when I get home.'

'Thanks. And Colleen didn't say any more?'

'No, only that he'd had a comfortable night, and they may do another scan later today or tomorrow.'

I thanked Nora again and we said goodbye. While it wasn't the good news I'd been hoping for – that Patrick was sitting up in bed eating and joking with the nurses – it wasn't bad news either. Aware that I should update Jill, I phoned her and told her what Nora had told me.

'Thanks, Cathy, I'll tell Stella. Let me know when you hear more. And Cathy?'

'Yes.'

'What I said earlier: obviously we're all hoping Patrick gets over this, but I have to be practical.'

'I know, Jill. Thanks.'

Chapter Nineteen

The Power of Prayer

With Paula strapped in her seat in the rear of the car listening to nursery rhymes, I drove to Michael's school for the 3.00 p.m. finish. As we waited in the playground with the other mothers and carers for the bell to ring and the children to come out, I considered what I should say to Michael about his father's condition. He was a sensible, honest boy who was very mature for his age, so he deserved an honest but age-appropriate response. Putting aside Nora's feeling that Patrick's illness had progressed further than he'd let on, which was simply her (and Jack's) view, I was left with the fact that Patrick's condition was unchanged from yesterday and he was still asleep, which is what I decided to tell Michael when he came out.

The bell sounded from inside the building and the main doors opened and were then hooked back by the school receptionist-cum-secretary. A couple of minutes later the children began streaming out, going to their parents and carers waiting in the playground. When Michael appeared the priest whom I'd met when I'd first collected Michael from school was with him. The priest had his hand lightly resting on Michael's shoulder and I saw a few of those waiting glance over and track Michael and the priest's path to us.

Paula gave my hand a little squeeze. 'I don't like that man,' she whispered. 'He's scary.'

'Sshh,' I said.

'Mrs Glass,' the priest said as he drew near.

'Hello, Father. Is everything all right?' I smiled at Michael, who wasn't looking sad, more embarrassed, which I guessed was as a result of the priest escorting him to me.

'Michael tells me his father is in hospital again and he's staying with you?' the priest said.

'Yes. Unfortunately Patrick collapsed yesterday and was taken to hospital.'

'And how is he today?' the priest asked. Michael looked at me.

I spoke to them both as I answered. 'Patrick's still asleep,' I said. 'They're doing some tests and also giving him a blood transfusion, which will help.'

The priest frowned, concerned, while Michael's face brightened.

'Dad had a transfusion last time,' Michael said. 'And he was well again after.'

'Let's hope it works this time, then,' the priest said cautiously.

'It will, Father,' Michael said. 'I'll ask for it in my prayers.'

The priest smiled and ruffled Michael's hair affectionately. 'You're a good lad, Michael. I'm sure God will hear your prayers.' Turning, he headed off across the playground to talk to another parent, the hem of his cassock kicking up as he went.

'I wish he wouldn't do that,' Michael said, flattening his hair, so that I thought he was referring to the priest ruffling his hair, which many adults do to children. But Michael added, 'First he calls my name out in assembly and tells me to wait behind so he can ask me how Dad is. Everyone stared. Then he comes out here with me. Come on, Cathy, let's go.' Picking up Paula's free hand, Michael began across the playground and towards the exit. I appreciated how Michael felt. Children hate being singled out, even if it is with good intentions as with the priest, who simply wanted to know how Patrick was. But at school Michael wanted to blend in with the other children and try to leave his worries behind, not be the boy with the sick father.

Once we were in the car I explained to Michael that his father was still asleep, and Colleen and Nora were visiting this evening, but I thought we should wait until his dad was awake before we went. Although this was my plan, if Michael had really wanted to visit his father that evening I would have taken him. With his level of maturity and close bond with his father I thought Michael could make this decision, but he accepted what I said easily.

'Yes. It's better if we wait until Dad is awake in a few days,' he said as though this would definitely happen. I had purposely been vague about the time-scale, for clearly we didn't know when Patrick would regain consciousness.

Michael and Paula came with me into the playground to collect Adrian from school and we then went straight home. Although the weather that morning had been clear, it was now showering, so the children amused themselves indoors while I made dinner. Despite the shadow of Patrick's illness hanging over us they played happily, focusing on the present and their play, as only young children can. Over dinner Adrian and Michael even managed a few 'knock-knock' jokes, some of which were almost funny: *Knock knock. Who's there? Ben. Ben who? Been knocking so long I've forgotten.* Then: *Knock knock. Who's there? Isabel. Isabel who? Isabel working? I had to knock.* And: *Knock knock. Who's there? Justin. Justin who. Justin time for dinner.* Then Adrian added with a crafty smile at Michael, 'Or Just in right.' The boys exploded into laughter.

'That's enough, thank you,' I said over their laughing, aware we were now heading for the more smutty knock-knock jokes.

'What does he mean?' Paula asked innocently, aware she was missing out on something but not knowing what.

'Nothing,' I said. 'Adrian's just being silly. Finish your dinner, good girl.'

At seven o'clock I began the bath and bedtime routine, knowing that Nora and Colleen would now be at the hospital with Patrick. I thought that if Patrick was still unconscious then they might not stay the whole two hours, which meant that Nora would probably phone me earlier. So that as the evening wore on and there was no phone call from Nora I interpreted her silence as good news – that Patrick was awake and Colleen and Nora had stayed to the end of visiting at 8.00 p.m., although I didn't voice these thoughts to Michael.

I parted Michael's bedroom curtains as he liked them so that he could see the night sky, and before he climbed into bed he knelt to say his prayers. He'd been in good spirits all evening and his prayer was light and chatty: 'Dear God, as you know my dad's in hospital. I know he needs to sleep to get better but could you wake him up in a few days, please? Wednesday or Thursday would be good, if that's all right with you? God bless Mummy, Daddy, Nora, Jack, Colleen, Eamon, Cathy, Adrian and Paula. Amen.'

'Good boy,' I said, holding back the duvet so that Michael could climb into bed. I wondered if I should explain to Michael the difference between being 'asleep' and 'unconscious', which had become confused, but decided against it. There'd be time later if necessary to explain, for now Michael had put his faith in his God and it was helping him through this difficult time. We said goodnight and I came out; then I went into Adrian's room and said goodnight to him before checking on Paula, who was fast asleep.

It was nearly nine o'clock when I went downstairs and, believing that 'no news was good news' and that Nora would phone shortly to tell me Patrick was awake and recovering, I settled down in front of the television. When the phone rang ten minutes later it was Nora, but she didn't have the good news I'd been anticipating.

'No change, I'm afraid,' she said, her voice subdued. 'And they've finished giving him the blood plasma.'

'So why's he still unconscious?' I asked. 'Did they say?'

'The nurse tried to explain that when the body is under trauma sometimes the mind shuts down to protect itself. Jack wondered if Pat had hit his head when he'd collapsed on Sunday but when I asked the nurse she said there was no sign of a head injury.'

'So what is the trauma, then?'

'His illness, I suppose.'

'I see,' I said slowly, not really understanding, but aware Nora didn't know any more.

'How's Michael?' Nora asked.

'He's all right. He firmly believes his dad will be awake in a couple of days. I hope he's right.'

'So do I,' Nora said. 'Or we'll all have some adjusting to do, very quickly.' I understood what she meant, for I was no better prepared to accept that Patrick might not regain consciousness than presumably she, Jack, Eamon and Colleen were, and certainly not Michael.

Nora promised she'd phone again as soon as she heard anything and, if not before, then the following evening after she and Colleen had been to the hospital. We said goodbye and I went upstairs to check on the children, wondering if they'd been woken by the ringing of the phone. Adrian and Paula were asleep but as I crept into Michael's room I saw his eyes were open; he was lying on his back and gazing towards the window at the darkening sky.

'Are you all right, love?' I asked gently, moving closer to his bed. He gave a small nod. 'That was Nora on the phone. She and Colleen have just returned from the hospital. Your dad is still asleep.'

Michael gave another small nod. 'He'll wake up on Wednesday or Thursday,' he said matter-of-factly. 'That's what I asked for in my prayers.' And while I was impressed by Michael's faith in the power of prayer I was concerned that if Patrick didn't regain consciousness Michael was going to find it even more difficult to cope. But for the same reasons I hadn't explained the difference between being asleep and unconscious I decided not to shake his conviction now by suggesting the alternative.

'I'm praying he'll be awake soon too,' I said, and left it at that.

But when Tuesday and Wednesday came and went with no change in Patrick's condition I began to start thinking the unthinkable: that I would have to prepare Michael (and Adrian, Paula and myself) for the possibility that Patrick might never regain consciousness. My eyes filled at the very thought. Nora phoned on Wednesday evening and couldn't hide her sorrow and sounded very depressed. She said that officially, according to the doctor, there was no change in Patrick's condition but she personally thought his colour looked even worse despite the blood transfusion. She said that if there was still no improvement in Pat's condition by Friday or if his condition worsened then she thought I should take Michael to see his father at the weekend to say goodbye. Her voice broke, and she added that

Jack and Eamon would be going with her and Colleen to the hospital the following evening, Thursday.

On Thursday morning when I woke Adrian and Paula they asked me how Patrick was, as they had done every morning that week, and I again said there was no change and he was still unconscious. After Nora's phone call I'd decided I'd better start using the word unconscious to make the distinction between Patrick's condition and natural sleep. Adrian and Paula looked sad but didn't say anything. When I woke Michael and told him he said forcefully, 'Dad would never leave me without saying goodbye.' I wasn't sure if it was a statement, a sign of his faith, or a desperate plea.

'No,' I said quietly.

Jill phoned on Thursday morning just after I'd arrived home from taking the children to school. She said she'd spoken to Stella, who had spoken to the doctor the day before, but Jill didn't really tell me any more than I already knew: that Patrick was comfortable but wasn't improving. Jill said the hospital would phone Stella if there was any change. Stella had scheduled a meeting with the doctor to review Patrick's case for the following week, when they would consider the options of moving Patrick to a nursing home or hospice. I put the phone down and cried openly. All week I'd been strong for Michael, hoping that his prayers would be answered and Patrick would regain consciousness, leave hospital and continue life where he'd left off. Now I was starting to think that the best I could hope for was that Michael and his father would get the chance to say goodbye to each other, although with Patrick still unconscious even that seemed unlikely.

On Thursday afternoon I was in the garden bringing in the washing from the line while Paula played in the sandpit when the phone began ringing from indoors. Leaving Paula playing, I dropped the towel I'd just unpegged into the washing basket and went in through the French windows, dreading answering the phone for fear of the news it could bring.

'Hello?' I asked tentatively, picking up the receiver in the sitting room. There was no reply, just an odd rustling sound. 'Hello?' I said again. 'Who's there?'

There was another small silence followed by a rustle before a croaky voice said, 'Hello, Cathy.'

I couldn't believe my ears. 'Patrick?' I gasped. 'Is that you?'

'Yes. Sorry, I dropped the phone on the bed. Look, I can't talk much: my throat is very sore. Will you bring Michael to the hospital this evening to see me?'

'Yes, of course. How are you? Oh, I'm so pleased to hear you.'

'I'm doing all right, thank you.' I heard his breath catch before he said, 'See you both tonight, then. Goodbye, love.'

Chapter Twenty

Hospital

I returned the receiver to its cradle, overwhelmed and hardly daring to believe. Patrick, who a few minutes ago I thought might never regain consciousness, was now awake and well enough to phone me. With my heart pounding and choking back emotion I immediately picked up the receiver again and dialled Nora's number. It was engaged. I pressed 5 for ringback so that as soon as she'd finished on the phone it would reconnect to me. Perching on the sofa, I kept an eye on Paula in the garden while I waited for the phone to ring. Patrick was awake: I could scarcely believe it. I couldn't wait to tell Michael! The first thing Michael always asked when I collected him from school was: 'How's Dad?' And now I could say, 'He phoned, and you are going to see him tonight.' I could picture his little face, so happy and relieved.

I jumped as the phone gave two rings, signalling ringback, and picked it up.

'Nora, it's Cathy.'

'Oh, Cathy, Pat's just phoned me. He said he'd spoken to you. Isn't it wonderful? I was so surprised. Wait until I tell Jack.'

'Yes, it's incredible,' I said. Pat's asked me to take Michael to the hospital this evening.'

Hospital

'I know: he said. So I think Jack and I, and Colleen and Eamon, will wait until seven to visit. It will give Michael a chance to spend time with his dad. Did Pat say anything else to you?'

'No, only to bring Michael. He sounded quite weak.'

'Yes. I think he just wanted to let us to know that he was awake and recovering. He asked me to phone Colleen and tell her.'

I smiled. 'I can't wait to tell Michael.'

'No. Bless him. See you later, then. I'm off to find Jack. He's pottering in the garden and didn't hear the phone ring.'

We said goodbye and I hung up.

For the same reason that Nora had decided that she, Jack, Eamon and Colleen would delay visiting Pat until 7.00 p.m. – so Michael could spend time with his father – I decided not to take Adrian and Paula to the hospital that evening. Also, I wanted to make sure Patrick felt well enough to have lots of visitors; children can be very tiring for an adult who's not feeling well. If Pat felt well enough I could take Adrian and Paula with me when I took Michael at the weekend. I assumed that as Pat had made the decision for Michael to see him in hospital, he would want me to take Michael every day.

Aware it was short notice and that I was asking a big favour, I picked up the phone again and dialled Jenny's number. She had children of her own, so whether or not she could babysit for me that evening would depend on Ben, her husband, being home to look after their boys. Jenny didn't know Pat was in hospital again and when I briefly explained what had happened, she was more than happy to sit for me and said she'd phone Ben to make sure he was home from the office by 5.30. I thanked her very much. As a single parent and foster carer, I'd be at a complete loss without friends like Jenny to help me out at short notice.

I went into the garden and told Paula that Patrick was awake and had just phoned me from hospital. 'That's good,' she smiled happily. 'I like Patrick. Michael will be pleased.'

We arrived at Michael's school ten minutes before coming-out time and waited in the playground for the bell to go. As soon as Michael arrived at my side I said: 'Good news! Your dad is awake. He phoned me this afternoon and I'm taking you to see him tonight.'

'Yippee!' he said, giving Paula and then me a big hug. 'I knew he would. I just knew it. My dad's awake!'

Michael held Paula's hand as we began towards the car and I explained to Michael what had happened: that the phone had rung an hour before and when I'd answered I'd been so surprised to hear his dad. I continued with the warning that he'd sounded very weak and we might not stay the whole two hours if he was tired and needed to sleep, which Michael understood.

'When can I see Patrick in hospital?' Paula asked, once we were in the car.

'Maybe at the weekend,' I said. 'If Patrick feels up to it.'

'When's the weekend?' Paula asked.

'The day after tomorrow,' Michael explained as he fastened first Paula's seat belt and then his own in the rear. 'I'll teach you the days of the week if you like.'

'Yes please,' she said, resting her head on his shoulder. So the journey to Adrian's school was to the sound of Michael chanting the days of the week and Paula making a good attempt to repeat them in the correct order.

The three of us then waited in the playground to meet Adrian, and as soon as he came out Michael told him the good news. 'Dad's awake and I'm going to see him tonight!'

'Cool,' Adrian said, which was his latest expression.

'And we're going at the weekend,' Paula added.

'If Patrick feels well enough,' I qualified.

Once we were home the time vanished. I made an early dinner and Jill phoned while we were eating to tell me what I already knew: that Patrick had regained consciousness. Apparently the hospital had notified Stella, who'd phoned Jill. I updated Jill – that Patrick had phoned me and I was taking Michael to see him tonight.

'I'll tell Stella,' Jill said. 'I'll phone you tomorrow to see how it went.'

'Yes, fine.'

Usually information about a foster child and their family comes from the social worker or support social worker (Jill) but in this case because I was in close contact with Patrick and his friends I tended to be aware of new information or developments first and pass them on to Jill and the social services.

I finished eating, fed Toscha, gave the children pudding, and while they ate I had a quick wash, changed my clothes, and then cleared away the dinner things. Jenny arrived at 5.40. She knew where everything was and I told her to help herself to whatever she fancied in the kitchen. I'd already explained to Paula that Jenny would be putting her to bed – Adrian would stay up later – so, giving Paula and Adrian a kiss and a hug, I thanked Jenny, and left with Michael. Michael was looking very smart in weekend casual clothes – navy trousers and matching sweatshirt. In the car he could barely contain his excitement: bobbing up and down in his seat, avidly watching the journey progress through the windows, and chatting away excitedly. 'It's been ages since I've seen Dad,' he said more than once. 'Sunday was such a long time ago. I knew he'd wake up. I knew it. My prayers were answered, weren't they, Cathy?'

'Yes, love, they certainly were.'

I parked in the hospital car park, fed one-pound coins into the ticket machine and then placed the ticket on the dashboard. As Michael and I crossed the car park to the main entrance I reminded him that his father might be very tired and may not be able to talk much. But nothing could dampen Michael's enthusiasm. 'No worries, I'll talk to him,' he said, beaming.

It was only when we entered the hospital and I saw the ward names displayed on the board with arrows pointing in different directions that I realized I didn't know which ward Patrick was on. When I'd collected Michael on Sunday Pat had just been admitted and was in casualty, but now he would be on a ward. I wondered if Nora had thought to ask Pat which ward he was on; probably not, or she would have told me.

'I'll just find out where your dad is,' I said to Michael, leading the way to the reception desk.

I gave Patrick's full name to the receptionist. She asked for the date Patrick was admitted and was then able to find him on the computer. 'Constable Ward,' she said. 'Go down the main corridor, up the flight of stairs on your right, and the ward is second on the left.'

I thanked her and, with Michael by my side, we went down the corridor and up the flight of steps, which opened on to a landing. 'All the wards up here are named after famous paint-ers,' I said to Michael, pointing to the board showing the first-floor ward names.

We approached the second set of swing doors, over which was a large plaque showing Constable Ward, and going in we found ourselves standing at the end of a long ward with a row of beds on either side. It was an all-male ward and all the beds were taken. Each bed was separated from the next by a bedside cabinet and curtains in the traditional hospital layout; some of the curtains were open and others were partially drawn. Michael and I began down the centre aisle, scanning the beds and the faces of the patients nestled on their pillows.

'There's Dad!' Michael cried, spotting his father halfway down the ward on the right. He rushed over and I followed. By the time I arrived at the bed Michael was already lying on the bed, hugging and kissing his father.

I stood to one side, waiting for my turn to say hello. Patrick had his arms around his son and his head buried in Michael's shoulder. A drip ran from Patrick's left arm and I was concerned Michael might accidentally catch it; I moved it slightly so that it was out of the way. For a few moments father and son didn't speak; they just held each other tightly as though they would never let go. I couldn't see their faces, as they were buried in each other's shoulders, but I could guess the emotion they showed.

Slowly Pat relaxed his arms from around Michael and, raising his head, looked and smiled at me. 'Hello, Cathy,' he said quietly. 'Good to see you again.'

'Good to see you too,' I said. Leaning forward, over Michael, I kissed Patrick's cheek.

Michael was still half-lying on the bed, hugging his dad for all he was worth. I pulled up the chair from beside the cabinet and sat as close as I could to the bed. Pat's free hand opened and sought mine.

'How are you?' I asked, taking his hand.

'Not bad. All the better for seeing Michael and you.' He smiled again and then paused to catch his breath. 'I can remember leaving church on Sunday and then nothing. The nurses tell me it's Thursday today.'

'That's right.'

'Doesn't time fly!' he joked, the old Patrick shining through.

I could see he'd lost weight in the four days he'd been unconscious. And while his skin wasn't as pale as it had been the last time I'd seen him on Sunday, when it had been almost grey, his breathing was laboured and talking clearly took a lot of effort; although that he was awake and talking at all was a minor miracle, I thought.

'We've all been so worried about you,' I said, stroking his hand. 'Adrian and Paula send their love.'

'Who's looking after them?' he asked, ever thoughtful of others.

'Jenny.'

He nodded.

'I understand Nora and Jack are coming later with Eamon and Colleen?'

'Yes. They've been so good to me.'

We continued talking, mainly about what Michael had been doing since Sunday. Pat had to pause between sentences to take deep breaths; Michael lay on the bed beside him, snuggled into his side. Every so often Michael lightly touched his father's face with his fingertips, as if checking he was still there and real. Presently Pat needed to change position to be comfortable and Michael climbed off the bed. Together we helped his father to sit more upright and I plumped the pillows behind him; then the two of us carefully eased him back on to the pillows.

'Ah, that's better,' Pat sighed. Then to me: 'You should have been a nurse.'

I laughed. 'I did think about it when I left school.'

'You'd have been good at it,' Pat said, smiling.

Michael now sat on the bed close to his father and told him more about his week at school, and then answered his dad's questions about whether he was doing his school work and able to concentrate with him being in hospital. Michael said he was and Pat praised him. Then Michael told his dad the Scalextric was at my house and I asked if that was all right.

'Of course,' Patrick said. 'Take whatever you need from the house to make him comfortable. Has he got enough clothes with him? I might be in here for a while.'

I saw Michael's face cloud at the mention of his dad staying in hospital; I suppose he thought that now his father was awake he would be able to go home very quickly, but I knew from seeing Patrick just how frail he was and that he wouldn't be discharged for a while.

'I might collect some more of his clothes over the weekend,' I said to Pat. 'When Nora arrives, I'll ask her when it will be convenient.'

Pat nodded. 'And remind me to ask her to check my fridge. Stuff will be going off by now.'

'Don't worry,' I said. 'A few bad eggs won't hurt. Just concentrate on getting better.'

'As long as you're not a bad egg,' Pat joked with Michael, ruffling his son's hair.

The three of us continued chatting generally – about the weather, the news on television, the games Michael had played with Adrian and then the homework Michael was supposed to be doing that evening.

'I'll explain to the school you saw your father this evening and you'll do your homework at the weekend,' I said to Michael. I knew there wouldn't be time when we arrived home to do it.

At exactly seven o'clock I saw Patrick's gaze shift to over my shoulder. 'They're here,' he said.

I turned to see Nora, Jack, Colleen and Eamon coming towards us. Chatting excitedly and carrying gifts of sweets, fruit and flowers, they were like a group of guests arriving at a house party. Other patients and their visitors turned to look at them as they surrounded the bed with 'Hi's and 'Hello's, and took turns to hug and kiss Pat. Pat smiled and thanked them as they laid the flowers, sweets and grapes on the bed beside him, and I saw his eyes mist.

Standing, I insisted Nora sit in my chair while Eamon said he'd find one for Colleen. He glanced around and then turned to a young man in his late teens in the next bed who didn't have a visitor. 'Could I borrow your chair if it's not being used?' Eamon asked him.

'Sure, mate,' the young man said. 'My girl can't get in today because of our kid.'

'Thanks,' Eamon said, sliding the chair over. 'Tell us to shut up if we're making too much noise.'

'You're all right, mate,' the young man said. 'This place could do with livening up. It's like a morgue.'

As we'd come into the ward I'd seen a printed sign on the door stating that only two visitors were allowed at a patient's bed at any time, but the nurses seemed to overlook the fact that there were now six of us around Pat's bed, and not being particularly quiet either. Michael sat on the bed beside his father, enjoying the attention he was now receiving, while Nora and Colleen sat on the chairs on one side of the bed and I stood between Jack and Eamon on the other side. There was a party atmosphere, with lots of joking and quick-witted repartee between Jack and Eamon, which set us all laughing. We ate some of the grapes and sweets and Pat's friends asked Michael about school and if he was behaving himself; then Nora retrieved a large bag which she'd tucked beside her feet. 'I thought Michael might need some more clothes,' she said, passing the bag to me.

'Thank you,' I said. 'You must have read my thoughts.'

'That'll save you a trip.' Pat smiled at me.

'Your house is fine,' Nora reassured Pat. 'I'm putting your mail on the hall table: I didn't think you'd want to be bothered with it in here. I've cancelled your milk and paper for now. I'll start them again when we know when you're coming home.'

'Thanks, love,' Pat said. 'I think I might be here for a while. I can't get out of bed at present without help, let alone walk upstairs.' This was the only time Patrick mentioned his condition and the conversation remained light and chatty. We were like a group of friends on a night out, and not for the first time I was touched by the depth of their friendship and that they had welcomed me into their group after knowing me for such a short while.

At eight o'clock a bell rang, signalling the end of visiting time.

'That went quickly,' Nora said. 'Eight already!'

She and Colleen stood to say goodbye as Eamon returned Colleen's chair to the neighbour's bed. 'Thanks,' Eamon said, and then gave the young man a handful of Patrick's wrapped sweets, which we'd all been tucking into.

'Cheers, mate,' the young man said. 'That's nice of you.' I felt sorry for him, having no visitors, and he looked very young to have a child of his own.

Nora and Colleen kissed Pat, and then Eamon and Jack shook his hand and hugged him. Pat was looking tired now, although his cheeks were flushed from talking and laughing, giving him a healthier glow.

'You get some sleep now,' Colleen said. 'We'll see you again over the weekend.' The four of them then left with waves and calls of goodbye as Michael began saying goodbye. He hugged and kissed his dad and told him over and over again he missed him and he had to come home soon. I saw Patrick's eyes well.

I said goodbye; leaning forward I kissed Patrick's cheek and felt his arms around me, holding me tight. 'Thanks for all you're doing, love,' he said quietly. 'I don't know what I'd do without you.'

I kissed his cheek again and slowly straightened. 'Shall we come again tomorrow evening?' I asked.

'Yes please.'

'I was thinking I might bring Adrian and Paula at the weekend,' I added. 'What do you think?'

He hesitated. 'To be honest, Cathy, I'd rather you waited until I'm up and about. It won't be much fun for them here. Do you mind?'

'No, of course not.'

'Send them my love.'

'I will.'

Michael hugged and kissed his dad again and then I slowly drew him away from the bed. We walked down the centre aisle of the ward, stopping every so often to turn and wave. Patrick waved back. We gave a final wave as we went through the double doors and out of the ward.

'All right?' I asked Michael, touching his shoulder reassuringly.

He nodded. 'Why do you think Dad doesn't want Adrian and Paula to visit at the weekend?' he asked thoughtfully.

'Because he wants to wait until he's feeling better.'

We continued along the corridor. Michael was quiet and then said, 'I hope that's the real reason.'

'What do you mean?' I asked, glancing at him, puzzled. 'What other reason could there be?'

Hospital

'I don't know.' He shrugged. 'It's just not the sort of thing Dad would normally say.'

'No, but he's ill. I can understand why he wouldn't feel up to it.'

But Michael was right: there was another reason his dad didn't want Adrian and Paula to visit him, although I didn't find out what it was until some time later, and when I did I was heartbroken.

Chapter Twenty-One
Support

It was after 8.30 p.m. by the time we arrived home and, leaving the bag of clothes Nora had packed in the hall, I sent Michael upstairs to wash and change, ready for bed, while I saw Jenny out. Jenny said Adrian and Paula had been fine during the evening and that Paula was asleep and Adrian was in bed reading. She asked me how Patrick was and I said he was weak but recovering. I then said, 'Jenny, I know this is asking a lot but I've got a bit of a problem. Pat doesn't feel up to having Adrian and Paula visit him, but he would like to see Michael again tomorrow. I won't keep asking you, but is there any chance that you could sit for me again tomorrow evening? It would be the same time. I'll understand if you can't.' I felt awful asking.

'No problem,' Jenny said easily. 'Of course I'll help you out. If Ben isn't home in time I'll bring the boys. It's Friday, so a late night won't hurt them.'

'Thank you so much,' I said. 'I'm very grateful.'

'Don't be silly,' she said. 'You're welcome.'

I thanked her again; we said goodnight and I saw her out. While I was relieved Jenny could help me out again the following evening, I knew I couldn't keep asking her and I would need to make other arrangements, although quite what escaped me. I could ask Rose, but like Jenny she had children of her own, as did most of my other friends, so asking for regular babysitting when they should be with their families seemed an imposition; and not knowing how long Patrick would be in hospital made planning more difficult.

Taking the bag of Michael's clothes upstairs, I left it on the landing and went into Paula's room. She was on her side and sound asleep. With her small delicate features relaxed in sleep and her long fair hair spread out on the pillow behind her, she looked angelic. I stroked a few strands of hair away from her face and then kissed her cheek and crept out, leaving the bedroom door slightly ajar, as she liked it. Michael had finished in the bathroom and was just disappearing into his bedroom. 'I'll be with you in a minute,' I called as I went into Adrian's room to say goodnight.

Adrian was propped on his pillows, reading by the light of his lamp. 'Everything OK?' I asked.

He nodded and glanced up from his book. 'How's Patrick?'

'He's doing all right. He sends his love. Finish the chapter and then I want you to go to sleep.' Adrian loves reading and I was sure he would read all night if I let him.

I kissed Adrian goodnight and came out, closing his bedroom door, as he preferred, although I would check on him later to make sure he had switched off his lamp. Taking the bag of clothes Nora had sent, I went into Michael's room. He was in bed, presumably having said his prayers, and was now lying on his back, gazing through the curtains at the darkening sky.

'I'll unpack these tomorrow,' I said, placing the bag of clothes to one side, out of the way.

'Cathy,' Michael said, 'how long do you think Dad will be in hospital?'

'I'm not sure, love, but I think it will be at least a week,' I said, perching on the edge of the bed.

'I was thinking,' Michael said. 'If you, Adrian, Paula and Toscha came to live at my house, we could all help to look after dad and then he could come out of hospital sooner. Dad says you'd be a good nurse and I think so too.'

I smiled. 'That's nice of you to say. And I shall certainly be helping you and your dad when he leaves hospital. But for now your dad needs to be looked after by qualified doctors and nurses who know what medicine to give him.'

'Or Dad and I could come here to live?' Michael persisted. 'We don't have a cat, so it would be easier.'

I laid my hand lightly on his arm. 'Michael, love, I don't want you to worry. Your dad is being well looked after. He is in the best place, honestly. When he comes out of hospital he'll want to go to home, and Nora, Jack, Colleen, Eamon and I will all help him. So please stop worrying. The adults will take care of him.' Which seemed to reassure Michael. He yawned, turned on to his side and asked for a kiss goodnight. When I looked in on him ten minutes later he was asleep; so too was Adrian, having switched off the lamp.

I sent a note into school with Michael the following day, explaining that Michael hadn't done his homework because he had been visiting his father in hospital and he would do it at the weekend. When I met Michael from school at the end of the day he handed me a folded note from his teacher. I read it as we walked to the car: *Dear Mrs Glass, thank you for your letter. The head has made me aware of Michael's father's illness. Of course Michael can do his homework whenever he has the time. Kind regards, Jane Wilson.* Michael had read the letter and said smartly: 'Miss Wilson says I can do my homework any time. It doesn't have to be this weekend.'

Support

'She says when you have the time,' I corrected, 'and you'll have time this weekend.'

'I might not,' Michael said, bobbing along beside me. 'I've got to see my dad.'

'Of course you'll see your dad,' I said, 'but you'll still have time to do your homework. I'll make sure of it.'

He pulled a face and then went quiet for a moment.

'I'll help you if it's difficult,' I added.

'It's not,' he grumbled. 'I just don't want to do it.'

Paula looked at him oddly, never having seen Michael sulk before.

'Your dad thinks school work is important and so do I,' I said, and opened the car door.

Michael climbed in, scowling; he sulked for five minutes and was then over the grumps. He wasn't a moody child but like most boys his age he'd rather have been playing than doing homework.

I sometimes find that when I have a problem to which I'm trying to find a solution, suddenly the answer appears and the problem is solved as if by magic. So it was with the problem of finding a sitter for Adrian and Paula while I took Michael to the hospital. I had Friday covered – Jenny was going to sit; and then driving home on Friday morning, having taken Paula to nursery, I hit upon the idea of asking my parents if they could sit on Saturday and then stay for dinner. They were due for a visit and Patrick had suggested that at the weekend Michael could visit in the afternoon session, 2.00–4.00, instead of the evening. Once home, I phoned Mum and put my suggestion to her; naturally she and Dad were happy to help and thanked me for the invitation to dinner. Then twenty minutes later the phone rang and it was Colleen. Having said

hello and asked how we all were, she said: 'I've just been talking to Nora about hospital visiting. We think it's better if we
take it in turns to visit Pat rather than all four of us go
together. Pat looked very tired last night by the time we left.
So Eamon and I are planning to visit on Sunday afternoon
and Nora and Jack will go in the evening. I was wondering if
it would help if we took Michael to the hospital on Sunday
afternoon with us? Eamon and I usually go to church on
Sunday morning, so we were thinking Michael could come
with us to church, then we'd have some lunch and go on to
the hospital for two o'clock. We could drop him off afterwards. What do you think?'

'Well, yes, if you're sure. That's very nice of you.'

'Not at all. Eamon and I would like the company and
Michael knows us well. We're his godparents, you know? We've
taken Michael to church before and he has stayed with us
sometimes.'

'I'm sure Michael will like that, and it will also help me out. I
was struggling to find someone to stay with Adrian and Paula
on Sunday.'

'Look, love,' Colleen said kindly, 'if we can be of any help let
us know. You only have to say. You've got a heart of gold doing
the fostering with two children of your own. I don't know how
you manage it.'

Neither did I sometimes, but as usual when someone praises
what I do I felt embarrassed and uncomfortable. 'Thank you,' I
said quietly.

'Church is at ten fifteen, so can we collect Michael at nine
forty-five?'

'Yes. But I don't think Michael has his suit with him, unless
it's in the bag Nora sent. I haven't had a chance to unpack it yet.
I know Pat likes Michael to wear his suit for church.'

Support

'Don't worry,' Colleen said. 'It won't hurt this once. It's our souls the good Lord is after, not our clothes.'

I laughed. 'OK. Thanks again. See you Sunday.'

Although I was sure Stella wouldn't mind if Colleen and Eamon took Michael to church, gave him lunch and then took him to the hospital, as Michael's social worker, I still had to have her consent. Michael was in care on a voluntary care order, so the usual constraints of fostering a child under a full care order didn't apply. Had Michael been taken into care on an emergency protection order it would have been very different: Colleen and Eamon and anyone else over the age of twelve with whom Michael spent time alone would have had to be vetted by the social services and police-checked, as I was. It might seem over-zealous but it is to protect the child.

I phoned Jill, told her how Patrick had been the previous evening when Michael and I had visited him in hospital and how Michael had been after the visit; then I asked her about Sunday.

'I'm sure it will be fine,' Jill said. 'I'll tell Stella and get back to you if there's a problem, which I'm sure there won't be. It was nice of them to offer to help out,' Jill added. 'And Michael will enjoy it.'

'Yes, he will,' I agreed.

Jill paused and then said, 'Cathy, I think you're going to need some more help, from the agency, if Patrick is staying in hospital and doesn't want Adrian and Paula there. Shall I arrange for some support? One of our carers could babysit Adrian and Paula in the evenings next week while you take Michael.'

I knew my fostering agency offered 'support', as it's termed, but I hadn't thought to ask. When I'd first started fostering I'd accepted all the support that was on offer, but once experienced

I hadn't really needed it, until now. Now I realized I needed help and should accept Jill's offer.

'Thanks, Jill,' I said. 'That would be a big help. Can it be a carer Adrian and Paula know?'

'I'll see who's available and get back to you.'

'Thanks,' I said again. I put the phone down and breathed an enormous sigh of relief. Now I could concentrate on looking after Adrian, Paula and Michael without the continual worry of finding sitters.

I went upstairs and unpacked the bag Nora had sent. She'd included the suit and tie Michael wore for church and I hung it in the wardrobe with the other clothes she'd sent: more casual outfits, trainers and another set of pyjamas. Jill phoned twenty minutes later and said that Helen Lewis could babysit Adrian and Paula every evening the following week. I was very pleased. I knew Helen, and so too did Adrian and Paula. Helen and her husband, Pete, were a lovely couple in their early sixties who usually fostered babies. Their last child had recently been adopted after living with them for nearly two years and they were now taking some time off before the next baby arrived. Their own children were adults and lived away from home. I already had Helen's phone number, so I thanked Jill and told her I'd phone Helen over the weekend to clarify the arrangements for the following week.

I collected Paula from nursery at twelve noon and on the way home I stopped off and bought a large box of chocolates as a thank-you present for Jenny. I then explained the plans for the weekend and the following week to Paula: that Nana and Grandpa were coming on Saturday to stay with her and Adrian while I took Michael to the hospital and would then stay for dinner, which delighted Paula. Then on Sunday Colleen and Eamon would take Michael to church and to the hospital; and the following week Helen Lewis would be sitting with her and Adrian.

'So we're not going to the hospital?' Paula asked, when I'd finished, remembering I'd said I might take her and Adrian at the weekend.

'No, Patrick is very tired and wants to wait until he's better before he sees you and Adrian.'

Paula accepted this and then asked: 'Can we have an ice cream every time you go out, like we did last night?' As a treat – to soften the blow of her and Adrian being left behind – I'd told Jenny they could have an ice cream when I'd gone.

'Yes, all right,' I said, smiling. 'But that's a lot of ice creams. I'd better stock up the freezer. How many will I need to buy altogether? Do you know?'

Paula looked thoughtful and then began counting on her fingers, adding up two ice creams a day to the end of the following week. 'Sixteen,' she announced proudly at last.'

'Fourteen,' I said.

She frowned, puzzled. 'No, it's sixteen, I'm sure.'

'It's fourteen,' I said, keeping a straight face. 'You and Adrian won't need an ice cream on Sunday because I won't be leaving you.'

'Oh Mum!' she said, realizing I was joking, and playfully tapped my arm.

Later that afternoon when I met Michael from school I explained the arrangements to him, and he was comfortable with spending most of Sunday with Colleen and Eamon and said he'd done a similar thing before when his dad had been unwell. When I met Adrian from school I repeated the arrangements; why I hadn't waited until all the children were together so I only had to explain once, I didn't know. I think it was because I tried to treat each child as an individual with their own personality and needs. Adrian, like Paula, was pleased at the thought of spending Saturday with Nana and Grandpa.

Friday evening followed the same routine as Thursday, with an early dinner ready for when Jenny arrived at 5.40. Jenny brought her sons, aged eight and six, with her and Adrian's and Paula's faces lit up. They were so excited at the prospect of playing with friends all evening that they nearly forgot to kiss me goodbye before rushing off. Michael looked a little disappointed that he couldn't stay and join in the fun, although of course he was pleased to be seeing his father.

'Send Patrick my best wishes,' Jenny called as she saw Michael and me off at the door.

'I will. Thanks again. Help yourself to whatever you want from the kitchen.'

We arrived in the hospital car park at exactly six o'clock; I fed the meter and then Michael and I joined the other visitors going in through the main entrance. I stopped off quickly at the small shop in the lobby and bought a newspaper and packet of biscuits for Patrick, and a bar of chocolate Michael fancied. I didn't buy sweets for Patrick, as I thought he would still have plenty of those Colleen and Nora had given him the night before.

As we entered the ward Patrick was watching the door and spotted us straight away. He was propped on his pillows and gave a little wave. Going over we both kissed him and I asked how he was feeling. 'Not bad,' he said. And I thought he looked much brighter.

Michael sprawled on the bed next to his dad as he had the evening before, while I pulled up the chair. I was pleased to see that the young man in the next bed had a visitor – a young woman with a child, whom I took to be his partner and son.

Support

Patrick thanked me for the newspaper and biscuits and for buying Michael the chocolate bar.

'I must give you some money,' he said. 'I know how much this lad eats.'

'There's no need,' I said. 'The social services give me an allowance.'

'I know, but it doesn't seem right. When I first approached the social services I offered to pay for Michael's keep but Stella said they couldn't accept it: that there was no provision to accept it, which seems daft.'

I agreed. I had sometimes thought that families with children in care should perhaps contribute to their children's keep if they had the means. But then again, given that most children in care weren't there on a voluntary basis, as Michael was, but had been removed from their parents (for abuse and neglect) it hardly seemed sensitive to take away the children and then ask their parents to pay to have them looked after. It was an uncomfortable issue and Patrick's case was unusual, as was his offer to contribute.

We were the only visitors Pat had that evening and if I'm honest conversation flagged after the first hour. Patrick tired easily and while he was obviously happy that we were there he was largely content just to sit and listen. Michael exhausted all his news by seven o'clock and then snuggled into his father with one eye on the television which hung from a central point on the ceiling. It was therefore left to me to keep the conversation going and I searched for things to tell Pat that might be of interest and I hadn't said already. After a while Patrick began to doze, his eyes closing and then suddenly opening with a start.

'Sorry,' he said. 'I must have dropped off. How rude of me!'

'Have a sleep if you want to,' I reassured him. 'Michael is happy to just be with you.'

'And you, Cathy?' he said taking my hand. 'Are you pleased to be with me?'

'Yes, of course.' I smiled.

Patrick dozed until eight o'clock when the bell woke him up. He came to with a start and apologized again; then said he'd make sure he was wide awake when we visited the following day. I told him again not to worry and then, checking he had everything he needed, Michael and I kissed him goodbye and came away. He waved until we went through the doors at the end of the ward and were out of sight.

When we arrived home all the children were in high sprits. Paula was in her pyjamas and still up and having so much fun she hardly noticed I'd returned. Michael immediately joined in the game of hide and seek while Jenny and I escaped to the kitchen, where I made a cup of tea. We told the children the kitchen was off limits in their game unless there was an emergency or we were needed. Then Jenny and I settled at the breakfast bar with our tea and a slice of cake each and had a good girly chat. It was nearly ten o'clock when Jenny finally said they should be going and called her boys. I thanked her again for helping me and gave her the box of chocolates.

'You shouldn't have,' she said.

'I'm very grateful,' I said. 'I couldn't have managed without you.' Which was true.

The four of us stood on the doorstep and waved goodbye to Jenny and her sons and I closed the front door. The children were exhausted, although they wouldn't admit it, and I took them straight up to bed. The evening had made a pleasant end to a week fuelled by uncertainty and anxiety and I was now looking forward to the weekend. My parents were coming on Saturday, and then on Sunday I would be able to spend time with Adrian and Paula while Colleen and Eamon took Michael to church and the hospital. I could relax now I knew Patrick was recovering from the setback and would leave hospital before too long.

Chapter Twenty-Two

Improving

We all had a lie-in on Saturday morning and weren't up and dressed until ten o'clock. After breakfast I suggested to Adrian and Michael that now would be a good time to do their homework.

'There'll be plenty of time later,' Adrian said. Michael agreed.

'So you're going to do it while Nana and Grandpa are here?' I asked Adrian. 'And you're taking yours to the hospital when you see your dad?' I asked Michael.

They took my point. 'Let's do it now and get it out of the way,' Michael said, and Adrian agreed.

'Excellent decision,' I said.

'Hurry up,' Paula said. 'Then we can play outside.'

It was a lovely warm June day and I knew the boys wanted to play in the garden, which they could do once they'd done their homework. Adrian and Michael fetched their school bags from the hall and settled at the table. Adrian had maths and some spellings to learn while Michael had an essay to write entitled 'Life in a Faraway Land'.

'Do they mean the Isle of Wight?' I joked to Michael.

He smiled. 'Africa,' he said. 'The church has missionaries there. We've been learning about them in RE [religious education].'

Improving

'What's a missionary?' Paula asked.

Michael explained: 'A person from the church who goes to faraway countries. They do good work and try and convert the people who live there.' So I thought he had been listening in his lessons.

'What's convert?' Paula asked.

Michael thought. 'Change people's minds,' he said after a moment.

'What? Like we try and change Mum's mind if we want more television?'

Michael and Adrian laughed. 'No,' Michael said. 'The missionaries try to change their minds about religion so they worship our God.'

'Are there lots of gods?' Paula asked.

'Possibly,' I said, intervening. I could see this conversation going on all morning to the exclusion of homework, so before we entered a theological discussion I asked Paula to help me while Adrian and Michael did their homework.

An hour later all the homework was finished. I checked it through and then the boys took their school bags to the hall, where they left them ready for Monday. The children then played in the garden while I did some of the preparation for dinner that evening, so that I didn't have it all to do when I returned from the hospital.

Mum and Dad arrived at 1.00 p.m. and as usual were overjoyed to see us. They hadn't met Michael before, although they'd spoken to him on the phone.

'What a lovely boy,' Mum said to me as we ate a sandwich lunch in the garden. 'He's so polite and respectful. It's so sad about his father.'

While I hadn't told my parents all the details of Patrick's illness – because of confidentiality and because I didn't want to

189

upset them – they knew enough to be worried and anxious for Michael.

'What have the doctors said?' Mum asked me quietly.

'That he needed a blood transfusion,' I answered, for this was as much as I knew.

At 1.40 Michael and I said goodbye to my parents, Adrian and Paula; Mum asked me to give Patrick her and Dad's best wishes. We were about to go out of the front door when Mum called: 'Are the children allowed an ice cream when you've gone? Paula is asking.'

'Yes, Mum,' I returned. Then to be fair I said to Michael: 'I'll buy you an ice cream or some chocolate from the shop at the hospital.'

We arrived at the hospital at exactly two o'clock and it was so busy it took me five minutes to find a free parking space. The lobby and the shop were busy too; clearly afternoon visiting at weekends was very popular, particularly for those with children. I bought the chocolate bar Michael wanted and a newspaper for Pat.

When we arrived on the ward Patrick was talking to the young man in the bed next to his. He finished as we neared and the young man said 'Hi' to Michael and me. I thought Patrick looked a bit sad as he greeted us and a few minutes later, when the young man had his earphones in and was listening to his music, Pat said quietly to me: 'He's only twenty-one and has a rare blood disease. He's waiting for a bone-marrow transplant. He can't work and has a baby to support. And I grumble!'

Pat didn't grumble, never, but I knew what he meant. When acute illness strikes the young it seems even more unfair than in someone older. I was pleased when a few minutes later the young man's partner arrived with their child; although they were young to be parents they seemed very responsible and loving.

I thought Patrick was gradually improving. His breathing seemed to be easier and he said he'd been out of bed a couple of times without help. 'I'm planning a shower tomorrow,' he said. 'The high point of my day! The nurse said I have to be able to walk up a flight of stairs before they will discharge me.'

'When will that be?' Michael asked.

'End of the week, I hope,' Patrick said.

'Is that what the doctors have said?' I asked. 'That you will go home at the end of next week?'

'More or less,' Patrick said, and changed the subject.

Patrick didn't tire so easily that Saturday afternoon, perhaps because it was the afternoon and not the evening or perhaps because the blood transfusion had taken effect. He was no longer receiving the blood plasma and saline solution and the drip had been removed. There was a small plaster on the back of his hand where the needle had been. Conversation flowed between the three of us and Michael and I found plenty to say. I explained that Colleen and Eamon had offered to bring Michael the following day and Patrick said he thought it was a good idea. He wasn't expecting any visitors that evening, Saturday, but assured me he didn't mind. I then said my parents sent their best wishes.

'That's nice of them,' he said, smiling.

'I hope you'll be able to meet them one day, when you're out of hospital,' I said. Patrick gave a slight, unenthusiastic nod, which I interpreted as lethargy brought on by being in hospital. I appreciated it must have been difficult for him to plan ahead when he wasn't feeling well and have been incarcerated in a hospital bed for nearly a week.

Michael ate some of his dad's biscuits and we continued talking about anything that came to mind: hospital food, the sunny weather, Michael's school work, the babysitting my fostering agency had arranged for the following week. 'Good, I'm pleased,' Patrick said, relieved and ever-thoughtful. 'I was wondering how you'd manage bringing Michael all next week.'

The two hours' visiting time flew by and at four o'clock when the bell sounded Michael was telling his father about Father Ryan, who was a new and trendy teacher at school. 'You'll have to tell me the rest next time,' Patrick said as visitors began to leave the ward.

We said goodbye and as Patrick kissed Michael he said: 'See you tomorrow, son. Say a prayer for me in church.' Then to me: 'I'll phone you tomorrow evening and see you Monday, Cathy. Thanks for everything. God bless.'

It was 4.30 when we arrived home and as soon as we entered Mum asked Michael how his dad was.

'Getting better, thank you,' Michael said politely, before scampering off to play with Adrian and Paula.

Mum helped me get the dinner ready while Dad pulled up a few weeds in the garden and kept an eye on the children. When we were alone in the kitchen Mum asked me if I thought Patrick was getting better as Michael had said. I said yes, and that he had seemed a lot brighter and he hoped to be out of hospital by the end of next week.

'That is good news,' Mum said. 'It's marvellous what they' – meaning doctors – 'can do now.' Like me, my parents were always optimistic and saw the positive whenever possible.

Saturday dinner was a lovely family occasion with my parents, my children and Michael seated around the dining-room table, tucking into the roast; although I have to admit that more than once I thought of Patrick lying in his hospital bed and wished he could have joined us. It was still warm outside after dinner, so we took our pudding and coffee into the garden, where I chatted with Mum and Dad as the children played. Later Mum insisted on helping me to clear up the dinner things before they left. It was nine o'clock when we all kissed goodbye and waved my parents off at the front door. Paula was nearly asleep on her feet and I put her to bed first while the boys washed and changed. They were exhausted too – from the late night before and also from being on the go all day. Adrian had his lamp off when I went in to say goodnight and Michael was yawning and taking his suit from the wardrobe, ready for the following day.

'I'll see to that,' I said. 'You get into bed. You're tired out.'

Yawning again, he went to the bed and before climbing in he knelt to say his prayers: 'Dear Lord, thank you for making my daddy a bit better. Can you do the same tomorrow, please? Then by the end of the week he will be well enough to go home. Thank you. Amen.'

'Perfect,' I said.

Stifling another yawn, Michael climbed into bed and I said goodnight and kissed his forehead. 'Straight off to sleep,' I said. 'You have to be up in the morning.'

'Night, Cathy,' he said, turning on to his side and snuggling down. 'Thanks for a nice day. I like your parents. I wish I had a nana and grandpa. You're very lucky.'

'Yes, we are,' I agreed.

The following day I was up and dressed by 8.30 and, leaving Adrian and Paula to sleep, I quietly woke Michael, as Colleen and Eamon were collecting him at 9.45. I suggested he showered and then came down and had breakfast in his dressing gown before he put on his suit ready for church. 'Yes, that's what I do at home,' he said. 'So it stays clean.'

We usually have a cooked breakfast on a Sunday and Michael said he'd like a bacon sandwich with tomato ketchup, so while he showered I went downstairs and cooked his bacon and my scrambled eggs. Presently Michael appeared in his dressing gown, followed by Adrian and Paula in theirs: they had woken to the smell of bacon cooking, so it was eggs and bacon all round.

Once Michael had finished he went upstairs to brush his teeth and change into his suit. He was downstairs again, ready and looking very smart, by 9.30. The suit, shirt and tie he was wearing were his 'Sunday best', and he'd been wearing them when he and Patrick had come to dinner straight from church the month before. I thought back to that day and the lovely time we'd all had with fondness. How well Patrick had been then. He certainly couldn't cope with all that now; but he will again soon, I told myself, when he's better and out of hospital.

Michael sat upright on the sofa while he waited for Colleen and Eamon. 'Do you want to play until they come?' Paula asked Michael from where she was sitting on the floor, surrounded by the farmyard set.

Michael looked at the game. 'I'm not allowed when I've got my suit on,' he said, which I hadn't told him, so I guessed it was Patrick's rule – to stop Michael spoiling his suit when he was ready to go to church, which seemed reasonable.

The doorbell rang shortly before 9.45 and Colleen was on the doorstep, looking very smart in a pale-blue matching skirt and jacket. Eamon was waiting in the car and gave a little wave. I knew they hadn't time to come in, so I called Michael, who was in the sitting room. Adrian and Paula, still in their dressing gowns, followed Michael to the front door. Colleen said hello to all three of them and asked how they were. 'Good,' Michael said. Paula grinned shyly while Adrian answered for them both: 'Very well, thank you.'

Colleen confirmed she would be returning Michael after hospital visiting at approximately 4.30 p.m. I thanked her, and Adrian, Paula and I waited on the doorstep as Michael got into the car and then waved as the car pulled away. I closed the front door and, telling Adrian and Paula they should wash and dress before they continued playing, I led the way upstairs. Adrian showered first and I then ran a bath for Paula. She played for a while in the water before I helped her out and to dress.

Sometimes, if I am fostering a child with behaviour problems who is very demanding and needs a lot of attention, I appreciate the time they are away and out of the house so that I can relax and also give Adrian and Paula some attention, but this wasn't so with Michael. As soon as I closed the front door I felt someone was missing. It was similar to the feeling I had when Paula or Adrian were out at friends or with their father: while I was pleased they were having a nice time, I missed them and the house didn't seem right without them. So it was with Michael, and I wasn't the only one who felt this. 'What time is Michael coming home?' Adrian and Paula asked every so often, glancing at the clock.

When Colleen and Eamon returned Michael they came in for a cup of tea. Having come straight from the hospital, Colleen said she was gasping and was grateful for the offer. Michael changed out of his suit and into casual clothes, and then the children played with his Scalextric while Colleen, Eamon and I took our tea into the sitting room. Colleen and Eamon both said how much they'd enjoyed having Michael's company and that he'd spoken fondly of us, which was nice. They said that at church the priest had included Patrick in their prayers and

Patrick's friends had asked Michael how his dad was. 'So there was some point in going to church,' Eamon put in, looking pointedly at his wife. I guessed Colleen was the more enthusiastic churchgoer and Eamon went along to keep her happy.

'Do Nora and Jack go to the same church?' I asked.

'No,' Colleen said. 'They're not Catholics.'

'Lucky Jack,' Eamon said, which Colleen ignored.

Colleen went on to say that Pat sent his love and best wishes to me, and she thought he had definitely improved since the last time she'd seen him. Eamon agreed. She said she was sure Pat would be home by the following weekend, but if he wasn't then they would be happy to take Michael to the hospital on Saturday and to church and hospital on Sunday. I thanked them.

'No need to thank us,' Eamon said. 'You'll be doing us a favour. We're pleased to have Michael any time.' And again I thought it was sad they hadn't had children of their own, as they were a lovely couple who would have made loving and caring parents.

I refilled their cups of tea and then at about 5.30 Colleen said they needed to be going, as they were going out later. I called the children downstairs to say goodbye and we saw them to the door. Colleen kissed and hugged Michael and he returned her affection. 'Remember,' she said again to me as they left, 'if you need help taking Michael to see his father give us a ring.' I said I would.

After Colleen and Eamon had left, the children continued playing indoors, as it was showering outside, while I made dinner. We ate at 6.30 and then at 7.30 I began the bedtime routine. I was aware it was nearing the end of hospital visiting time and as Patrick had said he would phone I guessed it would be after Nora and Jack had left, as before. But 8.30 came and went and there was no phone call, and by nine o'clock I had to admit he wasn't going to phone. Perhaps he was too tired or perhaps he was chatting with his neighbour and hadn't thought to phone, I speculated. Whatever the reason I was disappointed, for even a short phone call to say goodnight would have been nice.

At ten o'clock I settled Toscha in her basket for the night, switched off the downstairs light and went upstairs. I checked on the children who were all fast asleep; then I showered and climbed into bed. I was asleep as soon as my head touched the pillow and only woke when the alarm clock sounded at six o'clock the following morning.

Chapter Twenty-Three

Worry Mode

The evening routine that had begun on the previous Thursday now continued on Monday and for the rest of the week, although I didn't have the worry of finding a babysitter. In the afternoon Paula and I collected Michael and Adrian from school; I made an early dinner and then helped Paula into her pyjamas, ready for when Helen arrived at 5.40. Each evening Adrian and Paula had an ice cream after I'd gone, and I stopped off at the hospital shop to buy Michael a chocolate bar and Pat a newspaper. On Tuesday the young man in the bed next to Patrick was sent home for a few days and an elderly man who was very deaf took his place. Pat spent most of his day listening to the hospital radio, watching television or taking short walks up and down the ward to regain his strength in preparation for going home.

During the week I saw Patrick steadily improve, each day growing a little stronger as his colour and stamina returned. On Wednesday he was sitting on the bed when we arrived, rather than lying on it, and on Thursday he said the doctors had said he could go home the following day.

'Fantastic,' I said, while Michael threw his arms around his dad and just hugged him hard. 'Shall I collect you and take you home on Friday?' I asked.

'Thanks, but I'm sorted,' he said. 'Jack has offered to collect me. If you could bring Michael home in the evening that would be a big help.'

'Yes, of course,' I said. 'Adrian and Paula will be pleased to see you again.'

Patrick hesitated. 'Cathy,' he said quietly, turning slightly away from Michael. 'Would you mind if you didn't bring the children tomorrow? Could Helen look after them one more time?'

'Well, yes, she could,' I said, a little confused. While I appreciated Pat hadn't wanted to see Adrian and Paula while he was very ill in hospital, I didn't really understand why they couldn't come with me when I took Michael home.

'Perhaps you could stay for a cup of tea and we could have a chat,' he added. 'I'd like to speak to you alone.'

I looked at him carefully but there was nothing to be read in his expression. 'Yes, I can,' I said. 'Is everything all right?'

'Fine,' he said without meeting my gaze.

Pat then stretched out on the bed with his head resting on the pillows and Michael took up his usual position, sprawled next to his father. 'Looking forward to me coming home, son?' Pat asked him.

Michael nodded. 'Can't wait.'

'I'll pack his things tomorrow while he's at school, so we'll be ready,' I said. 'What time shall I bring him home?'

'As soon as Helen arrives, please,' Pat said. 'And Cathy, thanks for everything. It goes without saying I'm very grateful.' Leaning forward he planted a little kiss on my cheek.

I wouldn't say there was an atmosphere that evening as we continued talking – mainly about the next day and Patrick's homecoming – but something seemed to hang in the air. Perhaps it was my imagination but I thought Patrick wasn't making eye contact with me as much as he usually did, possibly avoiding my gaze like someone who has a guilty secret. Michael didn't notice any discrepancy in his father's behaviour and chatted away happily. In fact Patrick spent most of the two hours talking to Michael, which was obviously fine – Michael was his son – except it now seemed that it was possibly to avoid talking to me.

When the bell sounded at eight o'clock Pat and Michael got off the bed and Pat walked with us to the end of the ward. His walking and breathing had greatly improved and I thought once he was home he needed to try to put on some weight. We said goodbye at the doors leading from the ward; Pat kissed my cheek and then hugged and kissed Michael. 'See you both tomorrow,' Pat said. He then waved until we turned the corner and were out of sight.

Michael bobbed along beside me as we crossed the car park, but once in the car and going home he fell silent.

'Everything OK?' I asked, glancing at him in the rear-view mirror.

He nodded but didn't say anything.

'Sure?' I asked.

'Yes. I'm so pleased I'm going home with Dad, but I'm going to miss you guys. All the games I've played with Adrian and Paula, and not having to cook and clean. It's like I've been on holiday.'

I smiled sadly. While I couldn't have wished for a better compliment – a child telling me that staying with me was like being on holiday – it was an indication of the high level of responsibility Michael felt when he was at home helping his dad.

'I'm sure we'll all get together again soon,' I said.

'After church on Sunday?' Michael suggested.

'We'll see. Your dad is likely to be a bit weak, having just come out of hospital. He may not feel up to it, but I'll ask him when I see him tomorrow.'

When we arrived home Paula was still up, as she had been the last couple of evenings; I think Helen, with two boys, rather enjoyed playing with her and reading her stories. Michael told Adrian and Paula his good news – that his dad was going home – and I asked Helen if she could sit one last time the following evening while I took Michael home. She said she could and would arrive at the usual time. I thanked her and she left.

I could see that Adrian and Paula had mixed feelings about Michael leaving, just as Michael had done in the car. 'That's really nice for you, Michael,' Paula said carefully. 'Will you come and stay again soon?'

Michael shrugged. It was a difficult question for Michael to answer, for obviously if he did stay again it would mean his father was unwell again. I answered for him: 'When Patrick feels well enough he and Michael could come for Sunday dinner like they did before.' The children nodded.

Adrian then asked me, 'Will there be time for a game of Scalextric tomorrow before Michael goes home?'

'I should think so, but I'll have to pack away everything else so that we are ready to leave when Helen arrives.'

'We're not coming with you?' Adrian queried.

'No. Pat wants to get settled home first,' which the children accepted.

That night Adrian, Paula and Michael said a poignant and final goodnight to each other before going to their own rooms; tomorrow night Michael would be at home in his own bed. When Michael was washed and changed I went into his room to say goodnight. He knelt by his bed to say his prayers, which were touchingly full of thanks: 'Thank you, Lord, for making my daddy well enough to go home. Thank you for sending Cathy to look after me. Thank you for all the fun time I've had with Adrian and Paula. Thank you for keeping my mummy safe in heaven. Thank you, Lord, for everything. Amen.'

'And thank you for sending Michael to stay with us,' I added with a smile. 'He's a great lad and a pleasure to look after.'

Michael grinned and held his arms wide for a big hug before climbing into bed.

'Michael,' I said, as I tucked him in, 'remember, if you and your dad need any help phone me, OK?' He nodded. 'I know you have Nora and Jack next door, and Auntie Colleen and Uncle Eamon, but don't forget we're here if you need us.'

'I won't,' he said with another smile.

I kissed him goodnight and came out. I went downstairs, took the ironing board and iron from the cupboard under the stairs and set about the ironing so that Michael would have a case of clean and pressed clothes to take home with him. Once I'd finished, I watched some television before going to bed at 10.30. Any concerns I'd had about Patrick avoiding conversation with me during hospital visiting had faded, although I did wonder what he wanted to talk about alone. But Patrick and I often spoke in private – away from our children – as many parents do, discussing our children's development, schooling, eating and sleeping, etc., pooling knowledge and gaining reassurance from another parent's point of view. I therefore had no sense or foreboding that what Patrick wanted to tell me in private was going to shake us all.

On Friday morning as soon as I woke the children I could see that Michael was already taking on the responsibility that returning home would entail and with it the accompanying worry and anxiety. Even before he dressed he was worrying that he wouldn't have enough time to pack his belongings after school and saying he should do it now instead of having breakfast, although I'd already told him I'd do his packing.

'You get dressed and have your breakfast. I'll pack all your things today while you're at school,' I said again.

'But will you have enough time with everything you have to do?' he asked, which was something Adrian and Paula would never have dreamed of asking, assuming, as most children would, that as a parent I would make time.

'Yes,' I reassured him. 'Please don't worry. I'll have all your belongings ready, I promise.'

'Shouldn't I at least pack away the Scalextric?' he persisted.

'If you want to, but I thought you were going to have a quick game with Adrian and Paula this evening? It doesn't take long to pack away.' Which Michael finally accepted.

He washed and dressed, ready for school, but over breakfast he started worrying again. 'Cathy, perhaps we could stop at the shops on the way home. Dad might need milk and bread.'

Adrian and Paula looked at Michael with a mixture of awe and incomprehension, but then they'd never been in the role of a child carer – taking on the responsibility for the household that was usually the domain of the parent or adult in charge.

'Nora is seeing to that,' I reassured him. 'She's restarted the milk and newspaper delivery and she will make sure there is enough food in your fridge for the weekend. She and Jack will look in on you both regularly and if you need anything you know to knock on their door.'

Michael took a couple of bites from his toast and then said: 'I hope the hospital gives Dad his tablets. Once before I had to go to the chemist with a prescription and they wouldn't give me the tablets because I was under age.'

'I'll find out and if necessary I'll go to the chemist, although I'm sure Nora or Jack will have checked.'

Finally reassured – for the time being – Michael finished his breakfast and went upstairs to brush his teeth. A few minutes later he was downstairs again with his toothbrush and face flannel in hand. 'Shall I pack these now? He asked. 'I might forget them tonight.'

'If you want to,' I said. 'Put them in your wash bag and leave it in your bedroom.'

And in the car going to school Michael plagued himself with 'what if's and possible outcomes: 'What if Dad doesn't come home today?'

'Nora will phone me,' I said, 'and you'll stay with me for another night.'

'I think we need some more oxygen,' he said. 'The tank was showing 25 per cent full before I left.' Michael was referring to the oxygen cylinder his father kept beside his bed.

'I'll phone Nora and ask her to check it,' I said. 'Although your dad hasn't needed oxygen recently.'

'But he might in the night,' Michael said.

'OK. Don't worry, I'll ask Nora.'

I hoped that being in school would take Michael's mind off worrying.

As soon as I arrived home I began Michael's packing: emptying the wardrobe and drawers in his room and then checking under the bed and downstairs for any stray items. Once all his possessions were packed – apart from the Scalextric, which I left in his room – I phoned Jill to update her. She didn't know Patrick was being discharged.

'That's excellent news,' Jill said. 'What have the doctors told Patrick? Do you know?'

'That he is well enough to go home,' I said. 'He didn't say any more, so I'm assuming his test results were fine.'

'I'll phone Stella on Monday when she returns to the office and make sure she's aware Patrick is home. Have a good weekend and thanks for all you've done.'

Once I'd collected Paula from nursery and we'd had lunch and she was playing, I phoned Nora. Jack answered and said they had collected Patrick from hospital and had arrived home about thirty minutes ago. Nora was with Pat now, making sure he had everything he needed.

'Michael's been worrying about his dad,' I said. 'Do you know if Pat has all the tablets he needs?'

'He has,' Jack confirmed. 'He brought them with him from the hospital.'

'I'll tell Michael. And the oxygen cylinder? Michael seems to think it could need replacing.'

'Pat normally orders a new one in plenty of time but I'll check. If it's running out I'll order a new one. They deliver the next day. Tell Michael not to worry. We're all looking after his dad. There's food in the fridge and Nora's doing him dinner.'

'Thank you,' I said. 'I'll tell Michael. He can worry. Did Pat say anything to you about his test results or what the doctors said?'

'Yes, they told him his blood-cell count was fine and he should go home and carry on as normal.'

'Great,' I said, and this confirmed for me that Patrick was well on the way to recovering, for I was sure Pat would have been honest with Jack and Nora who, together with Eileen and Eamon, were his oldest and closest friends.

* * *

When I collected Michael from school that afternoon the first thing he asked was, 'Is Dad home safely?'

I smiled. 'Yes, of course. Nora and Jack collected him this afternoon. And he's got all the tablets he needs with him.'

'Did you ask about the oxygen?' Michael said, slipping into worry mode.

'Yes. Jack was going to check it and order a new one if necessary.'

'And have you've packed all my things?'

'Yes, everything except your Scalextric and we'll do that later.'

'What about Dad's dinner?'

'Nora's cooking it for him, and Colleen and Eamon are calling in tomorrow, so stop worrying. Everything is fine.'

Michael grinned and taking Paula's hand gave the back of it a big kiss, which made her giggle.

The evening went as planned: the children played while I made dinner; then after we'd eaten we all helped pack away the Scalextric and carried it, together with Michael's bags, downstairs. We were ready for 5.30, when Helen arrived, and the children said goodbye to each other. It wasn't a lingering and emotional goodbye, just a simple 'Bye, see you soon,' for they believed as I did that if not this Sunday (as Michael had suggested) then very soon we would meet up again as one big family.

Chapter Twenty-Four

The Night Sky

I parked the car outside Patrick's house at six o'clock, which was the same time we'd been entering the hospital all week and stopping at the shop in the lobby.

'Hey, I've missed out on my chocolate bar tonight,' Michael joked, in very good spirits. 'I bet Adrian and Paula are having their ice creams.'

'I bet they are too,' I said, smiling. 'I owe you one. Remind me if I forget.'

'I will!'

I got out of the car and then opened the rear child-locked door to let Michael out. He sprang on to the pavement and was up the front path and ringing the doorbell before I'd taken the first of his bags from the car. The front door immediately opened and Michael fell into his father's arms. As he hugged his son Pat looked at me and winked and I smiled back. Apart from being very thin, Pat had a good colour and looked well.

'Michael, go and help Cathy with your belongings,' Pat said after a moment.

Michael returned to the car and together we carried his bags and Scalextric box up the path while Pat held open their front door.

'Good to see you home, Pat,' I said as he closed the door and I put the bags down in the hall.

'It's good to be home,' he said, and lightly kissed my cheek. 'Let's go into the sitting room. Nora's just left. She's looking in again later with my dinner. Bless her.'

I followed Patrick and Michael down the hall and into their sitting room. Pat's breathing was good and he seemed to be walking very well. The house was warm and inviting now that Patrick was home, compared to the last time I'd come in with Michael and Nora when Pat had been in hospital. A large vase of fresh flowers stood in the hearth, and the newspaper which I guessed Patrick must have been reading prior to our arrival lay open on the sofa.

'Sit yourself down,' Pat said, folding the paper and dropping it into the magazine rack. 'Would you like a drink?'

'No, I'm fine, thanks. Can I get you anything?'

Pat smiled and shook his head. He sat on the sofa and Michael nestled in beside him as I sat in the armchair. Pat put his arm around his son and kept it there, hugging him as the three of us started chatting. Michael told his father about the school assembly that morning which he, with his class, had presented to the rest of the school, and I told Patrick that Michael had had his dinner, and his washing was up to date apart from the school uniform he now wore. Pat thanked me for this and for all I'd done while he'd been in hospital, and I said there was no need to thank me as I was only too happy to help. Yet while we were talking, and although Patrick was his usual kind, caring and polite self, I sensed a certain reserve in his manner, a formality, as if he was preoccupied or was putting some distance between us. After a few minutes he said, 'Michael, would you go up to your bedroom, please, and start unpacking, while I talk to Cathy?'

Michael immediately scrambled down from the sofa and went out of the sitting room to do as his father had asked. We heard the large holdall which was full to bursting being bumped up the stairs and then Michael's voice: 'Dad, can I put up my Scalextric when I've unpacked?'

'Of course, son,' Pat said.

Standing, Pat crossed the sitting room and closed the door; then he returned to sit on the sofa, which was at right angles to the armchair in which I sat. He looked down, away from me, and concentrated on his lap. Although I appreciated Patrick wanted to talk to me alone, I had no reason to believe I should be fearful of what he was about to say. He seemed relaxed, just a little bit preoccupied.

'Cathy,' he said, finally raising his gaze to mine, 'in the months we have known each other I have always respected your honesty and integrity. I trust you will now respect mine. I need to speak to you openly and I hope you will understand the reason for my decision.'

I felt a sinking feeling in the pit of my stomach. 'Decision? What decision?' I asked.

Pat took a moment and glanced down again, as though gathering his thoughts or summoning strength for what he was about to say.

'Cathy, I think I'm right in saying we have grown very close in the time we have known each other and our families have grown close too.' I nodded.

'In a different place and time,' Pat conyinued, 'when circumstances would have been different, I think we could have built on this and possibly even made a future together, but I have to be realistic. Ironically, I wouldn't have met you in a different place and time because my illness was the reason we were brought together: so that you could look after Michael while I was in hospital. Rightly or wrongly, we have become very close and part of each other's lives. Don't get me wrong: it's been lovely. But I think we have both forgotten how ill I am. I've now had a reminder and as a result I've made some very difficult and painful decisions.'

Patrick paused to take a breath and the sinking feeling I had in the pit of my stomach exploded into fear. I didn't say anything but sat motionless, concentrating on Pat and waiting for him to continue.

When he looked at me again I saw the pain of what he was about to say in his eyes, even before he spoke. 'Cathy,' he said slowly, 'I am a dying man. That has always been so since I first met you and it remains true today. I intend making the most of the time I have left, but I don't want you and your children hurt any more than you have to be. I blame myself for letting the three of you grow close to me, but it was so easy and so wonderful. I hope you will forgive me for wanting a last stab at happiness.'

I went to speak, but Pat raised his hand, gesturing for me to stay silent. 'Please hear me out, love,' he said. 'This is so difficult, but I have to say it.'

I felt my heart pounding and panic gripped me. I looked at Pat as he took another breath before continuing. 'I like to think that as you and your family brought added happiness to Michael and me, so I gave the three of you something, perhaps a warmth, a male presence that had been missing since John left. But I am acutely aware that Adrian and Paula have already lost a father, and you a husband. I do not want any of you upset by losing another family member, which is how I've come to view myself.'

He paused.

'I don't understand,' I said. 'What are you trying to tell me?'

He took a deep breath, 'Cathy, I've made the difficult decision that it would be for the best if we no longer saw each other.

210

I hope and pray you will still look after Michael but I will no longer be seeing you, Adrian and Paula socially. Michael doesn't have a choice in losing his father, but your children do. I hope that by putting distance between us now, when the time comes you will not feel my loss so acutely. That is my decision. I hope you understand.'

The room was quiet. Nothing could be heard save for the faint ticking of the clock on the wall. I felt hot and cold at once and couldn't speak for fear of bursting into tears. Pat looked sad but composed. I knew I should admire his selflessness – his wish to protect us – but I couldn't.

'So you are withdrawing from our lives completely?' I said at last.

'As much as I can. I know this has come as a shock to you, Cathy, but it is for the best. I've had plenty of time in hospital to think about it. It wouldn't be right to continue as we were – nice as it has been.'

I rested my head on the chair back and looked at him. 'Oh, Pat,' I began but couldn't continue as my eyes filled.

We were quiet again for some time; then I took a tissue from my pocket and wiped my eyes. My voice trembled as I spoke and I asked the question I didn't want to hear the answer to: 'What exactly have the doctors told you, Pat?'

'That I have three months maximum and should go home and enjoy the time I have left. Which I intend to.'

I held my voice steady as I spoke. 'And you can't enjoy it with us?'

'I could, very much, but I won't. If you want to help me, Cathy, you can do so by looking after Michael whenever I have to go into hospital. Knowing he is being well looked after means everything to me.'

Although my heart screamed that Pat's decision was wrong

and we should continue as we had been – all seeing each other – a part of me knew he was right. I recognized the truth in what he said – we had all grown very close – and Jill's warning came back to me.

'Is that why you didn't want me to bring Adrian and Paula to visit you in hospital?' I asked at length. 'Not because you didn't feel well enough but because you were starting to put distance between us?'

Pat nodded.

I took a deep breath, wiped my eyes again and blew my nose. 'Supposing you and I continued to see each other? Without Adrian and Paula? We're adults. Surely we can handle this?'

Pat gave a small smile. 'Let's wait and see. It's difficult for me too. For now I think we should try and get on with our lives and concentrate on our children. Please don't think I'm being ungrateful.'

'I don't,' I said.

Standing, I went to the sofa and sat next to Pat. I put my arms around him and we held each other tight. He didn't resist. But as we hugged I felt just how thin and frail he had become; there wasn't a bit of flesh on him. I could feel his bones jutting out, and I wanted to hold him and look after him and never let him go. I caught the faintest whiff of the soap he used, so poignant in its familiarity, felt the slight bristle of his chin on my cheek, and the rise and fall of his chest against mine. I knew there was nothing I could say or do to change Pat's mind or alter the prognosis. We were all at the mercy of his illness, and Pat's decision had been made selflessly – to protect me and my children.

'You'd best be going now, love,' he said quietly, after a few moments, his voice thick with emotion. 'I need to get Michael settled.'

I stood, and moved a little away from the sofa. Pat stood too. 'Cathy,' he said. I turned and met his gaze, his usually kind and smiling eyes were now full of pain and sorrow. 'Tell me you forgive me and that you understand,' he said, close to tears.

'There is nothing to forgive,' I said quietly. 'And yes, I do understand.'

'Thank you,' he said, and lightly kissed my cheek.

'Have you told Nora and Jack, and Colleen and Eamon?' I asked.

'Not yet. I will, closer to the time or when it becomes obvious, although little slips past Nora.'

'And what will you tell Michael?'

'That the two of us will be spending as much time as we can with each other. That's all he need know for now.'

I gave a small nod.

'Sorry,' Pat said, touching my arm.

I took his hand. 'Don't be. If I regret anything, it would be that we didn't meet sooner. You were right when you said you've given my children and me something. It's something very special: you've restored my faith.'

'In men?' Patrick asked with a slight smile.

'In one man,' I said. Pat's eyes misted and he waved for me to go before he broke down. I turned and began towards the sitting-room door.

Pat followed me down the hall to the front door. I paused at the foot of the stairs and, keeping my voice steady, called up: 'Goodbye, Michael! I'm off now.'

'Bye, Cathy,' Michael returned, and then appeared on the landing. 'Tell Adrian and Paula I'm putting the Scalextric up ready for when they come.'

I glanced at Pat. 'I'll explain,' he said quietly to me under his breath.

'Night,' I called to Michael.

'Night, Auntie Cathy.'

Pat opened the front door and I went out.

I didn't look back as I continued down the path. Concentrating hard, I looked straight ahead. I heard Pat close the door behind me, and taking my keys from my jacket pocket I opened the car door and got in. As I put the key into the ignition Nora came out of her front door carrying a cloth-covered tray, presumably Pat's dinner. She saw me and smiled enthusiastically. I managed a small smile in return and she continued up Pat's front path. I started the car and pulled away. I drove to the top of the street, out of sight of Pat's house, and parked. I turned off the engine and wept. I cried openly as I hadn't done in a long while: for Pat, our children and the unfairness of it all.

As I sat behind the steering wheel, my cheeks wet and my head lowered, shielding my face from any passer-by, my phoned bleeped with a text message. I mechanically took the phone from my pocket and opened it, fearing more bad news. I was surprised to see it was from Pat, and my heart skipped a beat wondering if he had changed his mind about us seeing each other. He hadn't, but what he said helped a little. A great one for quotes, he texted: *Stars are openings in heaven where the love of our lost ones shines through. Look to the stars Cathy and don't be sad. Pat x*

When I arrived home I put on a brave face.

'Did everything go all right?' Helen asked, coming into the hall.

'Yes, thank you,' I said.

Adrian and Paula were watching a video in the sitting room and called 'Hi, Mum,' as they heard me come in, and then goodbye to Helen as she prepared to leave.

I thanked Helen as I saw her out. 'I'm so grateful for all your help.'

'Any time,' she said. 'You're more than welcome.'

Having said goodbye to Helen I went into the sitting room, where Adrian and Paula were watching the last five minutes of the film *Beethoven*, about a very large and mischievous St Bernard dog. I joined them on the sofa and when the film had finished I switched off the television and announced in a bright positive voice: 'I thought we'd have a day out tomorrow at the zoo.'

'Great!' Adrian exclaimed.

'Great,' Paula cried, clapping her hands together.

'Great!' I said and hugged them hard.

I read the children a few stories and then began the bedtime routine. It was then that Michael's absence became really obvious.

'Is Michael staying with his daddy now?' Paula asked as I tucked her into bed.

'Yes, love.'

'Is his daddy better?'

'He's well enough to go home,' I said carefully. Then, preparing Paula for not seeing so much of Michael in the future, I said: 'I'm sure Michael and Pat will want to spend lots of time with each other – just the two of them, to make up for all the time Pat was in hospital.'

'Yes,' Paula agreed. 'I would if I was Michael.'

When I went into Adrian's room he asked, 'Is Michael coming to the zoo with us tomorrow?'

'No, love. Pat isn't up to it and Michael will want to be with his dad as much as possible.' Which was reasonable and Adrian accepted.

Although I put on a brave face and remained positive in front of the children that evening, inside my heart ached and I was very sad. Once I'd said goodnight I went downstairs and sat on the sofa in the sitting room with the television on low. But my thoughts were a long way from the television programme and I repeatedly gazed past the screen and through the French windows, watching the sky slowly darken. It was nearly ten o'clock before the sky was dark enough to see the stars. Standing, I crossed the room and quietly opened the French windows. I stepped outside. The late June air was warm and heady with the scent of flower blossom. I stood on the patio and gazed up at the sky. It was a clear night and the stars were twinkling brightly. I remembered Michael's first night with us, when he and I had stood side by side at his bedroom window, and the comfort he'd found in seeing the night sky. He'd said the stars made him think of heaven and the angels that were looking after his mummy, and who would one day come to fetch his daddy. Now, as then, I felt a lump rise to my throat and was truly humbled by Michael's strength and courage. I hoped Michael's faith stayed with him and would see him through the coming months, for never would a child's courage be tested more.

Chapter Twenty-Five

Staying Positive

We had a busy weekend. I had purposely made it so: a full day out at the zoo on Saturday and visiting my parents on Sunday. There was little time for wallowing in self-pity and Monday appeared very quickly; with it came the school and nursery run, only without the trip to Michael's school. I wondered how Michael was going to get to school because I didn't think Pat would feel up to taking him and neither would Pat let Michael go alone. I wondered if Nora and Jack might be helping out; retired and with a car, they had helped out Pat before, while Colleen and Eamon, in their forties, both had jobs so weren't so easily available during the working week. I hoped Pat knew that if he needed my help he only had to pick up the phone and ask.

Jill telephoned mid-morning and her voice was sombre and subdued. 'Cathy, Stella has spoken to Patrick earlier this morning and I'm afraid it's not good news.' I guessed what she was going to tell me but I let her continue. 'The scan and X-rays Pat had in hospital have shown the cancer has spread. The doctors have sent him home with pain relief only. There's nothing more they can do.'

'I know,' I said flatly. 'Pat told me.'

'I'm so sorry, Cathy.' I could hear the heartfelt sympathy in her voice and I knew she was really feeling for me. 'How are you and the children taking this?'

'I haven't told Adrian and Paula. There's no need to yet.'

'And how was Michael when you took him home?'

'Pleased to be home. But Pat isn't going to say anything to him until it becomes necessary.'

'That's what Stella said, although she thinks Michael has a good idea his father's condition has worsened.'

'Quite possibly. They're very close.'

'And how are you, Cathy?'

'OK,' I said with no commitment. 'It's Michael I feel for. He's such a lovely lad, it's so unfair.'

'I know.' Jill was silent for a moment. Sometimes silence can say more than hundreds of words. Then she said slowly, 'Patrick is being very brave, and concentrating on the practical issues. Stella said he's been in contact with St John's Hospice. He wants to go there rather than hospital when the time comes. He plans on staying at home for as long as possible and Stella has put him in touch with the Marie Curie nurses.'

The mention of Marie Curie nurses confirmed the inevitability of the outcome for me; in the UK these nurses are usually brought in only when someone is terminally ill. I didn't say anything as Jill continued: 'Cathy, given Pat's prognosis, we'll obviously be keeping you on standby for Michael. Hopefully Michael will be able to stay with his father for some while yet, but when the time comes we will need to have you ready. Stella will be staying in close contact with Patrick and will monitor the situation. I'll obviously keep you up to date. Do you and the children still see Pat regularly?'

'No, not any more. It was Patrick's decision.'

'It's probably for the best.' And our conversation ended as it had begun – sombre and subdued.

* * *

I didn't hear from anyone connected with Patrick and Michael for the rest of the week. Adrian, Paula and I continued as 'normal', although little time passed when I wasn't acutely aware that a short drive away a father and son were making the most of their last weeks together. Adrian and Paula asked about Michael: when would they see him again? But they accepted my reply that he was busy with school and spending time with his father. Having not seen Patrick since before he went into hospital Adrian and Paula's attachment to him was already starting to weaken a little, as Pat had hoped it would. They obviously asked about Michael, whom they had grown close to while he had lived with us, but not so much about Patrick, whom they hadn't seen for some weeks. On many occasions I got close to phoning Pat just to see how he was and if he needed anything, but aware – from the conversation we'd had – that he wanted to put some distance between him and me as well as between him and Adrian and Paula, I didn't. I thought that if Pat wanted to speak to me he would phone, and I was right.

On Friday morning while Paula was at nursery my mobile bleeped a text message. It was from Pat: *Is it ok 2 phone 4 a chat?*

I texted back: *Yes x.* Like me, Pat preferred to use the landline for chatting and kept his mobile for texting and for calls when he was away from the house.

I went into the sitting room and sat on the sofa. A minute later the phone ran and I picked it up.

'Hello, love,' he said cheerfully as soon as I answered. 'How are you today?'

'Good, thanks. All the better for hearing from you,' I said lightly.

'That's what I like to hear. How are the kids?'

'Fine. At school, unless they're truanting,' I joked. 'How's Michael?'

'He's doing all right.'

Patrick sounded bright and positive and I didn't think it was an act put on for my benefit. He sounded genuinely in a positive and meaningful place. We chatted easily about the usual things: the children, school, the weather, etc., and then he asked after my parents and I said they were well. Although Pat had never met my family he'd seen photographs of them and I'd mentioned them when we'd talked in the past. Pat said Jack was taking Michael to school and collecting him, while Nora kept popping in with meals and snacks on a tray and generally fussing.

'It's so good of her,' Pat said, 'but I keep telling her she's spoiling me. I'm not so ill I can't cook.'

It was the first reference Pat had made to his illness during our conversation and I took the opportunity to ask: 'How are you?'

'A bit wobbly sometimes, but I can stay upright most of the time,' he said, laughing.

'You sound good,' I said.

'Yes, I'm doing all right. As they say in AA [Alcoholics Anonymous] – which I would add I've never been a member of – "one day at a time". Every morning I wake up and give thanks for another day and concentrate on making the most of it. Cathy, it seems to me there are two ways of approaching life when you are in my position. One is to become angry and depressed at the unfairness of it all, and waste what time you have left. The other way is to be grateful for the wonderful life you've had and make the most of every minute you have left. This way is far better. I've also had time to prepare myself and those around me so when I go it won't be a shock and I'll be organized and ready.'

I swallowed hard and tried to stay as brave as Pat was. He'd made it sound as though he was about to go on a journey, which

I suppose in a way he was. He sounded so positive that there was little room for sorrow or regret, and I greatly admired his philosophy, dignity and self-respect. I think his faith helped keep him strong. We continued talking in the same positive and light manner for ten minutes or so. He told me he'd been out for a short walk with Jack the day before, and tomorrow, Saturday, Jack was taking him supermarket shopping while Nora stayed with Michael and played Scrabble. Then on Sunday Colleen and Eamon were taking him and Michael to church and giving them dinner afterwards.

'That sounds good,' I said. 'Say hello to Colleen and Eamon for me, please.'

'I will. They think you're an angel. I've told them they don't know the half of it,' he joked.

A few minutes later I heard him become slightly breathless and he began to wind up the conversation. 'Is it all right if I phone you again next week?' he asked. 'I'll text first.'

'Yes, of course. Any time. You know I'm always pleased to hear from you.'

'Well, goodbye for now, then, Cathy. Send my love to the –' I knew he was about to say children, but he stopped himself. Instead he said: 'Love to everyone.'

'And you, Pat. Take care. You and Michael are in my thoughts.'

'You're all in mine too, Cathy, more than you'll ever know. Bye, love.'

'Bye.'

After I'd hung up I sat for a few minutes on the sofa with the sound of Pat's soft Irish voice and his gentle words still singing in my ears. I was pensive but not miserable. It would have been unjust to Pat's positive attitude and dignity for me to feel sorry for him or be depressed. I greatly admired his courage and self-possession and I knew that with the help and support of his oldest and dearest friends he was making the most of every day before he began the next stage of his journey.

That evening Colleen phoned and apologized for not phoning sooner – she and Eamon had had a very busy week at work. I said I understood and it was nice of her to call, although she didn't really tell me any more than I'd learnt from Pat – that he was coping well and staying focused and positive. She said Nora and Jack were keeping an eye on Pat and Michael and making sure they had everything they needed, which I knew from Pat. Colleen also said that whereas previously Pat had been fiercely independent and rejected their offers of help he now recognized he needed help, which had resulted in some of the responsibility being taken from Michael. Colleen said Michael had had an invitation to go to tea at a school friend's during the week and Patrick had insisted he went; Michael had enjoyed himself immensely. Colleen asked after my children and finished by wishing us a pleasant weekend. She said she'd phone again the following week, or before if the situation changed.

The children and I had a relatively relaxing weekend, with a trip to a local park on Saturday, and mainly in the garden on Sunday. John phoned to speak to the children on Sunday evening and when he'd finished talking to them he asked to speak to me. He confirmed the arrangements for the following Sunday, when he would be seeing the children, and then confirmed his solicitor had received a letter from my solicitor starting the divorce proceedings. 'I'm pleased things are moving at last,' he said conciliatorily.

I didn't say anything. I suppose I could have agreed or even asked how he was but my generosity didn't stretch that far. We said a polite goodbye and then Adrian realized he'd forgotten to tell his father that he'd come top in the spelling test at school, and couldn't be persuaded to wait until the following Sunday to share the news, so I dialled John's number. A woman answered and for a moment I thought I must have misdialled; then it dawned on me it would be John's partner, Monica. I hadn't spoken to her before, as John preferred to phone us when he spoke to the children and on the few occasions I'd had reason to phone him, he'd always answered.

'Sorry to disturb you,' I said, recovering. 'It's Cathy. Could Adrian speak to his father, please? He's forgotten to tell him something.'

There was a second's pause and then, flustered, she said, 'Oh yes, of course. Just a minute, I'll get him.' I guessed she felt as uncomfortable as I did. And it was strange hearing her call John to the phone and tell him his son wanted to speak to him.

I passed the phone to Adrian and he told his father his good news; and then Paula remembered something she'd forgotten to tell him, so once Adrian had finished speaking he passed the phone to her. Paula told her father she'd been to nursery and had played in the home corner with Natasha and Rory, which wasn't ground-breaking news but just something she wanted to share with her daddy, which was nice.

That evening the children and I watched a video together; then I read them a story and they had their baths and were in bed at a reasonable time, ready for school the following day. I wondered if I should be writing up my fostering log notes, but there wasn't really much to say apart from the phone calls from Pat and his friends, which weren't directly relevant to Michael's care. I decided to suspend the log until such time as Michael stayed with us again.

* * *

The Night the Angels Came

The week disappeared with the usual school and nursery routine and included Paula spending half a day in the reception class of the primary school she would join in September. It was the same school Adrian attended, so Paula was already familiar with it, as were some of her friends who had older siblings there. The weather was changeable and on clear afternoons the children played in the garden when they returned from school, and when it rained they played indoors. They both had a friend to tea on Thursday. Then on Friday evening shortly after nine o'clock I was in the sitting room, having another attempt at reading a novel I'd started a month before, when my phone bleeped a text message from Pat: *Can I phone?*

Naturally I texted back: *Yes x*

I closed my book and picked up the phone as soon as it rang.

'Hi, lovely,' Pat said brightly. 'How are you?'

'Fine, and you?'

'Good. Still here.'

I smiled. We swapped our news and then Pat said, 'According to my calculations Adrian and Paula will be seeing their father this Sunday. Is that right?'

'Yes,' I said, slightly puzzled as to why he had thought of that.

'Cathy, if you're not too busy I was wondering if you could pop over for an hour. It's a while since you've seen Michael and I think it would be good for him.'

'Yes, I'd be happy to. Is Michael all right?'

'He's fine. I just thought he should see you again before too long.'

'You're not being admitted to hospital again?' I asked suspiciously.

'No, not yet. But I don't want Michael forgetting you. Is eleven o'clock on Sunday all right? We'll go to church in the evening for a change.'

'Fine. I'll see you Sunday, then.'

We said goodbye and I slowly replaced the handset. I appreciated why Patrick wanted Michael to see me – so he wouldn't lose the ease and familiarity he felt around me, gained from all the time he'd spent with us. But I would have to think carefully if and what I told Adrian and Paula of my visit. If I didn't tell them I was going and they found out they might feel I'd sneaked off without them, and if I told them they would ask why I hadn't timed the visit so that they could go. In the end I decided not to tell them I was going, and after I'd seen Patrick it was obvious what I had to tell them.

Chapter Twenty-Six

A Few Days' Rest

On Sunday, having seen Adrian and Paula off with their father, I arrived at Pat's house as arranged at eleven o'clock and Michael answered the front door. He was as pleased to see me as I was to see him. 'Hi, Auntie Cathy,' he cried, throwing his arms around me and giving me a big hug.

'Hi, love,' I said. Then drawing back slightly so I could see him properly, I said, 'I'm sure you've grown.' Michael appeared taller now than when I'd last seen him – two weeks before – and I knew from Adrian that boys his age had sudden growth spurts.

'Dad says I've grown too,' Michael said proudly.

I smiled. 'Where is Dad?'

'In the living room.'

I followed Michael down the hall and into their sitting room. I probably should have read more into the fact that Michael had answered the door rather than Pat. But it wasn't until I entered the living room and saw Patrick struggling to stand to greet me that I knew why he hadn't gone down the hall to answer the door. He couldn't. His health had deteriorated so much since I'd last seen him that it was now taking all his energy and concentration to get out of the chair. I hid my shock as he steadied himself against the arm of the chair and extended a hand to take mine.

'Hello, love,' I said, going over.

I took the hand he offered in mine and then put my arms around him and gently hugged him. We didn't speak. I was too choked and I think he was too. After a moment he drew back and slowly eased himself down into the armchair again. 'Thanks for coming,' he said with a small smile once he was settled.

I sat on the sofa next to Michael and looked at Pat and then Michael. Keeping a tight lid on my emotions, I said simply: 'It's good to see you both again.' I put my arm around Michael and gave him another hug.

Pat smiled. 'We're very pleased to see you too,' he said, his voice catching.

'So what have you been up to?' I asked lightly, looking at Michael.

'Tell Cathy your news,' Pat said slowly, resting his head on the chair back.

I looked at Michael as he began telling me that he'd been chosen to play for his school's basketball team and I congratulated him. Then he told me about his friend Simon – the lad he'd had tea with – who was now planning a birthday party to which Michael would be invited. As Michael talked I stole a glance at Pat. He was so frail and depleted by weight loss he looked like an old man sitting in his armchair and I could have wept. He was concentrating on everything Michael was saying, clearly taking enormous pleasure in Michael's achievements, and he was so very proud of his son. Pat returned my glance with a smile. I swallowed hard and knew I had to stay as positive and focused as he and Michael were.

Presently Pat interrupted Michael and said slowly, 'Sorry, Cathy, I'm forgetting my manners. Would you like a drink?'

'Just a glass of water, please,' I said. 'Shall I get it?'

'No, I'll get it,' Michael said, immediately jumping up. 'Do you want a drink, Dad?'

'Water, please, son.'

Once Michael had left the room Patrick looked at me in earnest. He spoke slowly and carefully, as though each word was an effort. 'Thank you so much for coming, Cathy. I know how difficult this must be for you: seeing me like this.'

I gave a small nod and smiled sadly. What could I say? Yes, Pat, it's absolutely dreadful seeing you like this and knowing there's nothing I can do to help. But if I admitted to my feelings now I knew the lid I was keeping on them would burst open and I'd dissolve into tears. For Pat and Michael's sake I wanted to be as brave as they were, so I smiled again and said, 'I'm very pleased I came to see you both.'

Michael returned with the two glasses of water and placed one on the coffee table within reach of his father and handed the other to me. I thanked Michael and took a sip of the water; then I asked Pat if there was anything I could do: the washing or ironing, maybe?

'No, love,' Pat said. 'Nora's taking care of it. Thanks anyway.'

Then Michael asked if I'd like to play a game of knockout whist with him. I said I would, although I wasn't very good at it, which he knew from playing while he'd stayed with me. Michael took a pack of cards from the bureau drawer and dealt us seven cards each and then placed the rest of the pack face-down on the sofa between us. Pat watched us playing, with his head resting on the chair back, smiling when one of us won a trick. Just after twelve noon, when I'd been there for nearly an hour and Michael had won three games to my two, the front doorbell rang.

'That will be Nora with lunch,' Michael said, leaping off the sofa to answer the door.

I smiled at Pat. 'I'll go and let you have your lunch, once I've said hello to Nora,' I said. 'Will you promise to phone if you need me?'

'Of course,' Pat nodded. 'Thank you, Cathy.'

I heard Nora's bright 'Hello, Michael' come from the hall. Then Michael's voice eagerly asking what she'd made for lunch. 'Homemade tomato soup, and egg salad rolls,' Nora said.

'That sounds good,' I said to Pat. He gave a small nod.

Nora came into the sitting room carrying a tray covered with a white linen napkin.

'Hello, Cathy,' she said, smiling. 'I thought that was your car outside. How are you, pet?'

'Very well, and yourself?' I stood and kissed her cheek; then I moved Pat's glass of water to the side of the coffee table to make room for the tray.

'I'm fine and Jack said to say hello,' Nora said, setting the tray on the table and removing the napkin.

A mouth-watering smell of tomato flavoured with basil rose from the two bowls of soup. Michael was already drawing up the footstool to the coffee table, ready to begin.

'Just a minute,' Nora said to Michael. Then to Pat: 'Are you eating in here or at the table?'

'In here I think,' Pat said with effort. 'It's easier than at the table.'

I watched Nora as she took one of the bowls of soup from the tray together with the plate of egg rolls and placed them on the coffee table in front of Michael. I supposed that having seen Patrick daily Nora had had time to adjust to the deterioration in his health and wasn't as shocked as I was by his appearance but carried on as normal. Pat heaved himself further up the chair so that he was more upright and in a better position to eat. Nora spread the napkin on Pat's lap and placed the tray with the soup and spoon on top of it.

'Thank you, love,' Patrick said gratefully. He steadied the tray with one hand and took a deep breath as though summoning the strength to begin eating. My heart ached. It was pitiful to watch – he'd always had such a good appetite – yet somehow even now his dignity shone through.

Michael, seated on the stool at the coffee table, was tucking into his soup. Pat looked at the soup and then at me. I wondered if he felt embarrassed eating like this in front of me. I thought I should leave now; I'd been here for over an hour.

'I'll be off, then,' I said. Pat nodded. I stood and, careful not to unbalance the tray, leant forward and kissed Patrick's forehead.

'Bye, love,' Pat said, smiling at me. 'Thanks for coming.'

'Take care and phone if you need me,' I said again.

'I will,' Pat said.

'Bye, Auntie Cathy,' Michael said, pausing between mouthfuls.

'Bye, love. I'll beat you at whist next time.'

Michael grinned. Nora came with me down the hall to the front door. 'I usually have a tidy-up while they eat lunch,' she said. 'Then I sort out their washing. When they've finished eating I take away the dishes and come back at three o'clock with tea and cake. Pat still likes his cake, especially my Victoria sponge. Then I bring them dinner about six thirty.'

'You're so good,' I said. 'I don't know how they'd manage without you.'

'It just allows Pat to say stay at home a bit longer,' Nora said. 'There's a nurse looking in now too.'

I nodded. 'I hadn't realized how much Pat had deteriorated,' I confessed. 'Pat didn't say on the phone.' I felt my eyes well.

'Don't be upsetting yourself,' Nora said quietly, touching my arm. 'Patrick wouldn't want you crying.'

'I know, but it's all so unfair. Why him? Why Michael? What have they done to deserve this?'

'That's what Jack says, but I suppose if you have a strong faith as they have, then leaving this world perhaps isn't the worst that can happen. Not if you believe you are going to a better place.'

'I suppose so,' I said, unconvinced. 'I can't share their faith but I will keep strong for Michael.'

'I know you will, love. We all will. Did Pat say anything to you about Colleen?' I shook my head, guessing it was about taking Michael to church when he stayed again.

'No worries,' Nora said.

'What are you two gossiping about?' Patrick called jokingly from the living room.

'We're talking about you, not to you,' Nora returned with a smile at me.

'Bye!' I called down the hall as Nora opened the front door. 'See you soon.'

'Bye, Cathy!' Pat and Michael called together.

I kissed Nora goodbye and left, swallowing back tears, for to let them fall would have been a great disservice to Pat and Michael's courage.

That evening when Adrian and Paula returned home from seeing their father and had finished telling me their news, I said briefly that I'd visited Pat, and Michael was fine. I said Nora was helping Michael look after his dad but I thought it wouldn't be long before Michael came to stay with us again.

'Goodie,' Paula said, happy at the prospect of playing with Michael and not understanding the wider implications.

Adrian, that much older and understanding, more asked seriously, 'Is his dad going into hospital again?'

I nodded. 'I think he will, before too long.'

Clearly I needed to prepare Adrian and Paula, as Michael was preparing himself, so that when Pat required full-time nursing and had to go into the hospice it wouldn't come as such a shock, but I would do it a bit at a time. What I didn't know was that I hadn't got much time to do it in.

Monday and Tuesday passed with the usual school and nursery routine and housework; then on Wednesday afternoon Pat phoned without texting first. I knew the moment I picked up the phone that change was happening.

'Cathy, I've decided to go into St John's Hospice for a few days,' Pat said evenly. 'Just for a rest. Stella, our social worker, will phone you soon with the arrangements but I wanted to let you know myself.'

'Oh, I see,' I said. 'Just for a few days?'

'Yes. It's all getting a bit much for me at present and they're very good at sorting out pain relief. I'm going in this evening. Jack will bring Michael to you and then take me to St John's. Is six o'clock all right? Nora will give us dinner first.' Apart from sounding slightly out of breath, Pat was positive, matter-of-fact and practical in the way he spoke.

'Yes, whatever suits you,' I said. 'Michael is welcome to have dinner here if it's easier?'

'Thanks, but I'd like to have dinner with him before he goes. We won't call it the last supper.' It was said as a joke but, worried as I was, I didn't appreciate Pat's flippancy. 'Sorry,' he said. 'That wasn't funny, was it?'

'No,' I confirmed.

'OK. I'll get off the line now. Stella will be phoning you soon to confirm the arrangements. Thanks for stepping in and helping out again.'

'Text me if you need anything,' I said quickly as Pat wound up.

'Will do. God bless.'

I replaced the handset and almost immediately the phone rang again. It was Stella, phoning as Pat had said she would with the 'arrangements', which I assumed would include the visiting times for St John's. However, from what Stella now said, I wouldn't be needing the visiting times because Pat had told her he didn't want Michael to visit him at all.

Chapter Twenty-Seven
Premonition

'What? Not visit him at all?' I asked Stella, surprised. 'Pat's just phoned me. I must have misunderstood him.'

'Pat's said that as he is only going to be in for a few days he doesn't want Michael to come to the hospice. He will be home again at the weekend.'

'I see. Well, if that's what Pat wants.'

'It is, so we have to respect his wishes.'

'Yes,' I agreed reluctantly.

'I understand Pat's neighbour Jack will be bringing Michael to you?' Stella confirmed.

'Yes, that's what Pat told me.'

'Fine. And you're all right to do the school run?'

'Yes. We'll continue as we did before. It worked out fine.'

'Good. Well, thanks, Cathy. I'll let you know if there is any change in the arrangements.'

'Stella,' I said carefully, 'if Pat does stay longer – over the weekend – then I think Michael should see his father, don't you?'

'Absolutely, but Pat is adamant he will be out again on Saturday, and he's such a fighter, I'm sure he will.'

* * *

Premonition

I told Adrian and Paula that Patrick was going into a type of hospital for a few days. They were pleased to be seeing Michael, although sorry that his dad was unwell again. At six o'clock when the doorbell rang they came with me to answer the door and welcomed Michael, as Jack lifted Michael's holdall into the hall. I offered Jack a cup of tea but he said he wouldn't stay as he was going straight back to take Pat to St John's. He gave Michael a hug, said goodbye to all of us, and left with a wave, saying he or Nora would be in touch. Michael only had the one holdall – enough for a few days – and hadn't brought his Scalextric. I saw Adrian's disappointment.

'It wasn't worth packing up the Scalextric just for a few days,' I said. 'It's a nice evening, so why don't the three of you play in the garden, while I unpack Michael's bag?'

Disappointment vanished and they scampered off down the hall, through the sitting room and out of the French windows, while I took Michael's holdall upstairs. Michael's room was at the back of our house, overlooking the garden, so I could see the children while I unpacked. They had gone straight to the sand-pit, Michael's favourite activity after Scalextric. He seemed relaxed and at ease as he played. Used to staying with us and assuming he'd be home again at the weekend, he was taking his visit in his stride.

I finished Michael's unpacking, and went downstairs and into the garden, where I was met with a chorus of: 'Can we have an ice cream, please?'

I went into the kitchen, took three Cornettos from the freezer and returned to the garden, where I handed them out. We stayed in the garden until just before seven o'clock, when I said it was time to come in and start getting ready for bed, as they had school the following day. I took Paula upstairs while Michael and Adrian covered the sandpit and put away garden toys. Michael was so familiar with our house now that he knew where most things were kept, just as Adrian did.

Later, when Michael was ready for bed and I went into his bedroom to say goodnight, he said: 'Cathy, I was wondering if we could stop off at my church on the way home from school tomorrow, so I can light a candle for my dad? I know you're not a Catholic, so you don't have to come in if you don't want to. But I'd like to light a candle for my dad.'

'Of course we can,' I said. 'What a nice idea!'

I was very touched by Michael's request, but I was also acutely aware of my ignorance in respect of the practice of lighting votive candles in the Catholic Church. The children and I occasionally went to our local Church of England, which like many Anglican churches didn't follow the practice of lighting prayer or votive candles. However, I wasn't going to let Michael go into church alone: it didn't seem right.

'I'd like to come into church with you, if that's OK?'

Michael nodded. 'We have to pay.'

I knew there was a small charge for the candle. 'No problem,' I said. 'I'll remember to bring my purse when I collect you from school. And you can show me what to do.'

Michael smiled, drew his curtains together, leaving a gap in the middle so that he could see the sky, and then knelt beside his bed, hands clasped together, ready to say his prayers. As usual I lowered my head and looked away out of respect for his devotion. 'Dear Lord,' he began, 'please take special care of my daddy. He's in St John's, you know. Please make him well so he can come home again at the weekend. I know you want him to be with my mummy, but please don't send your angels yet.'

It was similar to the prayer Michael had said when he'd first stayed with me and now as then my heart went out to him. He seemed so small and vulnerable, kneeling humbly beside his bed, hands together and eyes closed, that I wanted to pick him up and hold him tight and never let him go.

After a moment he crossed himself, opened his eyes and stood. 'Cathy,' he said, climbing into bed, 'I know Dad says he'll be home by the weekend, but if he isn't can we go and see him at St John's?'

'Yes, of course,' I said.

That evening I propped a note by my handbag to remind me to take my bag with me when I collected Michael from school the following day. Usually, if I was just popping to the school I took my keys and phone but not my purse, which I would need for the candles. I vaguely wondered what happened if someone didn't have money with them: were they still allowed to light a prayer candle? I'd no idea. But that wouldn't be our worry, for on Thursday afternoon as I entered Michael's playground with Paula I had my bag firmly over my shoulder. Adrian was staying behind at school for a rehearsal for the end-of-year production in which he had a part, so I would collect him at 4.30 after we'd been to Michael's church.

'Have you had a good day?' I asked Michael as he bounded out of school.

'You haven't forgotten!' he said, seeing my bag on my shoulder.

'Of course not,' I said, smiling.

'Mummy never forgets,' Paula put in.

A mother who was standing next to me in the playground and must have overheard Paula's comment looked at me and smiled. 'I wish,' she said.

'Me too,' I said, laughing.

* * *

The Night the Angels Came

I drove to the Sacred Heart Roman Catholic church, which was five minutes away and in the direction of home. The church fronts the main road and doesn't have a car park, so I parked down the side street closest to the church. Michael, Paula and I got out of the car and then walked round the front of the church and to the main entrance. I'd already explained to Paula that afternoon what we would be doing and naturally she'd asked if she could light a candle too. I'd said I wasn't sure, as we weren't Catholics, but if it seemed appropriate then we would. The Sacred Heart was an imposing stone building built about 150 years ago in a traditional, almost Gothic style, with a tall bell tower, and huge arched stone doorway over which was a life-sized stone statue of Mary, mother of Jesus. The intimidating grandeur of the building, plus my unfamiliarity with the church and its practice, combined to make me feel slightly nervous – apprehensive almost – about going in. Paula must have felt the same, for as Michael turned the large metal door knob and pushed open the wooden door I felt her hand tighten in mine.

The door creaked and we stepped inside. Michael closed it again behind us. On the right was a stone font containing holy water. Michael dipped his fingers into the water and made the sign of the cross before moving forward into the main body of the church. Paula and I followed him in. To my surprise the interior of the church was bright and airy with sunlight streaming through the large stained-glass windows. Old combined with new, with rows of modern pews, and new wooden exposed beams in the high-arched ceiling, while round the walls of the church were ancient religious statutes and paintings. The church wasn't empty; half a dozen worshippers were sitting in quiet thought or prayer in the first few rows of the pews at the front of the church. Paula looked at me and I put my finger to my lips to remind her to be quiet. Michael stood at the end of nave, facing the altar, and crossed himself; then, turning to me whispered, 'The prayer candles are over here.'

Paula and I followed him silently across the rear of the church and to a walk-in stone alcove in the corner. It was like a little room in itself, only without a door. Rows of candles were burning on three stone steps, beneath a statue of Mary holding baby Jesus in a small shrine. I saw the box of new candles to the left, beside the donation box with a printed note on the front: '50p'. I took my purse from my bag and gave Michael the money. He dropped the coin into the donation box and took a fresh candle.

Although the main body of the church was lit by natural light, this alcove was lit mainly by the candles. There must have been about thirty prayer candles in various stages of burning. Their light stirred and flickered in the moving air, dancing over the stone walls and flagstone floor. Organ music played discreetly in the background, creating a particularly special atmosphere in this corner of the church. It was serene yet powerful, as though the prayers of all those who had gone before us had united and been enriched by the light of the candles. The feeling was palpable: light shining into the darkness of people's souls, for without doubt those who had lit candles before us, like Michael, had been seeking extra help in a time of crisis.

Michael crossed himself again, lit his new candle from one that was already burning and placed it carefully on the stone step. Bringing his hands together he looked up to the statue of the Virgin Mary. I, too, drew my gaze up, for although I wasn't a Catholic I could feel and appreciate the spirituality of the moment. Paula, standing close beside me and still holding my hand, watched Michael in awe. Keeping his eyes on the statue of Mary, Michael said a silent prayer; the light flicked on his face and I saw his faith and solemnity. After a moment he lowered his hands, crossed himself and turned to me. His expression was relaxed and peaceful, joyous almost. 'I've finished,' he said quietly. And we began to move away.

Paula and I didn't light a candle. I felt that as I couldn't share Michael's faith it didn't seem right to perform this ritual, and Paula didn't ask. We made our way silently across the rear of the church towards the exit and before we left Michael faced the altar again and crossed himself.

We were silent outside as we walked down the path and joined the street, as though the peace and tranquillity of the church had come with us. Then Paula suddenly asked Michael: 'Now you've lit a candle will your daddy get better?'

It was an innocent question, understandable in a child her age, but I inwardly cringed at her insensitivity, for I was sure having to answer would upset Michael. I was about to say something, though goodness knew what, when Michael turned to Paula and said quietly, 'It won't make my daddy well, but it will make us both feel better. We know God is with us and we have nothing to fear.'

My eyes immediately misted and a lump rose in my throat. I quietly slipped my arm around Michael's shoulder and the three of us walked arm in arm and in silence to the car.

That evening, after I'd collected Adrian from school, the boys did their homework and Paula watched television while I made dinner; then the three of them played in the garden until it was time for bed. That night Michael's prayer was simple: 'God bless Mummy, Daddy, Colleen, Eamon, Jack, Nora, Cathy, Adrian and Paula, and all my friends. Amen.' He crossed himself and climbed into bed. I said goodnight and went downstairs, wondering exactly how Pat was, for I hadn't heard anything from anyone at all that day.

Premonition

Shortly after nine o'clock the phone rang and it was Eamon. His voice was flat and emotionless. Having asked how we all were, he said, 'Colleen can't come to the phone, she's too upset. She's asked me to phone you. We saw Pat earlier this evening; we took Nora and Jack but we only stayed an hour. Pat is very poorly: he's not in pain but he's unconscious. It's not looking good, Cathy.'

I was shocked, for it had only been the previous afternoon Pat had been well enough to phone me to say he was going into the hospice for a short rest and he'd be out by the weekend. Now it appeared he had deteriorated dramatically. 'What did the nurses say?' I asked, my mouth going dry and my heart pounding.

'That he was being kept comfortable, and resting. They're very nice. I suppose they must be used to it. They said we could visit any time. I told them Pat had a young son who was being looked after, which they were aware of, and I asked if we should bring him to see his Dad.'

'What did they say?'

'That the decision when to bring Michael should be made by him in conjunction with his family, which in effect is us and you.'

I hesitated, swallowed hard and asked quietly, 'Are we talking about Michael visiting his dad to say goodbye?' I heard the words and my eyes filled.

Eamon gave a small sigh. 'I don't know, Cathy. Pat's rallied before. And he's always been very protective of Michael – not wanting him upset unnecessarily. He won't be pleased if he recovers from this and is home again at the weekend, but I'm not so sure.' He paused. 'Look, let's see how things go tomorrow. The four of us will be visiting again tomorrow evening. Let's make a decision about Michael then. The hospice will phone us if there is any change and we'll phone you straight away. There will be time for you and Michael to get there if necessary.'

'All right,' I agreed. 'Although I'm not sure what I should tell Michael when he asks how his Dad is.'

'No, neither am I. Sorry, I can't help you there, Cathy.'

That night, as I put the cat out for her night-time run, I stood on the patio and looked up at the night sky. There was no moon and it was cloudy, so there were only a few stars, dimly visible far away. What lay beyond those stars was anyone's guess, but I could appreciate the comfort in believing, as Patrick and Michael did, that there was a better place waiting for us. And certainly if entry to heaven depended on leading a good life on earth then certainly Patrick would be there, at the front of the queue. A kinder, more thoughtful and selfless man I hadn't met in a long while.

The following morning my dilemma as to what I should tell Michael about his father's condition became redundant when I went into his bedroom to wake him. Michael was already awake, lying on his back, gazing into space and looking very sad. I approached the bed and before I had a chance to ask what was the matter, he turned his gaze to me and said. 'I think the angels will be coming for my daddy soon. Very soon. By the end of the weekend.'

I was taken aback. Certainly Michael couldn't have overheard the conversation I'd had with Eamon the evening before; he'd been asleep and his bedroom door and the sitting-room door had both been closed. And even if he had overheard our conversation there'd been no mention of the weekend.

'What makes you say that, love?' I asked gently, sitting on the bed beside him.

Premonition

Michael shrugged. 'I can't explain. I just have a feeling, that's all.'

While I was aware that loved ones can sometimes have premonitions about those they are close to, I needed to remain practical. 'Uncle Eamon phoned last night,' I said choosing my words carefully. 'He and Colleen visited your dad with Nora and Jack yesterday. He said your dad was sleeping most of the time. They are going to visit again this evening and then we'll see when you should visit. Is that all right with you?'

Michael nodded.

'Your dad was hoping to be home at the weekend,' I added to put it into perspective.

'I know,' Michael said, matter-of-factly, getting out of bed. 'But I don't think he will be.'

I straightened his duvet and then left him to get dressed, ready for school.

At breakfast Michael was quieter than usual, which was hardly surprising given what must have been going through his head. I asked him a few times if he was all right, and he nodded. Once I'd taken the boys to school and Paula to nursery, I phoned Stella and asked if she'd heard anything from St John's Hospice. She hadn't – not since Patrick had phoned her on Wednesday to say he was going in. I told Stella what Eamon had said and that I wasn't sure if and when I should take Michael to visit his father. I didn't want to go against Patrick's wishes, but on the other hand Michael needed to see his father if this was goodbye. Stella said she'd phone St John's straight away and get back to me. When she returned my call twenty minutes later she said there was no change in Patrick's condition and that he was still unconscious. I asked her again if and when I should take Michael to visit. Stella said that as Patrick was unconscious and couldn't talk to Michael there didn't seem a lot of point in taking him now.

'But surely Michael needs to say goodbye to his dad?' I said.

'Let's stay positive,' she said. 'We're not at that point yet.'

I wasn't so sure. What Michael had said that morning had stayed with me. Michael was very close to his father and if he'd had a premonition I wasn't going to dismiss it.

Chapter Twenty-Eight
Time with Dad

Colleen phoned that Friday evening before Michael was in bed and told me there was no change in Patrick's condition. I asked her what she and Eamon now thought about me taking Michael to see his father over the weekend and she said they thought I should. Colleen then offered to take Michael with them when they visited and I said that if she didn't mind I would like to take him, as I too wanted to see Pat. I didn't say I wanted to see him to say goodbye but that was the implication.

'Of course,' she said apologetically. 'Sorry, I wasn't thinking. You need to see Pat. Will you take Adrian and Paula?'

'No. I'll ask my parents to babysit. We'll probably go on Sunday afternoon.'

'Yes, there's no restriction on visiting, although they ask you to avoid twelve thirty to one thirty, as it's a quiet time. I expect we'll go as usual in the evening, and I think Nora and Jack are going on Saturday.'

Colleen then asked if she could speak to Michael, as he was still up and I called him to the phone. They chatted for about five minutes while I read Paula a bedtime story. When they'd finished Michael seemed relaxed and reassured by speaking to Colleen; she and Eamon were Patrick's oldest and dearest friends and Michael had known them all his life. I told Michael

245

we would be going to see his dad on Sunday and then I telephoned my parents. Mum answered and I explained that Patrick was now in a hospice and that I needed to take Michael to see him. Straight away Mum offered to look after Adrian and Paula, and then became upset because Patrick was so ill. I felt bad at upsetting Mum, but that's what happens in fostering: the whole family becomes involved and suffers the sadness and losses of the looked-after child, just as they would their own child or grandchildren.

That night Michael had said his prayers before I went into his bedroom to say goodnight. He was in bed, waiting for me to tuck him in and give him a goodnight kiss. I had suggested earlier in the evening that we all went swimming the following day and Michael was looking forward to it. 'I'm going down the chute with Adrian,' he said. 'Are you coming down this time?'

Michael was referring to our previous swimming trips, when he and Adrian had spent most of the time going down the water-chute ride while I'd stayed in the shallow end, using Paula as an excuse. 'I could look after Paula if you want a go on the chute,' Michael added.

'We'll see,' I said. 'You're a better swimmer than I am.'

'Do you remember when we all went swimming and Dad watched while you came in the water with us?' Michael said thoughtfully.

I smiled. 'I do, love. We had a great time, didn't we?'

'Yes. I just wish we could do it again.'

I hugged Michael, and then sat on the bed holding his hand until his eyes closed and he fell asleep.

Going swimming on Saturday, with lunch out, followed by the afternoon in the park, was a good idea. It filled up most of the day and kept everyone happily occupied, so there was no room for fretting or worrying about what Sunday would bring. It was six o'clock by the time we arrived home and we were all pleasantly exhausted. After dinner the children watched a short film on television and then I took Paula up to bed while the boys took turns in the shower. They were all yawning madly by the time they were washed and in their nightwear and no one objected going to bed. Adrian and Paula were looking forward to seeing their nana and grandpa the following day and Michael was looking forward to seeing his father. I'd already explained to Michael that his dad probably wouldn't be awake and Colleen had said something similar when she'd spoken to him on the phone, so Michael was realistic in what to expect when he visited his father.

'It will be nice if Dad wakes up while we're there,' he said thoughtfully as I tucked him into bed.

'Yes,' I agreed. 'Although Colleen did say he was sleeping a lot,' I reminded him.

We all had a lie-in on Sunday morning and weren't up and dressed until ten o'clock, when I cooked a big breakfast — sausage, bacon, egg, tomatoes and beans. My parents arrived at twelve noon as arranged, and as usual Paula and Adrian rushed to greet them in the hall, eager to see them and tell them all their news. I noticed that Michael didn't join them in the hall, although having met my parents before he felt comfortable around them and usually rushed to greet them as Adrian and Paula did. I found him in the sitting room, seated on the sofa and vaguely flicking through a book.

'Are you all right?' I asked, as my mum and dad followed me into the sitting room.

Michael nodded.

Mum became distracted by Adrian and Paula, who wanted to show her something, while Dad went over and sat on the sofa next to Michael.

'How are you doing, lad?' my father asked gently.

'OK, I guess.' Michael shrugged.

'When you see your dad will you say hello to him from Nana and me, please, and send him our love?'

'Dad probably won't be awake,' Michael said despondently.

Dad knew this. He nodded. 'Just because someone isn't awake doesn't mean they can't hear you. His eyes might be closed but his ears are still open. I want you to remember that when you talk to your dad. Tell him everything you want him to know: he can still hear you.'

Dad's message was so obvious I wondered why I hadn't thought of it, for I could see the comfort Michael now found in my father's words. I felt quite choked up because I knew Dad had shared something very personal which had come from his own experience: he'd spent hours by his father's bed in his last few days, comforting and reassuring him as he'd slowly passed away.

'I will,' Michael said, looking appreciatively at my father. 'I'll talk to Dad and tell him all my news, just like I do when he's awake.'

'Good lad,' Dad said. 'That'll make him very happy. And don't forget to tell him how much you love him.'

'I won't,' Michael replied, smiling.

Michael and I left the house at 1.30 p.m. and I drove to St John's Hospice with the radio on low and Michael looking through his side window at the passing scenery. I'd never been to St John's before but I'd driven past the building, so I knew where it was. The roads were clear and we arrived at 1.50. Built about fifteen years ago, St John's was a red-brick single-storey building, set back from the road and surrounded by beautiful gardens. There was a small car park nestled in the trees to one side and I drove in and easily found a parking bay.

'Isn't this lovely?' I said, referring to the gardens. Michael didn't reply.

'Are you OK?' I asked, making my voice light, as I opened the rear door to let him get out.

Michael nodded but still didn't say anything. I sensed his apprehension and anxiety. I felt it too. It wasn't so much seeing his father that was making us anxious but seeing him in the hospice rather than at the hospital, which we were both very familiar with.

Opening the outer door to St John's we passed through a bright spacious lobby with large potted plants, and then entered the reception area. It was also very light, and decorated in pale blue with carpet, sofa, armchairs, coffee table and a magazine rack, reminiscent of a comfortable sitting room. Reception was empty, apart from us and the lady who was seated behind a low beech-wood reception desk, straight in front. She smiled as we entered and then asked: 'Can I help you?'

We went over. 'We've come to see Mr Patrick Byrne,' I said.

'Patrick is in Room 8,' she said, without having to check. 'It's just along that corridor down there.' She pointed. 'His room is on the left. Would you like a member of staff to show you?'

'I think we'll be all right,' I said.

'Here's our little leaflet showing you where everything is,' she said, handing me a pamphlet of St John's. 'Tea, coffee and soft drinks are always available in the lounge: through that door over there. Let me know if you need anything or if you would like to talk to someone later.' She smiled at Michael and me.

'Thank you,' I said. The receptionist's friendly manner and the welcoming atmosphere of the place had put me more at ease.

'Would you sign the visitors' book, please?' she said, turning the open book to face me.

I signed for Michael and me, adding the date and time, and returned the book. I could hear classical music playing faintly in the background, adding to the relaxed atmosphere of the place, although Michael was still looking worried. As we began in the direction the receptionist had pointed Michael linked his arm through mine and I threw him a reassuring smile. A middle-aged man with a teenage boy, also visiting, came towards us and said a friendly hello as they passed, and I returned their greeting. The rooms were numbered consecutively, going up from one; some of the doors we passed were open, revealing large airy rooms with carpet, upholstered chairs and modern built-in furniture. The door to Patrick's room was closed and I felt Michael's hand tighten on my arm. Giving a brief knock, I slowly turned the door handle and pushed open the door.

We were in a large bright room at the back of the building, overlooking the gardens. A gleaming white en-suite bathroom led off through a door to our right. The bed, in the centre of the room, was positioned so that the person in it could look out and see the gardens. Pat was asleep in bed, on his back with his head slightly raised on two pillows. There were two armchairs by the bed and an oxygen cylinder. 'You sit here next to your dad,' I said, pushing one of the chairs up to the bed. 'And I'll sit beside you.'

Michael sat in the armchair and leant forward. 'Hello, Dad,' he said, appearing more at ease now we were in the room and he knew there was nothing to fear.

Patrick didn't stir and looked as though he was simply asleep. There were no tubes coming from his mouth or nose, no wires leading to monitors and no drip. His breathing seemed easier than it had been for a long while – he wasn't rasping, perhaps because his breathing was more shallow; and his colour, while not ruddy, was not unhealthily pale. His arms lay over the covers either side of him and his hands were relaxed and slightly open. The wedding ring he always wore on the third finger of his right hand in memory of his wife had become loose with weight loss and had slipped down to his knuckle. I gently moved it back into position so that it wouldn't slip off and be lost.

'Dad, it's Michael here,' Michael tried again, touching his father's arm. Patrick didn't move. As Colleen had said, he was deeply unconscious.

I glanced around the room. Furnished in beech wood with a built-in wardrobe, chest of drawers, television, telephone, radio, and curtains matching the bedding, it was very comfortable and like a four-star hotel room. The view through the window was truly beautiful and inspiring, and I knew when Patrick had arrived on Wednesday and had been able to appreciate the view how much pleasure he would have drawn from it. I just wished Michael and I had been with him when he'd been admitted and had still been conscious, but Patrick being Patrick had arranged his admittance and then told his social worker, friends and me.

'Dad?' Michael tried again, but Patrick still didn't stir. Only his chest rose and fell with his breathing. Michael looked at me, disappointed, and unsure what to do or say next.

'Remember what Grandpa told you,' I reminded him. 'Your dad can hear you, so talk to him.' Then I wondered if Michael felt a bit self-conscious, talking to his father and getting no response. 'Shall I start?' I suggested. Michael nodded.

Sliding my chair right up to the bed and leaning slightly forward, I said softly, 'Hello Pat, Cathy here. It's Sunday afternoon and a lovely summer's day. The birds are singing and through your window I can see a beautiful climbing rose with masses of pink flowers. You would know the name of the rose. You're good with flower and plant names. There's a large rhododendron bush too, but that's finished flowering for this year. It needs a trim. I've had a busy week, as usual. Adrian and Paula are fine. My parents are looking after them. They all send their love. Michael is here right beside me and I know he has lots to tell you.'

Now I had begun, Michael was clearly less self-conscious about talking to his dad. Folding his arms on to the bed and resting his chin on top, he began: 'Hi, Dad, Michael here. I love you. I played basketball on Friday and we won 38–35. The other side were good, though. It was a difficult game. All the team will have to stand up in assembly next week and everyone will clap. That always happens when a team wins. Father Murphy knows you are in here and he said he'd visit you this weekend. Perhaps he's already been? He asked me if I wanted to come with him so we could say a prayer together but I told him I was coming with Cathy. It's not that I didn't want to pray for you but I didn't want him telling me what to say. I say my prayers every night but they're personal – between me and God – although I don't mind Cathy hearing. I thought you'd understand. We had a maths test at school last week and I got 90 per cent, and a spelling test and I got them all right.'

Michael continued telling his dad his news from school, then about a television programme he and Adrian had watched about flesh-eating dinosaurs; and then he described how our cat, Toscha, had caught a bird and I'd rescued it from Toscha's jaws. He made me sound very brave. Now Michael had begun talking to his dad he found plenty to say and chatted as though his dad was awake and could hear every word.

Time with Dad

As Michael talked I flicked through the leaflet the receptionist had given to me and then I tucked it into my bag. I looked again at Patrick; there was little outward sign of the illness that ravaged him within; he just looked tired and old. Occasionally his arm moved slightly or a muscle twitched in his face but that, and the steady rise and fall of his chest, was the only movement he made. He looked very peaceful and at rest.

As Michael continued to talk, my thoughts went back to the first time I heard of Patrick, when Jill had said: 'Cathy, I need to ask you something, and you must feel you can say no'; when she'd told me that Michael had lost his mother as a small child and his father had brought him up but was now very ill. I remembered I'd said I needed time to think before I committed myself because I was concerned of the impact looking after Michael could have on my children. I also remembered how Adrian and Paula had told me they knew what it was like to lose a father and they could help and comfort Michael when he was sad. I thought back to the first time I'd met Patrick: at the council offices with Stella and Jill, and how impressed and humbled I'd felt by his strength and courage. In the meeting I'd agreed to look after Michael but afterwards I'd had doubts. Had I made the right decision, I wondered now as I had then? Would I make the same decision again? Yes, I would. For despite the sadness, and the grief I knew was to come, my family and I were better people from knowing Patrick and Michael, and I hoped Michael had gained something from knowing us.

Michael stopped talking; having told his dad all his news, he had finally run out of things to say. We sat side by side, quietly gazing at Patrick. Presently a knock sounded on the door and a nurse came in.

'Hello, I'm Mary. Do you need anything?' she asked kindly, going to the bed and checking on Patrick.

'No, we're fine, thank you,' I said. 'Patrick's still asleep. How long has he been like this?' I asked.

'Since Wednesday night,' Mary replied, smiling. 'He put himself to bed on Wednesday evening as soon as his friend Jack left, and has been asleep ever since. I think Dad is tired out,' she said, smiling at Michael. 'Now he's having a well-deserved rest.'

Michael nodded. It was comforting hearing Mary normalize Patrick's unconsciousness as a well-deserved rest, and I thought she was right: Patrick was tired out – from battling with his illness for so long. In here he could relax and be well looked after.

Mary straightened the bed covers. 'If you want to talk to someone before you leave, ask at reception. There is always someone on hand to talk to relatives and friends.'

I thanked her and with a cheery 'See you later' she left the room. I could see why Patrick had chosen to come to St John's. It was far more friendly and personal than a large hospital.

Michael and I sat quietly by Pat's bed for a while longer, sometimes looking at him and sometimes glancing out of the window as birds hopped on and off the rhododendron bush, catching grubs and insects. I glanced at my watch and was surprised to see it was nearly four o'clock; we'd been here for two hours. While I was happy to stay as long as Michael wanted to, now he'd told his dad all his news I wondered if he was nearly ready to say goodbye and go home.

'Michael,' I said after a moment, gently touching his arm, 'is there anything else you want to tell Dad today? I was thinking we might go soon. What do you think?'

'Are we having dinner when we get home?'

'Yes. Are you hungry?'

He nodded and rubbed his stomach.

'OK. Let's say goodbye to Dad, then, and we'll come again tomorrow after school if you like.'

Michael nodded. We stood and I pushed the two armchairs away from the bed, back to where they'd been when we'd come in. Michael leant over the bed and, kissing his Dad's cheek, said: 'Bye, Dad. I'm going now. I love you so much.' It was said naturally, as if he was just going out for a while.

As Michael straightened and moved away from the bed I leant forward and kissed Pat's forehead. 'Bye, love,' I said. 'You're in our thoughts. Michael is fine, so please don't worry. Just rest and get the sleep you need.'

'I'm fine,' Michael repeated. We stood by the bed for a minute longer and then Michael gave his dad another kiss on the cheek and we came away.

Later, I wished I'd told Pat how much he really meant to me, and shared the happy memories of the good times we'd had together. But then life is full of 'if only's'. What was more important was that Michael had spent quality time with his father and had shared all his news.

Chapter Twenty-Nine
The Stars Glow Brightly

When we arrived home Mum had made dinner and we ate outside, making the most of the glorious weather. It was after seven o'clock when my parents finally said goodbye and we waved them off at the front door. After they'd gone I began the children's bath and bedtime routine, ready for school and nursery the following day. With only a few weeks left before the end of the summer term the schools were doing fun things and Michael was looking forward to their pupil-versus-staff cricket match the following day, which he'd explained was a school tradition. He said it was great fun to watch the priests running around and trying to play cricket in their cassocks. 'I'll have to remember to tell Dad the score when I see him,' Michael added brightly.

But later, when I went into Michael's bedroom to say goodnight, I found him looking very sad. He had said his prayers and was in bed. Immediately I knew he needed to talk.

'Are you all right?' I asked gently, hovering by the bed.

His face crumpled and he burst into tears. 'Cathy, soon I won't be able to tell my dad about school or cricket or anything, ever again. It's not fair. Most kids my age have two parents; soon I won't have any.'

I sat on the bed and took him in my arms. I held him close as he cried openly. There was little I could say or do to minimize his pain. Michael was right: of course it wasn't fair he and his dad would soon be parted; but I wasn't about to offer unrealistic hope and tell him his dad would get better. I stroked Michael's head and tried to soothe him as best I could as he buried his face in my shoulder and wept. Michael had been so brave for so long and now all his sorrow, frustration and anger were finally being released, possibly as a result of seeing his father in the hospice that afternoon. I knew how he felt – I was close to tears myself. I held him and rocked him gently until finally his tears began to subside and he asked for a tissue so that he could blow his nose. I sat holding him a while longer; then I heard Adrian call me.

'Will you be all right for a moment while I see what Adrian wants?' I asked.

Michael nodded and snuggled down into his bed where he curled on to his side.

I went into Adrian's bedroom; he was sitting up in bed looking very worried, having heard Michael crying.

'Michael's all right, now,' I reassured him. 'He's going to get some sleep soon.'

Adrian nodded but didn't look convinced. 'Will he see his dad again tomorrow?'

'Yes. I'll take him after school. You don't mind if Helen comes to look after you and Paula again, do you?'

'No.'

I kissed Adrian goodnight, checked on Paula, who was asleep, and then returned to Michael's room. He was as I'd left him, curled foetally on his side. His eyes were open and he was gazing towards the window. The curtains were open as he liked them and the night sky could be seen, dark and clear.

'The stars are very bright tonight,' he said quietly as I sat on the bed.

'Yes, they are. It's a clear night.'

'They're burning bright for my daddy,' he said. It was a quaint thing for a child to say but I knew how much comfort Michael drew from seeing the stars, just as his father did. 'One is glowing brighter than all the others,' Michael added. 'That's my mummy waiting for my daddy.'

I stayed with Michael, sitting on his bed and quietly stroking his forehead, until his eyes slowly closed and he drifted into sleep. I then crept from his bedroom and checked on Paula and Adrian, who were asleep, before going downstairs. I made a mug of tea and took it through to the sitting room, where I wrote up my fostering log notes, including our visit to the hospice that afternoon. Then I wrote a note to remind me to phone Jill in the morning to ask her to arrange for Helen to sit with Adrian and Paula on Monday evening while I took Michael to see his father. I switched on the television, adjusted the sound to low, and watched a film while listening out for any sound of Michael. If he woke I didn't want him crying alone in the dark. I checked on him at ten o'clock and eleven o'clock and he was asleep. It was after midnight by the time I finally put Toscha out for her run and went upstairs to bed. I slept and woke when the alarm went off at 6.15, but later, when I found out what had happened, I felt guilty for sleeping so soundly.

Having showered and dressed, I woke Paula and Adrian and told them it was time to get dressed, ready for nursery and school. When I went into Michael's room he was already awake and standing by the window in his pyjamas.

'Oh, you're up,' I said, surprised. 'I was coming to wake you. It's time to get dressed. Are you all right, love?'

'Yes,' he said quietly. 'I'll get dressed now.'

The Stars Glow Brightly

When he came down for breakfast Michael was subdued but not visibly upset. Adrian and Paula were always quieter on Monday mornings, finding it a jolt to get back into the routine of school after a relaxing weekend. Michael began eating and then stopped and looked at me thoughtfully. 'Cathy, this morning, before you came into my room, I heard my dad. It was so real. He said, "Michael, it's time to get dressed. We can't be keeping the priests waiting." That's what he always says – every morning – when I have to go to school. It was like he was in the room. That's why I was up when you came in.'

Adrian looked at me questioningly, while Paula said to Michael, 'Your daddy is in hospital. He isn't here.'

I smiled at Michael as I spoke, for clearly he had taken comfort from hearing his father's voice. 'Sometimes, when we are very close to someone, we can still feel their presence – their warmth and love – even though they are not actually with us.'

Michael nodded. 'It was a nice feeling, just like he was close by.'

Adrian and Paula seemed satisfied with my explanation and all three children continued eating their breakfasts.

Once they'd finished they went upstairs to brush their teeth while I cleared the breakfast dishes from the table. I was about to start rinsing them through when the phone rang. I went into the hall to answer it, vaguely wondering who could be phoning me at 7.45 a.m. on a weekday.

'Hello?' I said, half-expecting to hear a friend's voice asking for a last-minute favour: to take their child to school.

It was a friend, but not one asking for a favour.

'Cathy, it's Colleen.'

I felt a tingle of fear run up my spine. 'Hello, Colleen,' I said evenly.

There was a small pause before she said, 'Cathy, a nurse from St John's has just phoned. I'm sorry to be the one to tell you but Pat passed away in his sleep last night.'

My eyes immediately filled and I felt cold all over. This was the phone call I had known would come eventually but it didn't make it any easier.

'Will you tell Michael, please?' Colleen said, her voice shaking. 'Tell him his daddy died peacefully in his sleep. He's at rest now.'

'I'll tell him,' I managed to say. 'I'm so, so sorry.'

'Give Michael our love,' Colleen said, in tears. 'Could he phone me later when he feels up to it? God bless you all.'

Replacing the receiver, I wiped my hand over my eyes and began slowly up the stairs. The children had finished in the bathroom and now appeared on the landing.

'Who was on the phone?' Adrian asked innocently.

I looked at Michael. 'I'm sorry, love,' I began, going up to him. 'That was Colleen.' I didn't have to say any more

'He's dead, isn't he?' Michael said, his face crumpling. 'I knew when I heard him this morning.'

I enfolded him in my arms as he wept. Adrian and Paula stood close, either side of me; I held Michael and we all cried openly. Usually, I try to be brave for the children, but at that moment our grief was raw and overpowering, as only the news of a death can be. 'He died peacefully in his sleep,' I emphasized as my tears fell. 'Daddy is at rest now.'

I held Michael and kept Adrian and Paula close; huddled together in a small group on the landing we all cried, oblivious to the time or the routine we should have been following.

'My daddy is with my mummy now,' Michael said through his tears.

'Yes, he is, love. They're together now.'

We cried and cried until our tears were spent. We would cry again but for now I knew I had to take control and think what I needed to do. With the children close beside me we went downstairs and into the sitting room.

'Are we going to school?' Paula asked.

'No, love, not today.'

Then I wondered if Adrian and Paula would be better off at school and nursery and wanted to go, but when I asked them they said they wanted to stay at home and help look after Michael. They sat on the sofa with Michael between them; Paula held Michael's hand while Adrian linked his arm. I think Michael drew comfort from having them close, for they seemed to instinctively know what to say and do. I remembered Adrian's reassurance: that because he and Paula had lost their father (through divorce) they were better able to understand how Michael felt when he was sad, and it was true.

At 9.00 I knew Jill would be in her office and I asked the children if they would be all right staying in the sitting room while I went into the hall to make a few phone calls. I didn't want to use the phone in the sitting room, as it would be upsetting for Michael to have to listen to me keep telling other people that his father had died. The children nodded and I told them to call me if they needed me; then I went down the hall and phoned Jill.

She knew from my tone and that I was phoning when I should have been doing the school run that something was wrong. I held my voice steady as I said that Patrick had died peacefully in his sleep. While the news wasn't a shock to Jill, as Patrick had been ill for a long time, she was obviously very sympathetic and asked how we all were, especially Michael. She asked if I needed any help and I said I didn't think so today, as we would all be at home, grieving. She said if I did need help to phone her straight away. She also said she would notify Stella of Patrick's death as soon as she was in the office and would phone me later.

It was now nearly 9.30 and I phoned Adrian's school and then Paula's nursery and told the secretaries that the children wouldn't be going to school today as a close family friend had died. I didn't elaborate on who it was – it wasn't relevant, as they didn't know the reason I was fostering Michael. However, when I phoned Michael's school it was very different, of course. I told the school secretary Michael's father had died during the night, and knowing Michael and Patrick personally she was upset. She said she'd inform the head straight away. I said I didn't know when Michael would be returning to school but I would phone her when I did. I then telephoned my parents and told them; they were obviously upset and asked me to give Michael their love and tell him he was in their thoughts. I was finding that each time I told someone of Patrick's death although I had a lump in my throat and tears in my eyes it was becoming very slightly easier to say the words, as I slowly adjusted to the fact that dear, dear Patrick was no longer with us and was now at rest.

I returned to the sitting room, where the children were as I'd left them – in a row on the sofa. They were snuggled close together, quiet but not crying. Paula was lightly rubbing Michael's hand as I did hers sometimes when she was unhappy. I told them I had phoned their schools, and then I asked Michael if he would like to speak to Colleen. He said he would, so I suggested to Adrian and Paula that they found something to do while Michael talked to Colleen on the phone. They went into the conservatory where the toys were. I dialled Colleen's number and once she was on the line I passed the phone to Michael. I sat next to him on the sofa as he said quietly, 'Hello, Auntie Colleen. How are you?'

I obviously couldn't hear what Colleen was saying, but it was clear Michael took comfort from her words, as she reassured him and asked how he was feeling. When they'd finished Colleen asked to speak to me. Michael passed me the phone and then, standing, slowly crossed the room and joined Adrian and Paula in the conservatory.

'He's such a brave little chap,' Colleen said.

I agreed wholeheartedly. 'Yes, he is.'

Colleen then told me that she and Jack would be organizing the funeral and would let me know the day and time once they had seen the undertaker later in the day. She said it would be a cremation, in line with Pat's wishes, and the priest from their church – the Sacred Heart – would be conducting the service. Colleen said she'd informed Nora and Jack of Patrick's death and was trying to contact Patrick's only relative, his aunt, who was living in Wales. She finished by thanking me for all I was doing for Michael and said she'd phone again later.

I replaced the receiver and, standing, crossed the room to where I could see the children in the conservatory-cum-play-room. They were sitting on the floor in a small circle around the many pieces of a jigsaw puzzle. Although Michael wasn't joining in, but watching Adrian and Paula, he was at least occupied and not crying. I watched him a while longer and then moved away, not really sure what I should be doing. When you receive the news of a death, after the shock and grief you reach a sort of numb plateau, where you return to the practi-calities of living which surround you. Checking on the children again, I wandered into the kitchen and continued washing up the breakfast dishes, which I'd begun when Colleen had phoned.

The Night the Angels Came

The phone rang again just after ten o'clock and it was Father Murphy from Michael's school. He asked how Michael was and then asked if he could visit him later today – after school today, at about four o'clock, he said. I said yes, although to be honest I didn't really feel I had the option of saying no, as he seemed to assume he would be coming. When I told Michael that Father Murphy would be visiting later he nodded, as though his visit was an expected formality, and then returned to the jigsaw puzzle, which he was now helping to do.

Stella phoned half an hour later, having just received the news of Patrick's death. She sounded very sad, having got to know Patrick well in the time she'd been working with him. She asked how Michael was and I said he was being very brave, although he was obviously upset. She said she wouldn't speak to him right now but to give him her love and that I should phone her if we needed any support. Later in the morning my parents phoned and offered to come over and help, which was kind of them, but there really wasn't much they could do. I reassured Mum we were coping and also told her we had the priest visiting later; Mum said she would phone again but obviously to call her if we needed any help. In fact the morning disappeared in phone calls with offers of support and help. I'd just finished speaking to Mum when Nora telephoned. She and Jack both spoke to Michael and then Nora told me to phone her if we needed anything. Everyone was being so kind and thoughtful; it was very comforting.

At one o'clock I made a sandwich lunch and called the children to the table. None of us had much of an appetite, but we ate a little, albeit without our usual chatter, and when I offered the children an ice cream they quietly accepted. I explained to Adrian and Paula that when the priest came later we would go into another room so that Michael could spend time alone with

Father Murphy. Paula, despite seeing the priests regularly at Michael's school when we took and collected Michael, still found the priests unsettling, I think because their full-length cassocks created the appearance of them gliding – 'like ghosts', Paula said. She now asked Michael: 'Will you be all right alone with a priest?'

Michael nodded and I reassured Paula that Michael would be fine and that the priest would be able to comfort Michael spiritually – in a way I could not.

'Well, if you need rescuing shout for us,' Paula said very seriously. And despite our grief we had to laugh, Michael the loudest. It was the first laughter of the day and it was a release.

When the doorbell rang just after four o'clock, signalling the priest's arrival, Paula fled upstairs to her bedroom, quickly followed by Adrian, so that when I showed Father Murphy into the sitting room Michael was sitting by himself on the sofa, looking very lonely.

'Hello, Father,' Michael said respectfully, immediately standing.

'It's all right, lad,' the priest said kindly. 'Sit yourself down.'

Father Murphy went over and sat on the sofa next to Michael and I asked him if he wanted something to drink, but he didn't. 'I'll leave the two of you alone, then,' I said, and the priest nodded.

Pulling the sitting-room door to I went upstairs, where I found Adrian and Paula hiding on the landing, wanting a glimpse of the priest but not wanting to be seen. 'Honestly! Look at you two!' I said, not best pleased. 'Fancy running off and leaving Michael alone like that! Goodness knows what Father Murphy thought. He's a priest, not an ogre.' But Paula didn't look convinced.

Father Murphy was with Michael for nearly an hour and I stayed upstairs with the children and occupied myself by tidying the children's clothes in their wardrobes. When I heard the sitting-room door open I went downstairs, followed by Adrian and Paula. Michael and the priest were in the hall and Michael was actually smiling.

'Michael would like to go to school tomorrow,' Father Murphy said to me. 'I think you should let him.'

'Of course,' I said. 'If that's what Michael's wants.'

Michael nodded.

'Good lad,' the priest said to Michael and then he shook my hand. We said goodbye and I saw him out and closed the front door.

Paula was now looking at Michael carefully, finally realizing that the priest wasn't the ogre she imagined and his visit had done Michael some good. She looked at him a while longer and then asked, 'What did that priest man say to you?'

'Lots of things,' Michael said, 'and we said some prayers for my dad.'

'What sort of things?' Paula asked.

'That's private,' I said to Paula. 'Between Michael and Father Murphy.' I wasn't having Michael pressed into disclosing his private audience with the priest to satisfy Paula's curiosity.

I suggested the children watched some television while I made dinner, which they did. We ate at six o'clock and again the meal was subdued and without our usual chatter, but I was pleased to see Michael was eating. I said that as Michael was going to school the following day I thought Adrian and Paula should go too and they agreed. After dinner we went into the sitting room and I read the children some stories for the best part of an hour; then it was time to start their bed and bath routine.

Upstairs, Paula was exhausted and after her bath fell asleep almost as soon as she climbed into bed, but Adrian and Michael had grown gloomy again now they were tired. I talked to them and then once they had showered, I said goodnight and tucked them into bed, but I checked on them regularly. When I went into Adrian's room at nine o'clock I found he had finally dropped off to sleep with his arms around his favourite soft toy, but when I went into Michael's room he was still wide awake.

'All right, love?' I asked gently, sitting on the bed

Michael gave a small nod. 'I've been thinking,' he said softly.

'Nice thoughts?'

He nodded. 'About Dad and Mum. I never really knew Mum. She died when I was very little. Dad was like a mum to me; him and Auntie Colleen.'

'And now Daddy and Mummy are together again,' I said, hoping it would help.

'Yes, that's what Father Murphy said.' Michael gave a small wistful smile; then I saw his bottom lip tremble. 'I just wish they could have both stayed with me.'

'I know, love,' I said, and wrapped him in my arms.

He cried for some time, and I sat with him, holding his hand and stroking his forehead. Eventually his tears stopped and his eyes closed and he drifted into sleep. I sat with him a while longer and then crept from his room; leaving his bedroom door slightly open so that I would hear him if he woke upset. I went downstairs and into the sitting room, where I sat on the sofa, physically and emotionally exhausted.

Five minutes later the phone rang and it was Colleen.

'It's not too late too phone you, is it?' she asked.

'No.'

'Sorry I didn't get back to you sooner, but there's been so much to do. How are you all?'

'Not too bad. Michael's asleep now. He'll be going into school tomorrow.'

'Good. We've spent most of the day arranging the funeral. If you've got a pen handy I'll give you the details now.'

I reached for the pad and pen by the phone. 'Yes?'

'It's next Monday at eleven a.m.,' Colleen said, and I made a note. 'The cortège will leave from Patrick and Michael's house at ten thirty. I'll have to get Michael into his suit first, so I think we will need to collect him from you at eight thirty. I hope that's all right with you?'

'So you and Eamon will be taking Michael to the funeral?' I said, slightly taken aback, for I'd assumed that Michael would be going to the funeral with me. Indeed I'd already asked Mum and Dad it they could collect Adrian and Paula from school and nursery on the day of the funeral.

Colleen paused and in that silence I felt her discomfort; that she was uncomfortable with what she had to say. 'Didn't Stella phone you?' she asked awkwardly.

'Only first thing this morning. I haven't heard from her since.'

'Oh, she must have been called away. She was supposed to phone you and explain. We agreed Eamon and I would take Michael to the funeral,' Colleen began and then stopped. 'Look, Cathy, there are some other things you need to know. I really think it's best if you speak to Stella tomorrow.'

'All right,' I said, too tired and emotionally drained to ask why she couldn't tell me now.

Colleen then continued to say that Patrick had said he didn't want flowers at his funeral but would like people to make a donation to cancer research instead. She said she was going to invite the mourners back to her house after the service for a light buffet and I was obviously included. She thanked me again for all I was doing for Michael and we said goodbye. Aware there was something Colleen wasn't telling me but too tired to worry, I went to bed. Tomorrow, once the children were at school, I would phone Stella or Jill and ask what was going on.

Chapter Thirty

The Meeting

As it turned out I didn't have to telephone, for the following morning, having just returned from taking the children to school and nursery, the phone began ringing. The digital display showed it was Jill's office number.

'How are you all?' Jill asked, showing her usual concern for our well-being.

'Not too bad, considering,' I said. 'The children are at school. Michael wanted to go. He's coping remarkably well.'

'I understand a priest visited you yesterday afternoon?'

'Yes, Father Murphy. How did you know?'

'Stella told me. She's been in touch with Michael's school. In fact I was supposed to phone you yesterday but I had to place a child and it was nearly nine o'clock before I finished. Stella wants to set up a planning meeting. Do you feel up to it? She suggested tomorrow at ten o'clock.'

'Yes, I can do that. But why the rush?'

'There are certain things she needs to discuss. It will be at the council offices, so I'll meet you in reception at nine fifty. Obviously if you need any help today phone me, won't you?'

'Yes, I will, Jill. Thank you.'

We said goodbye and I hung up. I wasn't unduly surprised that Stella was setting up a planning meeting. These meetings are not unusual and are arranged to plan short- and long-term care for the foster child – with whom and where the child will live. However, given that Michael was already with me I didn't see the urgency; all we needed were some more of his clothes from home.

The house was unhappily quiet with the children at school and I telephoned Mum for a chat. I told her the funeral had been arranged for eleven o'clock the following Monday and asked her if she could collect Paula from nursery and look after her until I returned. She said of course she would and she would make lunch. I also mentioned that Michael would be going to the funeral with Colleen and Eamon, and Mum said that she thought that was appropriate given they were Patrick's oldest and closest friends. She then asked me if I wanted Dad to accompany me to the funeral, as I would be going alone. I thanked her but said I'd be all right as I knew the church and others I knew would be there.

Having finished speaking to Mum, I loaded the washing machine and then pushed the vacuum cleaner over the carpets. A couple of times I felt my eyes well as I thought of Patrick. I wondered how Michael was faring at school, and indeed if Adrian and Paula were all right. Clearly Adrian and Paula's bond with Patrick was only slight compared to the love (and loss) Michael was feeling, but nevertheless they were having to come to terms with losing someone; death is difficult for adults to cope with, and even more so for children. I was pleased when it was 11.50 and I could leave to collect Paula from nursery. As I went into nursery, Farah, one of the assistants, said quietly to me: 'I'm sorry to hear you've had a bereavement. Paula's been telling us that Mummy's friend has gone to heaven.'

I smiled sadly. 'Thank you. I suppose it's good that Paula is talking about it.' Farah agreed.

But outside, Paula asked, 'Is it all right to tell people that Patrick has gone to heaven?'

'Yes, of course, if you want to,' I said.

'It's not a secret?'

'No.' I looked at her carefully. 'We don't have secrets, do we?'

She hesitated and then said, 'Adrian told me not to tell the kids at nursery about your divorce. He said it's embarrassing.'

I gave her hand a little squeeze. 'It's OK for you to tell people if you want to. It's nothing to be ashamed of. I'll talk to Adrian later.'

It's surprising what a throwaway comment like the one Paula had made can reveal. I was surprised and saddened that Adrian felt as he did. Later that evening when Adrian was in bed I asked him why he didn't want his friends to know that his father and I were divorcing. Eventually, after much reassurance, Adrian admitted he felt ashamed because all his close friends were from happy two-parent families. I reassured him as best I could and said our family was a happy one-parent family. To which he agreed. But the bottom line was that, like me, Adrian would have to adjust and deal with the divorce because there was nothing I could do to change the outcome. Paula, that much younger, and without Adrian's social awareness, didn't really feel the stigma so much. I wondered yet again if John had truly considered the impact his leaving was having on the children.

When I collected Michael from school that afternoon Father Murphy accompanied him across the playground. 'Michael's had a good day,' the priest said. 'Let me know if he wants me to visit again.'

I thanked him and said I would, although I could see that Michael was embarrassed by the priest escorting him across the playground, watched by the other mothers. Michael had said previously to me that he didn't want to be singled out as the boy whose father was ill and now he certainly didn't want to be the boy whose father had just died. Like Adrian and most boys his age, he just wanted to blend in with his peer group.

The children were quieter than usual in the car going home and when we arrived they didn't want to play in the garden, so they watched television instead, while I made dinner. I kept popping into the sitting room and checking on them, especially Michael, who unsurprisingly was very subdued and clearly deep in thought. I asked him a few times if he was all right and he nodded. At bedtime when I went into his room to say goodnight he was looking out of his window, hoping to see the stars, but at 8.30 p.m. in July the sky was still light so no stars were visible.

I stood beside him at the window and we both gazed into space. 'The stars are still there, even though you can't see them,' I said, but it didn't help. A moment later Michael was in tears. I held him and soothed and told him it was all right to cry, until his tears subsided, and he said he was tired and wanted to go to bed now. He climbed in and curled on to his side. I asked him if he wanted to talk, but he didn't. Closing his eyes, he pulled the duvet up high although it was a warm night, gaining comfort from being enfolded. I sat with him, stroking his forehead until he fell asleep, and then I crept from his room.

I checked on him during the evening and then again before I went to bed, and he was asleep. I eased the duvet down from his face so that he wouldn't be too hot. In the morning when I went into his room he was still asleep and I had to wake him for school, so I guessed he had slept well, which would be good for him.

Once Michael was up and dressed he seemed a bit brighter than he had the day before. Indeed I felt it was becoming a little easier for us all as we fell into the school routine. Over breakfast

Michael asked if we could collect his Scalextric from home at the weekend and I said, most definitely; that I would phone Nora and ask when she would be at home to let us in. I was pleased Michael was taking an interest in his Scalextric again but I knew returning home would be difficult for him. I thought if he didn't want to go into his house he could wait with Jack, while Nora and I went in and fetched the Scalextric and anything else he needed.

Having taken the boys to school and Paula to nursery, I went straight to the council offices for the planning meeting. Jill was already in reception and greeted me warmly with a hug, and then asked how the children were. As we talked I saw Colleen and Eamon come into reception. 'Those are Patrick's friends, Colleen and Eamon,' I said to Jill, as she hadn't met them before. 'Are they coming to the meeting?' For it seemed an unlikely coincidence otherwise.

'I believe so,' Jill said.

We went over and I introduced Jill to Colleen and Eamon. They asked how Michael was and I said he was coping very well and was at school. We continued chatting as Jill led the way up the stone stairs to the floor where the committee rooms were. She showed us into Room 3, one of the smaller meeting rooms, where five chairs had been arranged in a circle in the centre of the room. We sat down and then Stella came in with a quiet 'Good morning' and sat in the vacant chair.

'Thank you for coming,' she said with a small smile, and took out a notepad and pen, which she held on her lap. 'Can we start by introducing ourselves? I'm Stella, Michael's social worker.'

After we'd introduced ourselves Stella opened the meeting: 'We all know why we're here,' she said evenly. 'Sadly Patrick passed away on Sunday after a long illness and we now need to look at the arrangements for Michael's care.' She paused. 'Cathy,' Stella continued, looking at me, 'you are Michael's foster carer and I know Patrick would want me to thank you for doing such a wonderful job. Your sensitive support and care of Michael has helped him through a very upsetting and difficult time. I should also like to add my own personal thanks for all the help you have given Michael.' Eamon and Colleen nodded and murmured their agreement.

I looked away, embarrassed. 'Michael is a pleasure to look after,' I said and a lump immediately rose in my throat.

Stella checked the notes on her pad and then looked up, ready to speak again. 'As you all know, Patrick became aware he was very ill some time ago and he sensibly planned for his son's care. I have been in regular contact with Patrick since he first approached the social services asking for help and I am therefore aware of his wishes. The department also has a copy of Patrick's will, which now has a codicil.'

Eamon and Colleen nodded again. I knew they were the executors of Patrick's will because Patrick had mentioned it to me a while back – at one of our first meetings – when he'd said he'd sold his car and had been putting his affairs in order to make it easier for Colleen and Eamon when the time came. I didn't know the contents of Patrick's will, nor that there was a codicil; there was no reason why I should know.

'Cathy,' Stella said, again looking at me as she spoke. 'Patrick told me you offered Michael long-term care and I know it was much appreciated. He has only one relative, his aunt, and she cannot look after Michael. However, there is now a second option for Michael which the department is seriously consider-ing.' I glanced sideways at Jill, who was concentrating on Stella, her face serious, clearly no more aware of this second option than I was.

'A month ago,' Stella said, concentrating on Jill and me, 'Colleen and Eamon told Patrick that they would very much like to look after Michael long term if it ever became necessary, and hopefully be allowed to adopt him.'

'Oh,' I said.

Stella nodded. 'But Patrick, always sensible and level-headed, told them to give it more thought. For although they are his oldest and closest friends, and have known Michael since he was a baby, Pat was concerned that with all the emotion surrounding his illness they might have made the offer without thinking through the far-reaching implications, and then find they couldn't fulfil their commitment to Michael. As we all know, Patrick's first concern has always been for Michael and he didn't want him going to live with Colleen and Eamon and then having to move if it didn't work out. He knew that if he stayed with you, Cathy, that wouldn't happen, as you are aware of the practicalities of caring for someone else's children from fostering. So Patrick told Colleen and Eamon to think carefully about their wish to look after Michael, and if after his death they were still fully committed then they should tell me, which they have. Patrick also said that Michael should be asked what he wanted and his decision should be final.'

Stella stopped speaking and the room was quiet. I looked from Stella to Colleen and Eamon, who were staring at the floor, perhaps not wanting to meet my gaze. I felt Jill's eyes on me and then her hand touch my arm.

'I think this has come as rather a shock to Cathy,' Jill said to Stella.

'Yes, I'm sorry. I appreciate that,' Stella said, 'but in keeping with Patrick's wishes – that Colleen and Eamon think carefully about their offer to look after Michael – I couldn't say anything before. Once Colleen and Eamon told me, I thought it was better if we met to discuss this in person, not for you to be told over the phone.'

Eamon nodded and looked up at me. 'Cathy, I hope you don't think we have been going behind your back in this,' he said. 'Pat asked us not to say anything until after his death when we had considered our offer carefully and were absolutely certain it was right and we could fulfil our commitment. As you know, we don't have any children of our own, although we would have liked them very much. Pat wanted us to be aware of how life changing our decision would be. We have thought about it long and hard and are convinced it is the right thing to do. Michael has known us all since he was little and we always played a part in his life and love him dearly. Pat knew that. It would mean so much to us to have Michael as our son, assuming he feels the same way. Colleen would give up her job so that she could be at home for him – to take him to school, have his dinner ready, and do all the things that mothers do.'

Eamon stopped and Colleen looked at me and added: 'If I can be half as good a mother as you are, Cathy, I shall be very pleased.'

I smiled weakly and looked away. Jill was right: it had come as a shock to me and I was still recovering.

Jill then asked Stella, 'What is the legal position regarding moving Michael to Colleen and Eamon?'

'Michael is accommodated on a voluntary care order so we don't need a court order to move him. It's the department's decision.' Stella then looked at me. 'What are your thoughts on this, Cathy? You know Michael well. Do you think it would be right for him to live with Colleen and Eamon?'

All eyes turned to me. I knew I mustn't let my heart rule my head when thinking what was best for Michael. I knew I needed to put aside my love for him and give an honest and objective opinion, which wasn't easy. I took a deep breath before I began. 'I've often thought Colleen and Eamon would make good parents and that it was a pity they didn't have children of their own,' I said. 'They clearly think the world of Michael and already have a strong bond with him, stretching back to when he was a baby. By comparison Michael has only known me for a short time. I am also aware Michael's faith is very important to him, just as it was for his dad. Colleen and Eamon are Catholics and therefore share the same faith. If Michael wants to live with Colleen and Eamon, then I'm sure it's the right thing to do. I will obviously support Michael and do all I can to make the move go smoothly.' I stopped just in time, for I could feel my bottom lip tremble.

There was a small silence before Jill asked Stella: 'When will you ask Michael?'

'I think the sooner we make a decision the better. Michael needs to be settled,' Stella said to Jill. Then to me: 'Could I visit you both tomorrow after school, about four o'clock?'

'Yes,' I said.

'Thank you.' Stella made a note on her pad.

'If Michael does go to live with Colleen and Eamon,' Jill asked, 'will he still be able to see Cathy and her children? I think we all recognize the bond that has developed between them and it would be in Michael's interest to continue.'

Colleen answered, 'Yes, definitely.' Then with a smile at me said: 'And I shall be asking Cathy for lots of advice on looking after Michael.'

I returned her smile.

The meeting ended as it had begun, with Stella thanking us for attending. She thanked me again for all I was doing for Michael, and then asked Colleen and Eamon to wait behind, as

The Meeting

she needed to talk to them. Jill and I said goodbye and left the room.

Outside we were quiet as we went down the stone steps and then crossed the reception. I think Jill realized I needed time to myself. I had gone to the meeting believing I would be making plans for Michael staying for good and instead I was having to face him leaving. I wondered what Paula and Adrian would say, for like me they had assumed Michael would be staying with us.

'What do you think Michael's wishes will be?' Jill said at last, breaking into my thoughts, as we left the building.

'I'm not sure. He has known Eamon and Colleen all his life but he's never lived with them. What if he doesn't know what he wants?'

'Then Stella, as his social worker, will make the decision,' Jill said. 'I think I should be with you tomorrow when Stella visits. Is that all right?'

'Yes please. I'd be grateful for your support.'

Jill smiled. 'I'll see you tomorrow, then, and try not to worry. Whatever the outcome we know Michael will be greatly loved and well looked after, which can't be said for all children.'

Chapter Thirty-One
The Right Decision

I t wasn't appropriate for me to tell the children the reason Stella was coming the following afternoon, so I simply said that Michael's social worker would be visiting us after school on Thursday. Adrian and Paula – used to social workers visiting as part of fostering – saw nothing unusual in this, while Michael just nodded and said, 'OK.' It was Wednesday evening, and after dinner Nora and Jack, and then Colleen and Eamon, phoned. After talking to me they asked to speak to Michael; Colleen and Eamon knew not to mention the reason for Stella's visit to Michael. I assumed Nora and Jack knew what was going on, for Nora said to me: 'I'd like to stay in touch with you, Cathy, wherever Michael's living.'

Michael and Adrian both had homework that evening, although Michael's teacher had sent a note in his reading folder saying that if Michael didn't feel up to doing it to leave it for another week, which was thoughtful of her. However, Michael said he would do his homework tonight as his dad always said he should do it when it was set so that he didn't forget it or rush through it at the last minute.

I smiled. 'Yes, I remember him telling me that,' I said. 'A very sensible man, your dad.'

Michael smiled too. He had mentioned his father a few times that day, which I took as a good sign that he was starting to work through the grieving process. I knew it was more difficult for those who lost a loved one and couldn't bear to talk about them or have their name spoken, as had happened with a friend of mine at school. It had been years before she'd been able to confront her loss and start to heal.

While Adrian and Michael did their homework I helped Paula with her bath and saw her into bed. I read her a bedtime story, kissed her goodnight and then came downstairs, where I checked the boys' homework. Adrian had maths and Michael had spellings to learn. They had done their homework well and decided to play cards before bedtime. And while Michael's pleasure when he won a game was subdued, I thought it was a good sign that he was able to play and was smiling sometimes.

The boys went up to bed at their normal bedtime and when I went into Michael's room to say goodnight he was again standing by the window, gazing at the sky. Like the previous night it was still too light to see the stars. 'The stars are still there,' I said as I'd said the night before, 'even though you can't see them.'

Michael left the window and knelt by his bed to say his prayers: 'God bless Mummy, Daddy, Colleen, Eamon, Nora, Jack, Cathy, Adrian, Paula, and all my friends. Amen.' He climbed into bed.

'All right, love?' I asked as I adjusted the duvet around him. 'You're doing very well.'

He nodded but his face was serious. 'I miss my daddy so much,' he said quietly. 'I wish he didn't have to die. It's not fair.' It was such a simple and heartfelt statement, I could have cried.

'I know, love,' I said, sitting on the bed. 'Sometimes life doesn't seem fair, does it?'

Michael looked at me thoughtfully. 'Do you think it's OK for me to think that sometimes – that life isn't fair? I mean I know I was lucky to have my daddy for all the time I did. And I know

Jesus wanted him, but I wish he hadn't taken my daddy. Will God forgive me for thinking that?'

'Of course he will,' I said. 'Your God is good and understanding. Of course you would rather have your daddy with you; anyone would. You have a right to feel hurt and maybe even angry. I would if I was you.' Which seemed to help Michael and he looked at me a little relieved. I didn't want him to beat himself up with guilt and conscience, which I think can sometimes happen with religious conviction. Michael was a small boy who'd lost his dad; of course it wasn't fair.

'I've told God I don't want him taking any more people I love,' Michael added, as he snuggled down into bed. 'Not Colleen and Eamon, Nora and Jack, or you and Adrian and Paula.'

'Don't you worry, he won't,' I said firmly. 'We're all staying here for a long while,' which made Michael smile. And while I obviously couldn't see into the future I felt sure destiny would never be so cruel as to take another of Michael's loved ones.

Before Michael fell asleep he talked some more about his dad, sharing happy memories of the fun times they'd had together. He mentioned the last time he'd seen his dad – at the hospice – and how he'd somehow known that could be the last time. He said he was pleased he'd talked to him and told him his news. Michael then asked me if he'd really heard his dad telling him to get dressed ready for school on the morning he'd died and I said it was certainly possible. I stayed with Michael, sitting on the bed and holding his hand, as his eyes finally began to close and he slowly drifted off to sleep. Once he was asleep I crept silently from the room and checked on Adrian and Paula, who were also fast asleep.

* * *

The Right Decision

The following morning, Thursday, Paula didn't go to nursery. She said she wasn't well. She had been fine when I'd woken her but once she was up and dressed she said she had a bad tummy ache and didn't feel able to go to nursery. Paula wasn't a child who had regular tummy aches and she usually liked nursery, so I kept her off, and she came with me in the car when I took the boys to school. However, once we were home again Paula immediately brightened and said she was feeling much, much better now. She also told me how much she loved me, and missed me when she was at nursery; then proved it by following me around the house and not letting me out of her sight. I began to wonder if her 'tummy ache' had more to it and was possibly emotional rather than physical. Sometimes when young children haven't the words to express complex emotions their feelings come out through minor illness, for example, tummy aches and headaches, which every parent knows. I thought that with all that had been happening recently it would hardly be surprising if Paula's tummy ache was symptomatic of something deeper.

'Is there anything worrying you?' I asked her a little later as I returned from hanging the washing on the line with Paula one step behind me.

'No,' Paula said adamantly. 'I'm a big girl now. I'm going to big school in September.'

'I know you're a big girl, love,' I said, 'but even big girls can worry and be upset. I am a very big girl and I still worry sometimes.'

'Do you?' she asked, amazed, as though this was a revelation. I suppose I always appeared so strong and in control I must have seemed invincible.

'Yes. I do worry sometimes,' I said. 'Everyone does. So what's worrying you? I think it may help if you tell me.'

She looked at me for a moment and then taking my hand in hers said seriously, 'I'm worried that God might want you in heaven like he wanted Michael's mummy and daddy.'

Clearly she'd got this idea from hearing Michael talk, but without his religious faith the prospect was more threatening than comforting.

'No, he doesn't,' I said firmly. 'And I'm not ill. I'm in very good health. I will grow old just like Nana and Grandpa, so please don't worry.'

'Do you eat lots of fruit and vegetables?' Paula asked. 'At nursery they give us fruit each day so we stay healthy.'

'Yes, you've seen me eat fruit and veg every day, so stop worrying, all right?'

'OK,' Paula said, finally reassured. She gave me a big hug and added, 'I'll be well enough to go to nursery tomorrow.'

'Excellent,' I said.

It was hardly surprising Paula had been fretting about losing me but I was pleased she'd been able to share her worries. I knew I needed to make sure Adrian wasn't internalizing his worries; with all the attention I'd been giving to Michael it was possible I hadn't been as sensitive as I should to Adrian's anxieties. Adrian and Paula, albeit on a different level to Michael, were having to deal with losing Patrick just as I was.

That afternoon as I drove home from collecting the boys from school I reminded the children Stella was coming. Once home we had time for a cool drink and a biscuit before Jill arrived at 3.50, and I made her a drink. Stella arrived at four o'clock and she too accepted the offer of a cold drink. We all went into the sitting room and Stella asked the children how school was and if they'd had a good day. After a couple of minutes she said she'd like to talk to Michael alone, which I'd expected. Social workers usually spend time alone with the looked-after child, and I also thought that Stella would want to seek Michael's opinion on where he wanted to live without me and the children present: having us there could have inhibited him from expressing himself if he felt he was being disloyal. The weather was good, so I suggested we went outside, and Adrian, Paula, Jill and I filed out through the French windows and into the garden, where we played a game of catch as Stella talked to Michael in the sitting room.

'What are they talking about?' Paula asked after a while, as she threw the ball to me.

'About Michael's future,' I said. 'Where he's going to live.' It was now time to prepare Adrian and Paula for the purpose of Stella's visit. I hadn't been able to say anything prior to Stella coming, but now she was with Michael and they were discussing his future, I needed to prepare my children.

'Stella is talking to Michael about where he will live permanently,' I said, glancing at Jill. 'They will have to decide if he is going to stay with us or live with his Auntie Colleen and Uncle Eamon. They also love him and want to look after him.'

'I hope Michael stays with us,' Paula said easily.

'If Michael does go to live with Colleen and Eamon, we shall still see him regularly,' I said and threw the ball to Jill.

'It's nice that so many people want to look after Michael,' Jill said positively, throwing the ball to Adrian. 'Some of the children you look after don't have anyone, do they?'

Adrian nodded and threw the ball to me.

'All right, love?' I asked Adrian, and he nodded.

I think because Adrian and Paula had grown up with fostering they were better prepared than most children their age for a child they'd grown close to suddenly leaving, although of course they always felt sad when the child left, and missed them after they'd gone. We continued to play catch for another fifteen minutes or so; then Stella opened the French windows and called: 'We've finished. Would you like to come in now?'

Paula and Adrian went in first as Jill and I fell into step behind them – up the garden, across the patio and in through the French windows. Michael was sitting on the sofa with Stella beside him and I knew immediately from his expression what his decision had been. Jill and I sat in the armchairs as Adrian and Paula squatted cross-legged on the floor in front of the sofa, as though giving Stella an audience. Stella looked at Adrian and Paula as she spoke:

'I'd like to thank you both for taking such good care of Michael,' she said. 'You've made him feel very welcome and have looked after him so well. Michael tells me he feels like you're a brother and sister to him.'

'That's all right. Michael's nice,' Paula said cutely. 'Not like that boy who stayed last year: he bit me.'

Adrian and Michael stifled chuckles. 'Well, he did!' Paula said indignantly. 'I had a mark on my arm for a week. My teacher saw it.'

'I know you did,' I said conciliatorily, 'but let's listen to what Stella has to say.'

Stella smiled at Adrian and Paula and put her arm around Michael and gave him a little hug. 'So a big thank-you for taking such good care of Michael, in the happy and sad times. Michael and I have had to make a difficult decision – about where he should live in the future. I know you would like Michael to stay and live with you but Michael's godparents, Colleen and Eamon, would like him to live with them. They haven't any children and they know Michael very well, so he would be like a son to them.' I knew what was coming next; I could feel the pull of Stella's words, guiding us towards the outcome. 'Michael and I have therefore decided it would be right for Michael to live with Colleen and Eamon, so they will be his for ever family. You will still see Michael. Colleen and Eamon will make sure of that and I know they will look after Michael and love him as you have done.'

Michael, who'd been unable to meet my gaze until now, finally looked at me. I smiled. 'We'll miss you, love,' I said, 'but I know you're as special to Colleen and Eamon as you have been to us. It is the right thing to do.' I saw his expression change from guilt to relief.

'When are you going?' Adrian asked.

'Sunday,' Michael said.

Jill and I looked at Stella for confirmation. 'I suggested Sunday,' she said. 'I thought that as Colleen and Eamon are taking Michael to the funeral on Monday it would make things easier for everyone if Michael moved in with them on Sunday. It also seemed appropriate for Michael to leave for the funeral with Colleen and Eamon – his family.' I nodded. I could see the logic in this.

'Michael will just take the belongings he has here to Colleen's on Sunday,' Stella added. 'I'll sort the rest out – his things from home – later. Is Sunday all right for you, Cathy?'

'Yes. We were going to my parents but we can go on Saturday instead. What time were you thinking of making the move on Sunday?'

'I've yet to confirm that with Colleen, but I should think about one o'clock?'

I nodded and threw Michael, who'd gone quiet again, another smile.

There wasn't much to say after that. Michael had made his decision in conjunction with Stella and I knew how much Colleen and Eamon loved him and how special he was to them.

I also knew that as an only child they would be able to invest the time that would be needed to see Michael through the grieving process and go on to lead a full and rewarding life. With Colleen and Eamon Michael would have the two-parent family he had never known and I knew the decision would have Pat's blessing.

Stella thanked us again for all we'd done for Michael and, making a move to go, said she'd ask Colleen to phone me to confirm what time she would be coming on Sunday. I left Adrian and Paula with Jill in the sitting room while I saw Stella to the door. As I returned to the sitting room I heard Michael say: 'I've always known Auntie Colleen and Uncle Eamon, ever since I was little.'

'You have, love,' I said. 'And if I was you I would want to make my home with them. I'm sure that's what your dad would want too.'

Michael smiled.

'Are you looking forward to visiting Michael in his new home?' Jill asked Adrian and Paula positively.

They nodded, and then Paula added, 'I wish Michael was staying. We might get another child who bites me.'

'Hopefully not,' Jill put in smartly.

'Will we still collect my Scalextric on Saturday?' Michael now asked me.

'Good point,' I said. 'It hardly seems worth bringing it here if we have to pack it away again for Sunday. Wouldn't it be better if Colleen and Eamon took your Scalextric straight to their house?'

Michael nodded and Jill agreed.

'I'll speak to Colleen about it when she phones,' I reassured Michael. 'She has the keys to your house.'

Jill stayed for another ten minutes while the children played in the garden. It was the first time Michael had felt like playing outside since we'd received the news of his father's death, and I was pleased to see he was starting to enjoy himself again.

'Once the funeral is over with on Monday,' Jill said, standing, ready to go, 'it should start to get a bit easier for Michael.' I nodded. 'You're going to miss him, aren't you?'

'Yes,' I said, 'and Patrick. He was such a good kind man. He was one of those people you feel better for knowing. I just wish I'd known him for longer.'

Jill called her goodbyes to the children and I saw her out and then went into the kitchen to make dinner. We were subdued over dinner, thinking, I suppose, of all that would be happening over the next few days. I was pleased we were going to visit my parents on Saturday; not only would it keep us occupied but it would also give them a chance to say goodbye to Michael, for although the children and I would be keeping in contact with Michael I wasn't sure if it would be practical for my parents to keep in touch or see him again.

That night, Paula, who was aware Michael said his prayers every night, decided she wanted to say her prayers. After I'd read her a bedtime story she sat upright in bed and, clasping her little hands together, screwed her eyes tightly shut: 'God bless Mummy, Daddy; Nana, Grandpa; my brother Adrian; Mummy's brother Uncle Tom; Michael; Michael's mummy and daddy; and Michael's new mummy and daddy who are Colleen and Eamon. I hope they will be very happy together. Amen.'

Chapter Thirty-Two
Heaven

Funerals are never easy and I knew Patrick's would be very upsetting and, as Jill had said, a hurdle to overcome, as well as a turning point for Michael. On Friday I told Michael's school's secretary that Michael wouldn't be in school on Monday as it was his father's funeral. The secretary said she'd inform the head, and that Father Murphy would be representing the school at the funeral. I also told Paula's nursery that my parents would be collecting Paula on Monday; they had asked us to inform them in advance if a different person to usual collected a child.

In the past when children we'd fostered left us we had usually given them a small leaving party, but that hardly seemed appropriate given Michael's bereavement. So on Friday evening the four of us watched a children's video together, with microwave popcorn and an ice cream each; then Adrian and Michael played cards while I took Paula to bed. Later, when the boys were upstairs washing and changing, ready for bed, Colleen phoned. She asked how we all were and then clarified the arrangements for collecting Michael on Sunday.

'Stella said one o'clock. Is that all right with you?' she said.

'Yes, fine. I'll have Michael's belongings packed and ready. He'd really like his Scalextric with him. I was going to collect it tomorrow but it hardly seems worth it as he's moving to you on Sunday.'

'No problem,' Colleen said. 'We'll collect it. Eamon and I are going to the house tomorrow to bring back as many of Michael's possessions as we can so that they are here when he arrives on Sunday. I've spoken to Nora and we both think that Michael will feel more at home if his things are here with him.'

'Yes, absolutely,' I agreed.

'His bed is made up ready,' Colleen continued, 'but I might change the duvet cover and use his from home – the one with a picture of Superman; that's his favourite. Eamon is going to redecorate Michael's bedroom once he's settled in, so Michael can choose the wallpaper; there are some lovely designs for boys' rooms now.'

'Yes, there are. He'll like that.'

'And I've been to the supermarket today and stocked up on all the food Michael likes. I hope I haven't forgotten anything.'

'He'll be fine,' I reassured her.

I could hear Colleen's tempered excitement, for while she and Eamon were obviously heartbroken at losing their dearest friend they were also excited at the prospect of beginning a new phase in their lives with Michael. As Michael would be gaining a two-parent family so Colleen and Eamon would gain the family they'd never thought they'd have. And I thought that Michael's story would eventually have the happy ending I wished for all the children I looked after.

On Saturday the children and I spent the whole day at my parents' house. We arrived at 10.30 a.m. and didn't leave until after 7.00 p.m., so there was little time for fretting about Michael leaving or him worrying about the funeral on Monday. My parents, sensitive to Michael's feelings, pitched the tone and mood of the day just right. My father kept Adrian and Michael occupied by having them help him with little jobs in the shed, garden, greenhouse and garage; while Paula, as usual, hardly left her nana's side. I even had time to read the newspaper. It was a pleasant day, but I knew how difficult it was going to be for Mum and Dad to say goodbye to Michael, aware it would probably be their last goodbye to him.

'Keep your chin up, young man,' Dad said to Michael, shaking his hand and putting on a brave face, as we finally stood in the hall ready to go. 'You're a good lad and I know you'll do very well for yourself. Send my regards to Colleen and Eamon.'

'I will,' Michael said.

Mum had tears in her eyes even before we'd begun to say goodbye; and she now hugged Michael as though she would never let him go. 'Hopefully we'll see you again one day,' she said, and then gave him a wrapped present.

'Thank you,' Michael said, surprised. 'Can I open it now?'

'Yes,' Mum said.

Michael tore off the paper and his eyes lit up. It was a copy of *The Guinness Book of Records*, which Mum knew Michael liked from reading Adrian's copy. 'Thank you so much,' Michael said. 'It's just what I wanted! And it's not even my birthday,' which made Mum well up even more.

We said a last goodbye and Mum and Dad stood at their garden gate and waved until we were out of sight. I then drove home with the children in the back of the car, the book spread open between them, gasping at the pictures of the world's biggest, fattest, tallest, longest record-breakers that filled the pages.

* * *

Heaven

The children were late going to bed that Saturday night but it didn't matter as we could all have a lie-in on Sunday. It was after 9.30 when I finally took Paula up to bed; she was exhausted after a full day at Nana and Grandpa's. I gave her a quick wash and helped her change into her nightdress and climb into bed. She yawned, curled on to her side and was asleep as soon as her head touched the pillow. I came out of Paula's room and went in search of Adrian and Michael, whom I had left to wash and change while I saw to Paula. I found them both in Michael's room, in their pyjamas, standing by the window and gazing up at the night sky.

I went over and stood between them; putting an arm around each of their shoulders we looked out at the sky. Because we were late going to bed it was dark. It was a cloudless night and the stars were clearly visible, twinkling brightly in the night sky. There was also a waxing moon glowing in a perfect crescent shape. It was a beautiful image of the sky at night and for Michael it was heaven.

'My daddy is with my mummy now,' he said quietly after a moment, not taking his eyes from the sky. 'And soon I shall be living with Colleen and Eamon. I'm going to miss you guys.'

'We'll miss you too,' Adrian said. 'But you can come and play here any time you like.'

'And you can come to my new house,' Michael said. 'I'm sure Auntie Colleen and Uncle Eamon won't mind.'

I agreed. 'I'm sure they will be very happy for you to have your friends to play. We'll look forward to it.'

It was after ten o'clock when the boys were finally in bed and asleep. I went downstairs and put Toscha out for her evening run, locked up and then went to bed myself. That night I had a strange dream: that Adrian and Paula and I were living with

Colleen, Eamon and Michael in a big house in an idyllic country setting and we were all very happy. I suppose it was my subconscious giving its seal of approval to Michael's new family and expressing the hope that we would stay in contact for many years to come.

The following morning, as predicted, we all slept in, and then once we were up and showered and dressed, I cooked us a big brunch. No one mentioned Michael's leaving but it hung unspoken in the air. When we'd finished eating I encouraged the children to play in the garden while I went upstairs and packed Michael's bags. I took his toothbrush, flannel, sponge and towel from the bathroom and tucked them in; then I stowed the bags downstairs out of sight in the front room.

I gave the children a drink and snack at midday and then at exactly one o'clock the doorbell rang. The children were still in the garden and didn't hear the bell, so were unaware Colleen and Eamon had arrived. Colleen and Eamon were both very smartly dressed, having come straight from church. I welcomed them in and we hugged and kissed in the hall. Then I showed them through to the sitting room, where the open French windows led on to the garden. We stood quietly for a while at the French windows, watching the children play; then Colleen said, 'I hope we can make Michael as happy as you have. He'll be an only child with us.'

'Don't worry,' I smiled. 'Michael's already planning on asking you if he can invite friends home – including us.'

'Of course he can!' Colleen exclaimed happily. 'That would be wonderful.

'The more the merrier!' Eamon agreed.

After a few moments Adrian spotted us and, pointing, said to Michael, 'Look. Your auntie and uncle are here.'

Heaven

Michael turned and the second he saw Colleen and Eamon he ran up the garden path and straight into Colleen's arms. It was the first time he'd seen them since making his decision to live with them. It was a wonderful warm welcome and just what Colleen needed to give her confidence in her new role as Michael's adoptive mother. I could see how touched she and Eamon were.

I offered Colleen and Eamon a drink but they said they really needed to be going, as they wanted to get Michael settled before tomorrow. Eamon loaded Michael's bags into the boot of the car and then returned to the house. We kept our goodbyes brief. I would be seeing Colleen, Eamon and Michael the following day at the funeral and I didn't think it would be long before we all met up again in happier circumstances. Adrian told Michael to phone him, and Paula gave Michael a big kiss, jumping up to reach his cheek. Then she said very cutely (and copying something she must have overheard an adult say): 'You're a nice boy, Michael. I'm sure your dad will be very proud of you.' Which made Michael and Adrian giggle, Colleen and me misty-eyed, and Eamon clear his throat with emotion.

Eamon went out first, and Michael followed with Colleen, linking his arm through hers. On the pavement Eamon opened the rear door of the car for Michael to get in and then checked his seat belt was fastened, before closing the door. Colleen got into the passenger seat and Eamon gave a little wave before climbing into the driver's seat. He started the engine and Colleen and Michael waved through their side windows as the car pulled away. The three of us stood on the doorstep and waved until they were out of view; then we went inside and I closed the front door. The children were looking very glum.

'How about we take a picnic up to the park?' I suggested. They liked the idea, so the three of us went into the kitchen and put together an impromptu picnic, which we then carried to the local park.

The afternoon was pleasant and it passed. I wouldn't say we were ecstatically happy but neither were we miserable or moping. Although we would miss Michael and feel sad for him at this time of loss, he was going to live with good people whom he already knew and loved. We bumped into some friends in the park and the children played together while I chatted to the parents, so it was after five o'clock before we returned home. I made dinner and then once we'd eaten I began the children's bath and bedtime routine, ready for school and nursery the following day.

'I like Michael,' Paula said pensively, as I tucked her into bed. 'He was like another brother to me.'

'I know, love. But we'll see him again soon. And you've got Nana and Grandpa collecting you from nursery tomorrow,' I reminded her, which cheered her up.

When I went into Adrian's room he wasn't in bed but was standing at his window with the curtains parted, looking up at the night sky.

'All right, love?' I asked gently, joining him at the window. It wasn't dark enough to see the stars, although the crescent moon was just visible.

'Do you think Michael's daddy is really in heaven with his mummy?' Adrian asked thoughtfully.

I smiled. 'If there is a heaven then I am sure they are there.'

'You have to be good to go to heaven, don't you?' Adrian asked, not taking his eyes from the sky.

'Yes, that's what people believe.'

'So will we go to heaven when we die?'

'Yes. We're good people, aren't we? Or we try to be.'

'What about Dad? Will he go?' Adrian asked.

Heaven

I should have seen this coming, I thought. 'Yes, I'm sure he will. God is most forgiving, just as I will be one day.'

Adrian turned from the window and threw me a knowing smile; he was old enough to appreciate my sometimes dry humour.

'Good,' he said, jumping into bed. 'I know Dad shouldn't have left us but I wouldn't want him burning in hell.'

'No, he won't,' I reassured him, although there were times when I might have wished for it, I thought. 'Your father loves you and Paula, just as I do.'

Chapter Thirty-Three

Leaving Michael

The following morning the school routine took over, so there was little time for me to dwell on the funeral later that morning. But it was strange not waking Michael, hearing him in the shower, seeing him at the breakfast table or taking him to school. I wondered how he was feeling on his first morning in his new home and I consoled myself that Colleen and Eamon would be on hand to hug and comfort him. Without the need to take Michael to school first I now drove straight to Adrian's school, where Paula and I waited in the playground until the bell rang and Adrian went in. It was the last week of the summer term, so on Friday the schools would break up for the long summer holiday. There wouldn't be much work done this week in class but lots of fun activities. Already I could hear the excitement of the children who ran around me in the playground, which was a strange contrast to what I was feeling, about to go to a funeral.

It was the same at Paula's nursery – lots of excited chatter as parents saw their children in for what would be their last week at nursery before they began 'big school' in September. I reminded Farah, the nursery assistant, that my parents would be collecting Paula; then, giving Paula a big hug, I said goodbye to her and that I would see her later in the afternoon.

Leaving Michael

It wasn't until I returned home and was alone that I started to feel down and worried about how I was going to cope at Pat's funeral. I hadn't been to many funerals, fortunately, only my grandparents' and that of a close friend, but I knew how upsetting I had found the services and the difficulty I'd had in controlling my emotions. Other mourners had seemed so brave and composed while I'd snivelled into a tissue and fought to hide my emotions and tears.

Reigning in my thoughts, I washed up the breakfast dishes and then wrote a note for Mum and Dad. They had keys to my house, so after they'd collected Paula from nursery they would let themselves in. Mum had insisted on cooking lunch, so my note said simply: *Thanks very much for your help. Take whatever you need from the freezer. See you later. Love Cathy. X* I propped it in front of the coffee jar and, steeling myself, went upstairs and into my bedroom, where I opened my wardrobe door. I took out my grey two-piece suit, light-grey blouse, new stockings and black court shoes and laid them on the bed. Concentrating on changing and not the reason why, I dressed in my smart outfit and then checked my appearance in the mirror. Looping my handbag over my arm, I went slowly downstairs and let myself out of the front door.

It was 10.40 when I arrived in the crematorium car park and parked in a bay by the hedge. I cut the engine, tried to silence my racing heart, and looked around. There were a dozen or so other cars parked; some of the cars were empty and others had occupants, presumably also waiting for Pat's funeral. A group of about five men and women about Pat's age stood together in one corner of the car park. I didn't recognize anyone. Releasing my seat belt, I lowered my window a little for some air. It was a dry warm day, humid almost, but with a grey overcast sky. As I waited, other cars arrived and parked. I looked out of the

window and concentrated on the neatly tended gardens awash
with flowers, and listened to the birds singing in the trees over-
head. My stomach churned. If I was feeling anxious, what must
poor Michael be feeling? A lump rose to my throat.

Ten minutes later the cortège, led by a shiny black hearse,
slowly pulled into view and on to the forecourt; I felt my eyes
start to fill. Patrick's coffin on display in the rear of the hearse
seemed even more pronounced with no bouquets of flowers
covering it and therefore shielding it partly from view. Pat had
asked that donations be made to cancer research rather than
sending flowers. The hearse drew to a halt in front of the chapel
followed by two shiny black limousines carrying mourners. As I
looked at the first car I saw Michael's little face peer out of the
side window. He looked so small and sad as he anxiously
scanned the unfamiliar scene outside the car. Colleen was seated
next to him and slipped her arm around his shoulder and whispered something in his ear. Eamon was sitting next to her, and
on the seat behind were Nora and Jack. There were other
mourners in the second car but apart from Father Murphy from
Michael's school I didn't recognize anyone.

Taking a deep breath to steel myself, I opened the door and
got out. Other mourners were also getting out of their cars.
Small groups gradually formed and then moved forward to wait
a short distance from the hearse. I too went forward. Jack saw
me and came over with Nora, and shook my hand warmly.

'How are you, love?' Jack asked.

'All right, thank you, and yourselves?'

'Not too bad,' Jack said. I noticed Nora didn't say anything
and looked very close to tears.

My gaze went again to Michael, who was now out of the
limousine and standing between Colleen and Eamon near the
back of the hearse. Eamon had a reassuring hand on Michael's

Leaving Michael

shoulder and Colleen was holding Michael's other hand. Michael looked so smart in his Sunday suit and I knew Pat would be proud of him.

The pall-bearers began raising the rear door of the hearse, and then slowly very slowly slid out the coffin. I felt my pulse quicken and I looked at Michael, who was staring at the coffin, his face sad and empty. With one movement the pall-bearers effortlessly lifted the coffin on to their shoulders and, turning, faced the chapel. The mourners moved forward in pairs, ready to form a procession and follow the coffin into the chapel. Jack offered me his arm so that I wouldn't have to walk into chapel alone, which was thoughtful of him. Nora took his other arm, and Jack guided us to stand behind Eamon, Michael and Colleen. I felt touched and honoured that I was being included at the head of the procession with the other chief mourners.

Michael turned and looked at me and I managed a reassuring smile. What an ordeal for a child of eight to have to go through, I thought. I wanted to reach out and hug him. We waited in silence as the other mourners lined up behind us; then the chapel doors opened. Organ music came from inside and our procession began to move slowly forward. The coffin rode high in front and appeared to lead the way. We went to the front of the chapel and the pall-bearers placed the coffin on the raised plinth. Michael, Eamon and Colleen crossed themselves and then slid into the first row of chairs. Nora, Jack and I, together with Father Murphy, slid into the second row. Once all the mourners were in the chapel it was full, with some standing at the back. I estimated there were over a hundred people present: a sign of just how popular and liked Patrick had been. The organ music stopped and the service began.

Having never been to a Roman Catholic funeral before and therefore not knowing what to expect, I found I was soon caught up in the relative formality of the service, which placed emphasis on the resurrection of Christ. It wasn't until the priest leading the service, who was also the priest from the Sacred Heart Church where Pat and Michael worshipped, began a tribute that I felt my eyes well and my lip tremble. Because the priest knew Patrick and Michael personally his words were warm and sincere as he spoke. He spoke of Pat as being an honest, kind and trustworthy person as well as a good practising Catholic. The priest praised the way Pat had brought up Michael and said he was a fine example of what a father could and should be. As he spoke I reached for my tissue; so too did Colleen and Nora, and I could hear other mourners behind me clearing their throats and blowing their noses. It was the personal tribute in an otherwise formal ceremony that stood out and was so poignantly touching.

Michael was very brave until near the end of the service when the priest gave the final blessing and Michael realized it would be the last time he would be with his father. He buried his head in Colleen's side and sobbed; Colleen had her arm around him and held him close. The doors opened and mourners were starting to leave. Colleen said something to Michael and I saw him nod. With her arm around Michael the two of them took the few steps to where the coffin rested. Michael put his hands together and closed his eyes and his lips moved in silent prayer. Opening his eyes, he crossed himself and taking a stop forward he kissed the coffin. I felt my eyes well and Nora, standing beside me, cried openly. The image of Michael standing so small and reverent beside his father's coffin is one I shall carry with me for ever.

I followed Nora and Jack out of the chapel and once outside I walked away to a corner of the shrubbed car park to compose myself. I wasn't the only one; others were taking a few minutes out – walking or standing alone – and those who smoked had formed a small group and were lighting up and inhaling deeply.

Presently Jack came over to me. 'Are you all right, love?' he asked kindly, touching my arm.

'Yes, thank you. Is Nora?'

'She's in the car waiting. You are coming back to Colleen and Eamon's for refreshments?'

'I told Colleen I would,' I said.

'Good. You know where they live?'

I nodded.

'We'll see you there, then.'

Jack went over to the limousine and climbed in beside Nora. Colleen and Michael were already in the car and Eamon was now getting in, having been talking to other mourners. I went to my car and waited inside for the two limousines to leave; then I started the engine and reversed out of the parking space. It was nearly 12.30 p.m. and Paula would be at home now, enjoying the attention of her nana and grandpa. I wished I was with them.

It was a fifteen-minute drive to Colleen and Eamon's house and when I arrived their street was already full of cars. I found a place to park in the next road and, getting out, I straightened my skirt and then made my way round to their house. Arriving alone instead of in a couple was something I was having to get used to, but it was at times like this – when I could have done with a reassuring arm – that I really felt it. Had it not been for Michael I think I would have gone straight home.

I rang the doorbell and someone I didn't recognize, but who clearly knew me, answered. 'Hello, Cathy,' the man said warmly. 'Come in, love. I'm Sean, Eamon's brother.'

We shook hands as I stepped into the hall. The house was teeming with people and the air buzzed with conversation. It was more like a party than a gathering after a funeral, and I guessed most of those who had been at the crematorium were now crammed into the house. Sean showed me through to the front room, where small groups of people with glasses in their hands were chatting and even laughing. A drinks table with bottles and glasses, and another table with a cold buffet, stretched round the bay window. Sean introduced me to his wife and grown son and daughter, and also to another brother and sister-in-law, who were together talking in one group. They all shook my hand warmly and said how pleased they were to meet me.

'What can I get you to drink, love?' Sean asked me.

I don't usually drink at lunchtime but after the morning I felt 'in need' of a drink. 'A small white wine, please,' I said to Sean.

Sean poured me a generous measure and I stood chatting with him and his family. As with many people I meet, once they know I foster they ask about fostering, as often it's something they've considered doing. We talked for a while about the ups and downs of fostering and children in general and then Colleen entered the room, and came to me. 'If you don't mind, Cathy,' she said, 'Michael would like to show you his room. Is that OK?'

'Of course,' I said. 'I haven't seen him since I arrived.'

Leaving my wine glass on a coaster on the bureau, I followed Colleen out of the front room, squeezed past people standing in the hall, and to where Michael was waiting, near the foot of the stairs at the rear of the house. He grinned when he saw me, and was clearly relieved the ordeal of the funeral was over. He threw his arms around my waist and hugged me hard.

'Good to see you again,' I said, kissing the top of his head.

'Come and see my room,' he said after a moment. 'It's great. I've got all my things here.' Colleen, who was standing beside us, smiled with pride.

Leaving Michael

'Lead the way,' I said.

'I'll leave you two to it,' Colleen said, and went off to tend to her other guests as I followed Michael upstairs.

The house appeared to be a three-bedroom townhouse which had been extended into the loft to make a fourth bedroom. Michael's room was at the very top, up two flights of stairs, but as we entered his room I gasped. It wasn't so much a bedroom as a suite. Colleen and Eamon had never boasted about Michael's room, but it was huge; the room together with the en-suite bathroom took up the entire top floor.

'This is amazing,' I said looking around the room. 'Aren't you lucky?'

Michael nodded.

As well as being a very big room it was light and airy, with a large dormer window overlooking the garden. The window was open and guests' voices could be heard floating up from the garden below. Colleen had said Eamon was going to decorate Michael's bedroom but it was already well decorated, although perhaps a little young for Michael now. The wallpaper, which matched the curtains and lampshade, were dark blue with cartoon characters from pre-school television programmes.

'I used to stay here when I was little,' Michael said, grinning. 'I think I'm going to have Batman wallpaper now like Adrian.'

'Sounds good to me,' I said.

The wardrobe was in the same wood as the bed frame, as were the chest of drawers and work station, which would be ideal for Michael when he had homework to do. But what impressed me most wasn't the size of the room, nor that it had its own bathroom, but that it was full of Michael's belongings. Colleen and Eamon must have worked very hard to bring all Michael's possessions here and arrange them, so that when Michael arrived he would feel at home and settle more easily.

His Superman duvet was on the bed, two large teddy bears – clearly old favourites – sat on the pillow, and Michael's dressing gown hung on a hook behind the door. As Michael proudly opened the wardrobe doors I saw his clothes hanging neatly on the rail, and likewise his drawers contained his underclothes, socks and T-shirts, all neatly folded. His books lined the bookshelves, and four large toy boxes at one end of the room brimmed with his toys. But most important of all, in the very centre of the room was his Scalextric – set up and with two cars at the finishing line. 'Uncle Eamon's been playing with me,' Michael said. 'But he's nowhere near as good as Adrian. Will Adrian come over and play some time soon?'

'I'm sure he will,' I said.

I sat on the bed while Michael showed me more of his toys, games and puzzles, obviously already feeling very comfortable in his new home. I admired everything he showed me and stayed positive, but I was acutely aware that the reason Michael was in this splendid room was that he'd lost his own home and father, as I'm sure Michael was aware. Clearly he would have swapped it all in a flash if he could have reversed the situation and had his dad back.

After a while Eamon came up to find us. 'Sorry to interrupt,' he said, 'but my brother has to go now. Could Michael come down and say goodbye?'

'Of course,' I said, standing. 'I really think I should be off now too.'

'Can't you stay a while longer?' Eamon asked. 'Colleen would like to introduce you to some of her family.'

I followed Eamon and Michael downstairs, where Colleen intercepted us, so that as Eamon took Michael to say goodbye to his brother and family, I went with Colleen into the sitting room and the garden to be introduced to her family. Unlike

Leaving Michael

Patrick, Colleen and Eamon came from large families with lots of nieces and nephews, which would be nice for Michael. It become apparent I was well known, for every time Colleen introduced me to one of her family the response was similar: 'Good to meet you at last, Cathy. I've heard so much about you. You're the foster carer who looked after Michael, aren't you?' And they began asking me about fostering.

Presently Eamon appeared with a plate of food for me and my glass of wine, which he'd retrieved from the front room. I thanked him and suddenly realized I was hungry; it was a long time since breakfast. For the next hour or so I mingled with the guests – friends of Patrick's and close friends and relatives of Colleen and Eamon, all of whom were lovely warm people and had known Patrick. Colleen assured me that Michael was fine and was playing Scalextric in his room with the neighbour's children, who had just come in. Although it may seem a strange thing to say I felt it had actually turned into a pleasant afternoon. Everyone I met was very, very friendly and we were all there for the same reason – out of love and respect for Patrick.

Eventually three o'clock approached and, while I knew Mum and Dad would collect Adrian from school, I felt it was time to go. I said goodbye to the couple I was talking to and then, leaving my plate and glass in the kitchen, I found Colleen in the garden. I told her I really needed to be going now and she understood.

'I'll fetch Michael to say goodbye,' she said, and we went into the house. I waited in the hall while Colleen went up the first flight of stairs and called Michael. He appeared with Eamon beside him and we made our way to the front door.

'Thanks again for everything,' Eamon said, shaking my hand warmly. 'We won't say goodbye as we'll be seeing each other regularly, I hope.'

'Yes, most definitely,' I said.

Colleen also thanked me and then kissed my cheek. I hugged and kissed Michael. 'See you soon,' I said.

Eamon opened the front door and the three of them came down the front-garden path with me and on to the pavement. 'See you soon,' they chorused, as I began walking down the street. I waved, and then before I turned the corner to the road where my car was parked, I looked back. The sun had at last broken through and was shining down on them. Michael stood between Colleen and Eamon and was waving madly. I gave a final wave and then turned the corner; it was time to leave Michael safely with his family and return to mine.

Epilogue

We saw Michael regularly – every couple of weeks for the first year, and then as time passed and the boys went to secondary school and then to college less frequently, but we still kept in touch. When the boys were younger Michael slept over at our house sometimes and Adrian slept at Michael's house. Paula was always pleased to see Michael when he stayed and the boys included her in their games. Sometimes we all went on family outings together: Colleen, Eamon, Michael, Adrian, Paula, me and the child(ren) we were fostering at the time.

Approximately three months after Patrick died I was opening the morning's mail when a cheque fell out of the envelope I'd just opened. I picked it up and saw it was for £200, made payable to me and drawn on the account of E. Doyle. Puzzled, I read the handwritten note, which I saw was from Colleen:

Dear Cathy,

As you know, Eamon and I are the executors of Patrick's will. All the monies from his estate, including the sale of his house, will go into a trust fund for Michael for when he is older. However, Pat added a codicil to his will. It was Patrick's wish that you be given £200 to buy your children an electric racing car set. He knew how much Adrian and Paula liked playing

with Michael's Scalextric and he hopes you will all have years of
enjoyment from one of your own. Please find enclosed cheque.
See you soon. Love and best wishes Colleen, Eamon and
Michael. xxx

Needless to say, I was so touched I was in tears by the end of the letter. 'Thank you, Pat,' I said out loud. 'How very kind and thoughtful of you! But then of course you always were.'

When I collected the children from school that afternoon (Paula had left nursery and was now at Adrian's school) I explained about Patrick's bequest. They were as touched as I was, and also very excited when, the following Saturday, we went shopping and brought the Scalextric. As Patrick anticipated, it has given my family (and me) many years of enjoyment – we still play with it now sometimes all these years later.

Then one cold evening in late January the following year I was in the sitting room, feeling pretty low. Adrian and Paula were ill in bed with flu, and the child I was fostering was also in bed but had been very naughty during the day and I'd continually had to tell him off. To make matters worse I was trying to make sense of the wad of papers that had arrived that morning from my solicitor in respect of my divorce. There were forms that had to be filled in; a lengthy letter from my solicitor with lots of legal terms; his interim bill, which was a shock; and an affidavit outlining the grounds for my divorce. It was all getting on top of me. Then my phoned bleeped with a text from a friend asking if I'd like to meet up for coffee. I replied: *Yes please!* and pressed send. As I did, a message popped up saying my inbox had 198 read texts and was nearly full. I decided to clear it out in preference to doing the legal paperwork. I began running down the texts quickly, deleting them one at a time, until I got to Patrick's, when I opened and read each one.

Epilogue

It was strange and very moving seeing his texts, almost as if they'd just been sent, although most were trivial and run-of-the-mill: *C u l8 x* or *Have u had a good day?* or *How are u?* etc. Then I came to the message Pat had sent after he'd made the decision not to see my children again and I'd been forced to acknowledge just how ill he really was; when I'd sat alone in my car crying and the text had come through. It read: *Stars are openings in heaven where the love of our lost ones shines through. Look to the stars Cathy and don't be sad.* I read it now as I read it then and felt my spirits lift. It was as though I was receiving the message afresh and with it Pat's philosophy to make the very best of life.

Dumping the legal correspondence from the solicitor to one side, I stood and crossed to the French windows and looked out at the night sky. It was a cold clear night and the stars and moon shone brightly against the inky-black sky. I thought of Michael and all the times we'd stood side by side at what had been his bedroom window and gazed up at the heavens. I remembered the comfort and strength he had drawn from seeing the stars: the little boy who'd firmly believed his daddy was going to join his mummy in heaven. I thought of Michael's strength and courage, and all my previous worries evaporated as I heard Patrick's mellow voice with its soft Irish accent saying: 'Look to the stars, Cathy, and don't be sad.'

I still have that text. When I bought a new phone I transferred it to the new SIM. If I'm feeling low or need to put things in a better perspective, I go to the window and look at the night sky. The glittering stars are so beautiful that I can believe they are indeed the love of our lost ones shining through. And of course the brightest star of all is without doubt Patrick's love for Michael and possibly a little for me too.

The Night the Angels Came

May joy and peace surround you,
Contentment latch your door,
And happiness be with you now,
And bless you evermore.